# Spider Webb's

# Classic Tattoo Flash 2

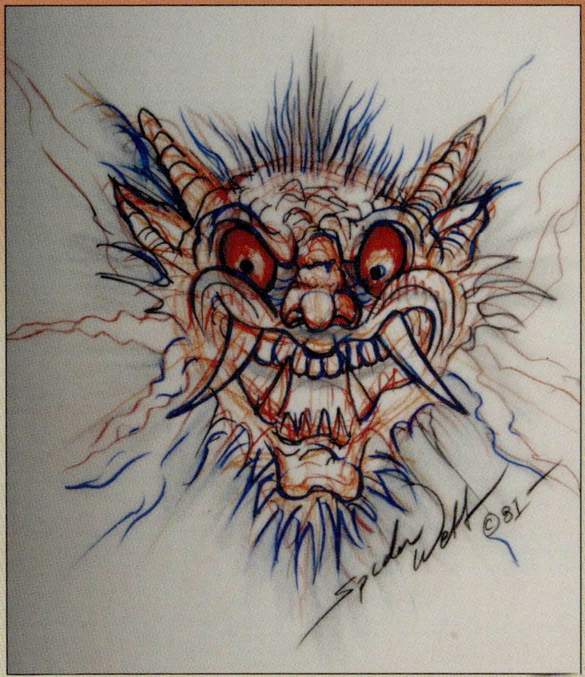

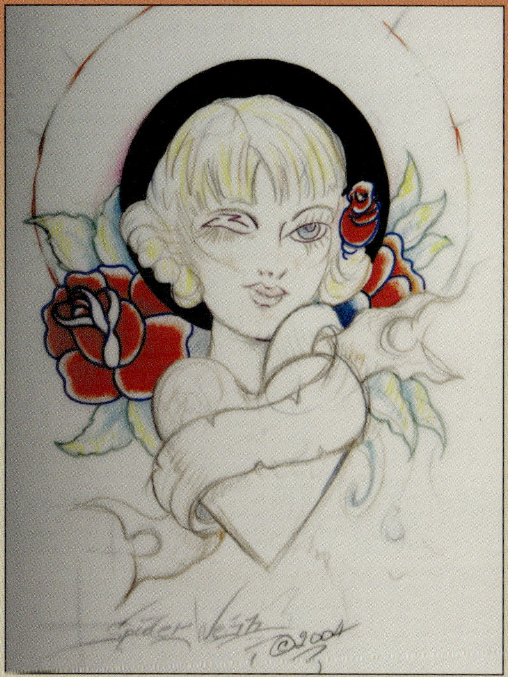

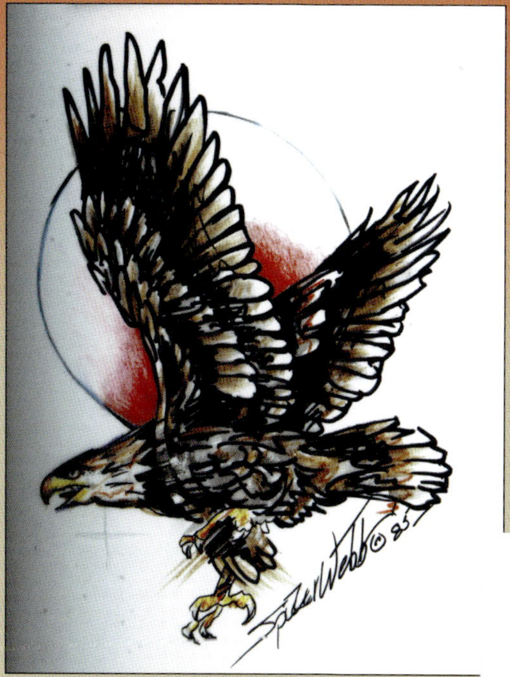

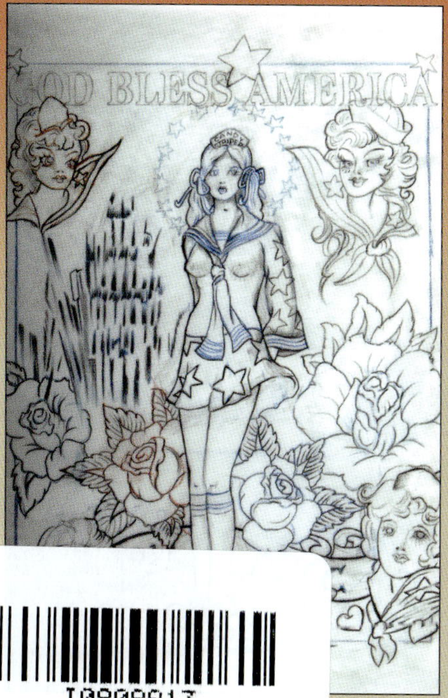




Schiffer Publishing Ltd®

4880 Lower Valley Road, Atglen, Pennsylvania 19310

Spider Webb

# Dedication

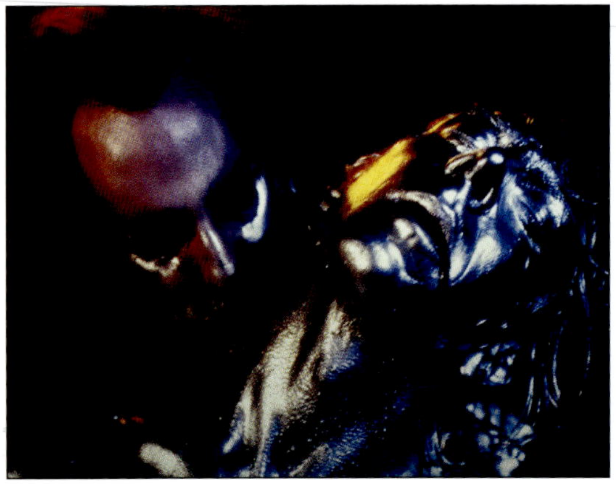

Spider Webb performing the "Vampire Tattoo" with Marc "10 1/2" Stevens, New York City, 1982.

—With love and respect Marc, R.I.P.
Spider Webb



**Front cover:** Spider Webb Classic Tattoo Flash © Spider Webb 1995.

**Other Schiffer Books by Spider Webb**
*The Big Book of Tattoo.* ISBN: 0764315609. $24.95
*Butterfly Flash.* ISBN: 0764315056. $19.95
*Dragon Flash.* ISBN: 076432504. $19.95
*Flash Dragons: The Art of Spider Webb.* ISBN: 0764325590. $19.95
*The Great Book of Tattoo.* ISBN: 0764316044. $24.95
*Heavily Tattooed Men & Women.* ISBN: 0764316052. $14.95
*Historic Flash.* ISBN: 0764316060. $25.00
*Military Flash.* ISBN: 0764315382. $25.00
*Pushing Ink.* ISBN: 0764315390. $19.95
*Tattooed Women.* ISBN: 0764315404. $19.95

**Other Schiffer Books on Related Subjects**
*Bushido: Legacies of the Japanese Tattoo.* Takahiro Kitamura & Katie M. Kitamura. ISBN: 0764312014. $29.95
*Life as a Sideshow Tattoo Artist: Stoney Knows How.* Alan Govenar. ISBN: 0764318322. $39.95
*Marked for Life: A Gallery of Tattoo Art.* Steve Bonge. ISBN: 076431436X. $29.95
*Sailor Jerry's Tattoo Stencils.* Kate Hellenbrand. ISBN: 0764315625. $25.00
*Street Shop Tattoo Stencils: Creating New Designs for Skin Art.* Brian Johnson & Chris Alexander. ISBN: 9780764330599. $24.99
*Tattoo Road Trip: The Pacific Northwest.* Bob Baxter. ISBN: 0764315226. $39.95
*Tattoos from Paradise: Traditional Polynesian Patterns.* Mark Blackburn. ISBN: 0764309412. $69.95


Library of Congress Control Number: 2008928557



Designed by Mark David Bowyer
Type set in Americana XBd BT / News Gothic BT

ISBN: 978-0-7643-3079-7
Printed in China



Published by Schiffer Publishing Ltd.
4880 Lower Valley Road
Atglen, PA 19310
Phone: (610) 593-1777; Fax: (610) 593-2002
E-mail: Info@schifferbooks.com

Please visit our web site catalog at **www.schifferbooks.com**

We are always looking for people to write books on new and related subjects. If you have an idea for a book, please contact us at the above address.

This book may be purchased from the publisher.
Include $5.00 for shipping.
Please try your bookstore first.
You may write for a free catalog.

In Europe, Schiffer books are distributed by:
Bushwood Books
6 Marksbury Ave.
Kew Gardens
Surrey TW9 4JF
England
Phone: 44 (0)208 392-8585
Fax: 44 (0)208 392-9876
E-mail: Info@bushwoodbooks.co.uk

Website: www.bushwoodbooks.co.uk
Free postage in the UK. Europe: air mail at cost.
Try your bookstore first.

# Contents



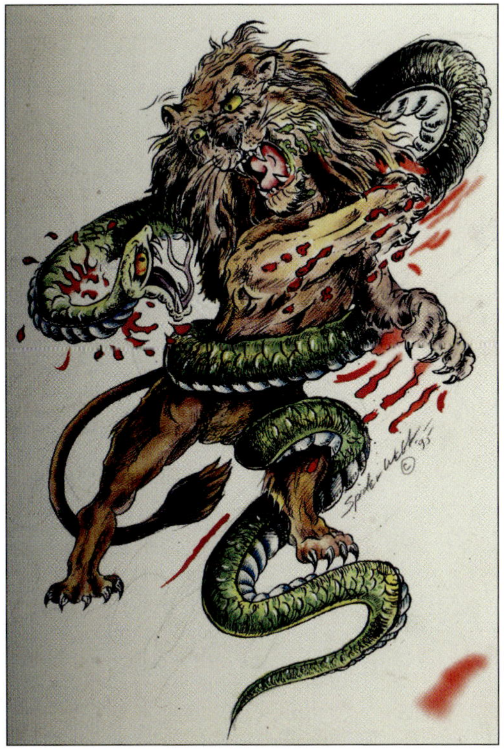

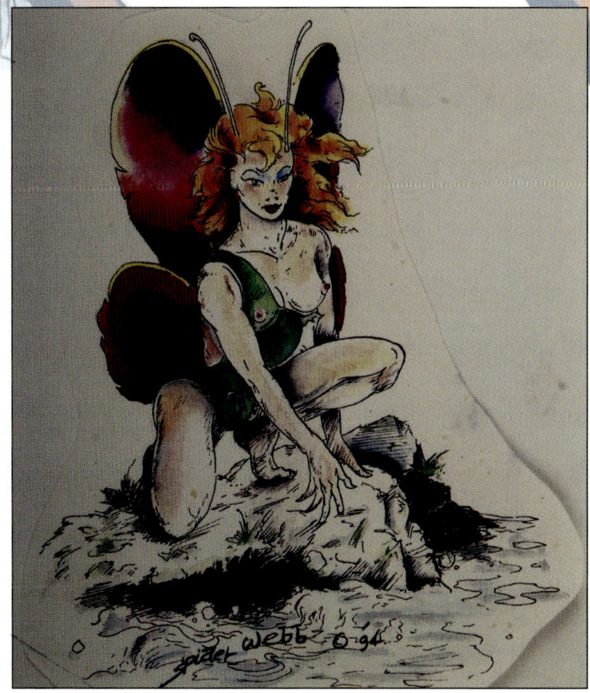

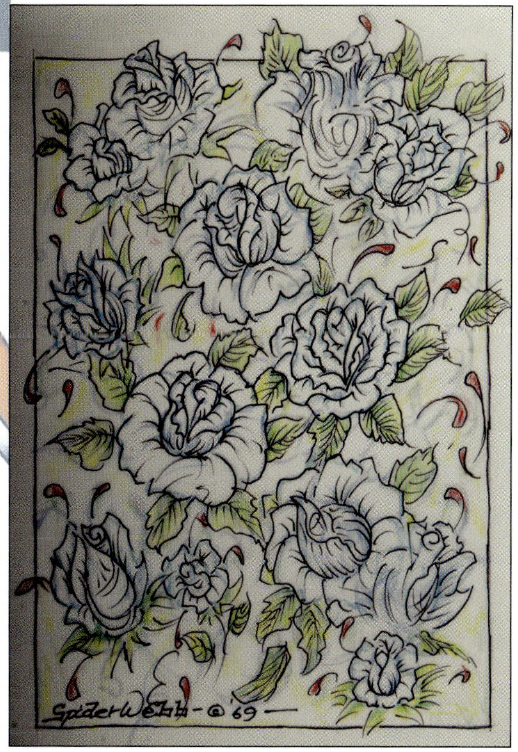

# Acknowledgments

Thanks to Chicago Chris and all the Bottom Rats – Ride on.

—Spider Webb
2007

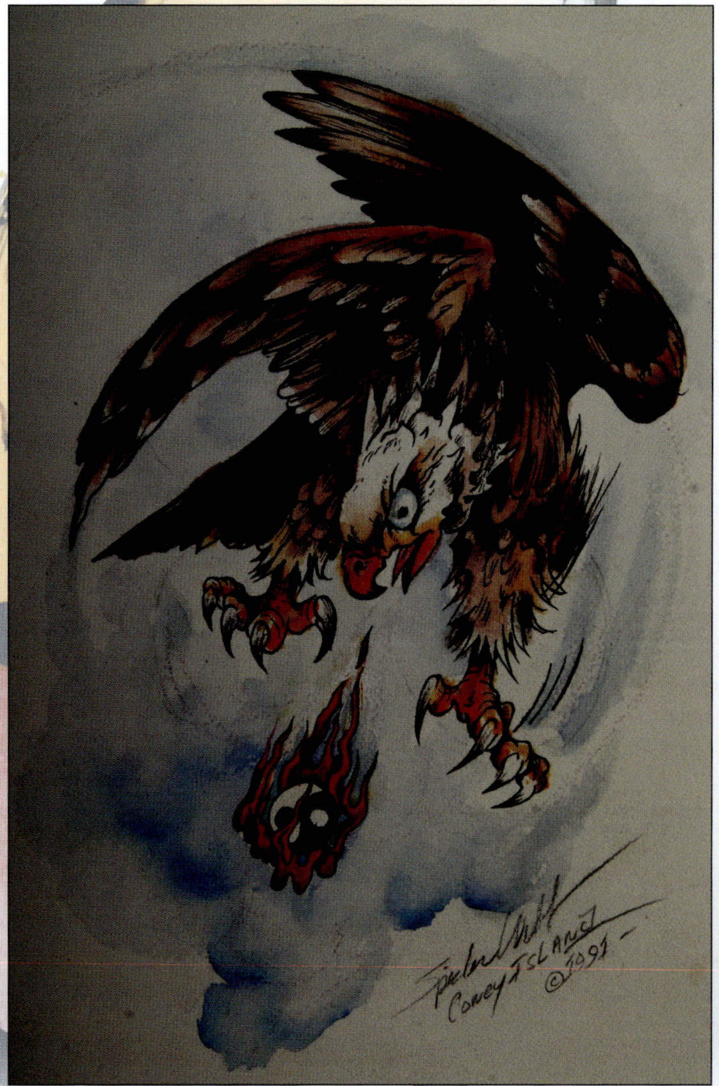

Dancing with Death tattoo
by Spider Webb, 1985.
*Spider Webb Archives*

# Preface

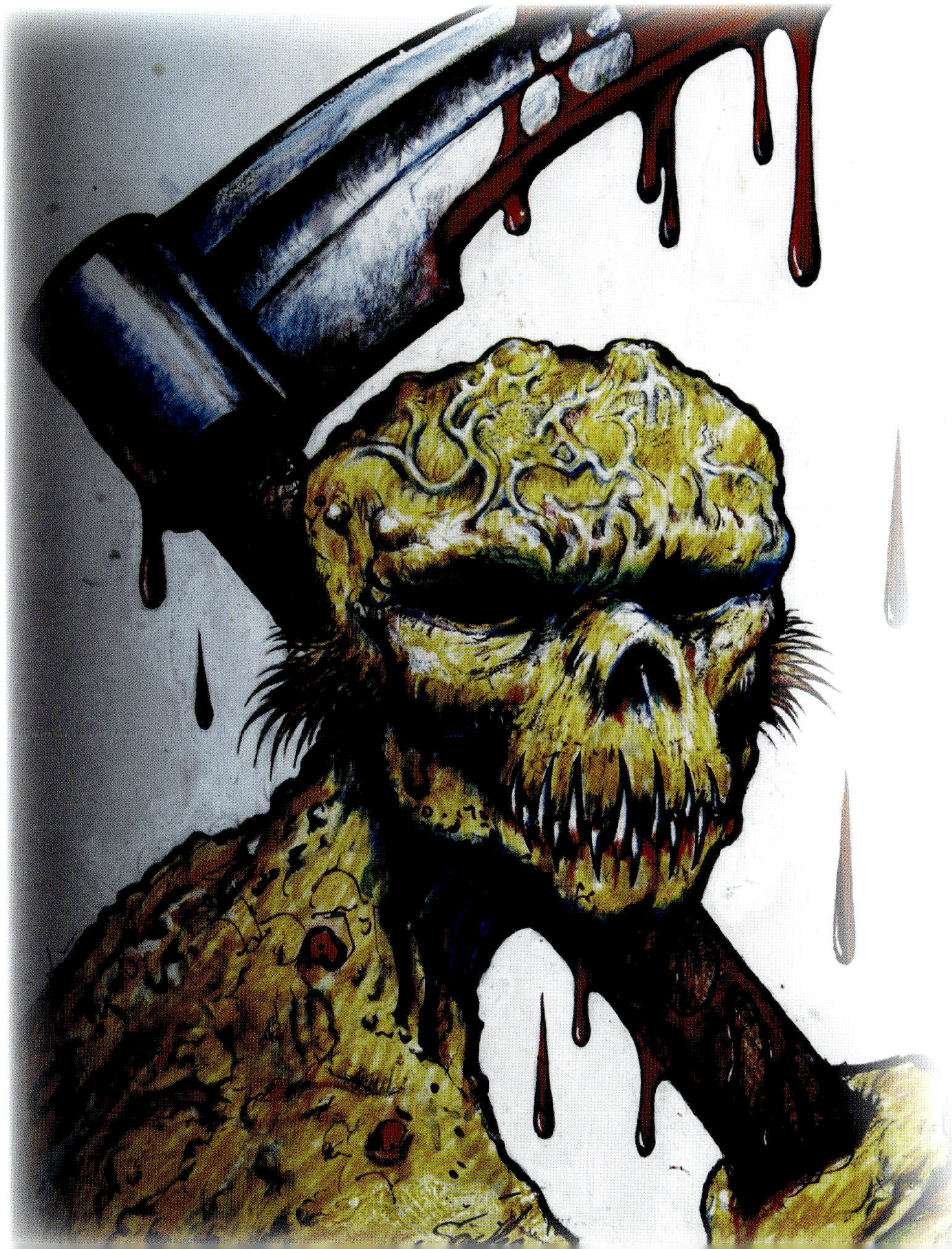

The work in this book was compiled and edited by SOS. She also added the quotes throughout the book, and for that I am eternally grateful. Mark D. Bowyer designed this book and I thank him for a job well done. Enjoy.

—Spider Webb
3 March 2007

"My books are water; those of the great geniuses are wine. Everybody drinks water."

—Mark Twain

# Foreword

The best thing about Spider Webb is that he is a magical guy. I have never met anyone who enjoys life with the intensity of emotions that he does. He is a grown man, yes, with all of the responsibilities that go along with that, and yet, he still has a child's sparkle in his eyes. Those whom are close to him have doubtless heard him exclaim after a great dinner, "that was the best meal of my life!" or on a sunny morning, "this is going to be the best day of my life!" and he means it, every time. If anyone suggests to him some good hearted mischief, whether it is taking photos with outrageous costumes or a funny phone call to an old friend, you will see a slow smile spread across his face as he enthusiastically answers, "yes, yes, yes!"

That is the Spider Webb I know and love. He is the type of person who grabs life by the balls and lives it, no matter what the situation. However, it is not always fun and games. There are serious times, and sad times. He experiences those periods just as intensely and deals with them in the only way he knows how...through his artwork. And what a body of work it is, taking shape in many forms. There are drawings, paintings, books, tattoos, tattoo machines, a magnificent chess set sculpted from tattoo machines, and even music. He plays an electric crutch.

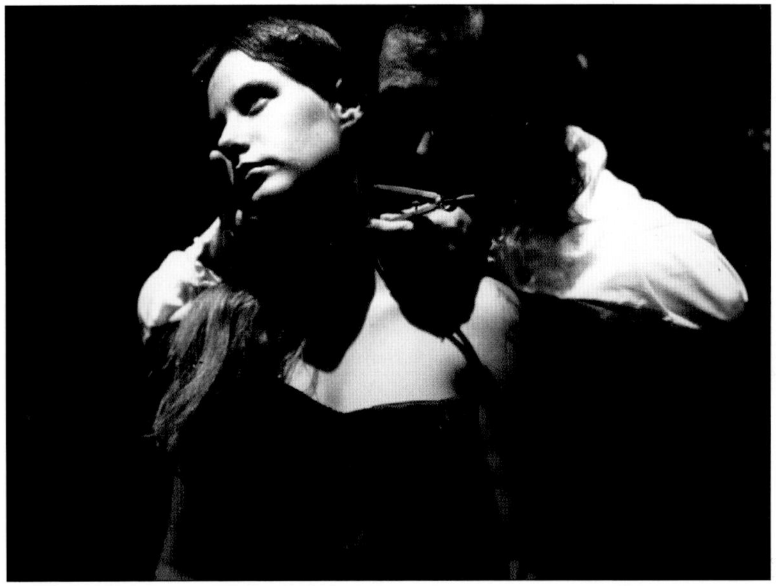

Spider Webb and Polar Bear Patty performing the "Vampire Tattoo," Woodlawn Cemetery, Bronx, New York, 1981. *Photo, © Melba Toast*

I had a chance to experience a very special moment with Spider a few years back, at one of his 9-11 art shows. We were on stage at Am-Jam and there was a big crowd. It was Memorial Day weekend and we wanted to remember those who were no longer with us. I had my bagpipes and Spider was on his electric crutch. We started to play "Amazing Grace" and a silence befell the crowd. As we finished there was a pause and then tremendous cheers. People told us afterward that they were very touched. I was glad to be a part of it.

And I'm glad to write an introduction for Spider's book. Different cultures across the world see him in different ways. In fact, each person has his own beliefs about Spider. Mine are that he is magical. He gets your imagination juices flowing, and I like that feeling.

—Polar Bear Patty
Ashville, NC
2007

# Introduction

The year was 1976. The place, the prestigious Levitan Gallery in New York City. A tattooed leather man was playing "Amazing Grace" on the bagpipes as I walked into the glittering space to see Spider Webb's latest work. Hanging on the gallery walls were huge blow-ups of conceptual tattoos. There were pictures of geometric shapes adorning human body parts, plus a six foot enlargement of "tattoo brush stroke," a homage to artist Roy Lechtenstein.

The crowd was as interesting as the art. Magicians and groupies, witches and priests, tattooed women with skimpy costumes, gay men with tattooed snakes slithering into secret places. Adding to the frenzy were TV crews with cameras, lights, and microphones, plus a hoard of flashing photographers, all circling the star, Joseph Patrick O'Sullivan, the celebrated artist known as Spider Webb.

Spider's revolutionary artwork blew me away. Most tattooists were still in the Stone Age. A few artists were discovering the popular Japanese styles, but tattooing wasn't considered a "fine art." Spider changed all that. Though he too did Japanese tattooing by request, his contribution was inventing a whole new style – part fantasy, part magic, part hallucination. Spider Webb, it turned out, had studied at the Art Students League and the School of Visual Arts, and had earned an MFA degree in art. "Artists like Marcel Dunchamp," he said, "taught me to look at the human body in fresh ways. Sculptors like Brancusi and Calder were freeing sculptures from their pedestals, allowing them to move. That excited me."

Spider Webb had a vision. He would bring tattooing into the modern age, and make it a legitimate and respectable art form. "Tattooing was 50 years behind the other arts," he said. "I put a rocket up its ass."

Spider also led the fight to legalize tattooing in New York City, his home town. The ban, which followed a hepatitis scare in 1961, had driven tattooists underground or out of town. Through legal work and media events (he tattooed porn star Annie Sprinkle on the steps of the Metropolitan Museum of Art) Spider, with help from friends and colleagues, was able to legalize tattooing. It was a big step toward making one of the world's oldest art forms safe, available, and respectable.

I did three books with Spider Webb. Our first, *X-1000*, showed Spider tattooing a thousand X's on a man's leg. Conceptual tattooing! "An interviewer asked me," he said, "if there were any limits to tattooing as an art form. I told her the only limit was the size of the human body. But my answer bothered me, so I came up with X-1000 the World's largest tattoo. I tattooed a tiny X on 999 different people. Then I tattooed 1000 Xs in the shape of one big X. Each book contained a blood print from the still fresh tattoo. The book quickly sold out and is a rare collector's item."

Our next collaboration was *Pushing Ink: The Fine Art of Tattooing*. Simon and Schuster published this one, and the reaction was hugely positive. There were no books on tattoo art at the time, no magazines, no videos, nothing. Spider had single-handedly brought tattoo art into the mainstream of modern art.

Spider and I also worked together on *Tattooed Women*, a collection of old-time tattoo photos he'd acquired from a Florida collector. It was tough work making prints from the old negatives but the experience of working with such important vintage material was priceless.

Spider Webb has produced many more books, each containing ground breaking ideas and images. Recently his book *Butterfly Flash* – water color paintings of butterflies – threw a curve to all of us who have known the flamboyant "clown prince of tattooing." The old blood boiler was now painting – pretty butterflies. Always ahead of the curve, this guy.

Ancient knights who sought to slay dragons were told "Watch out for the tail. Even when the dragon looks finished, his tail can still kill you." The same goes for Spider Webb and his amazing art. Keep your eye on this artist. He ain't finished yet!

—Charles Gatewood<br>San Francisco, California<br>2006

# Classic Tattoo Flash

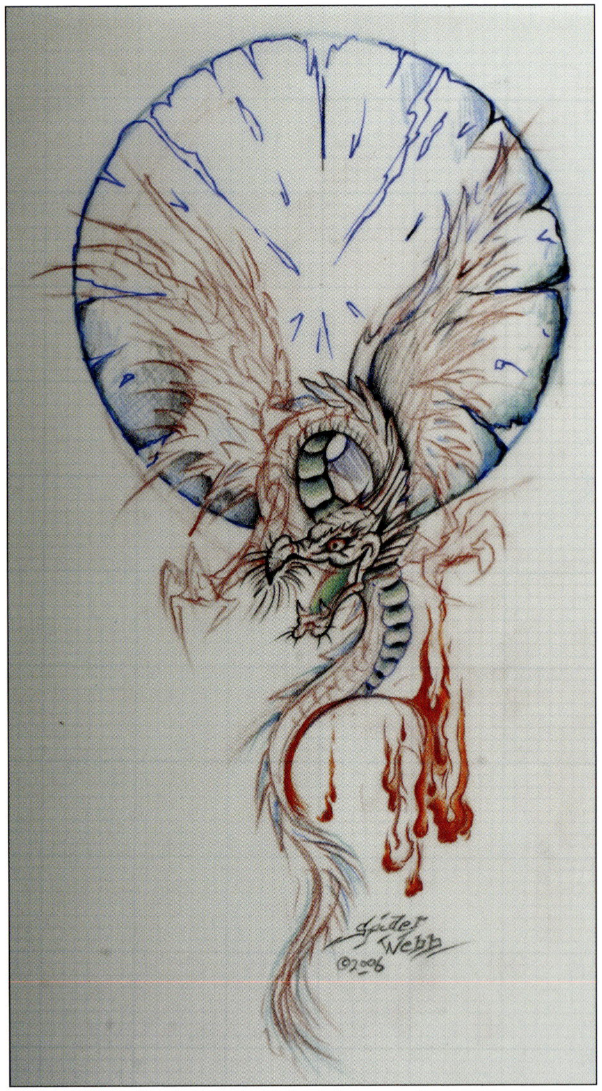

"Replacing Fear for Reason." Pencil on Vellum paper, 11" x 17". 2006.

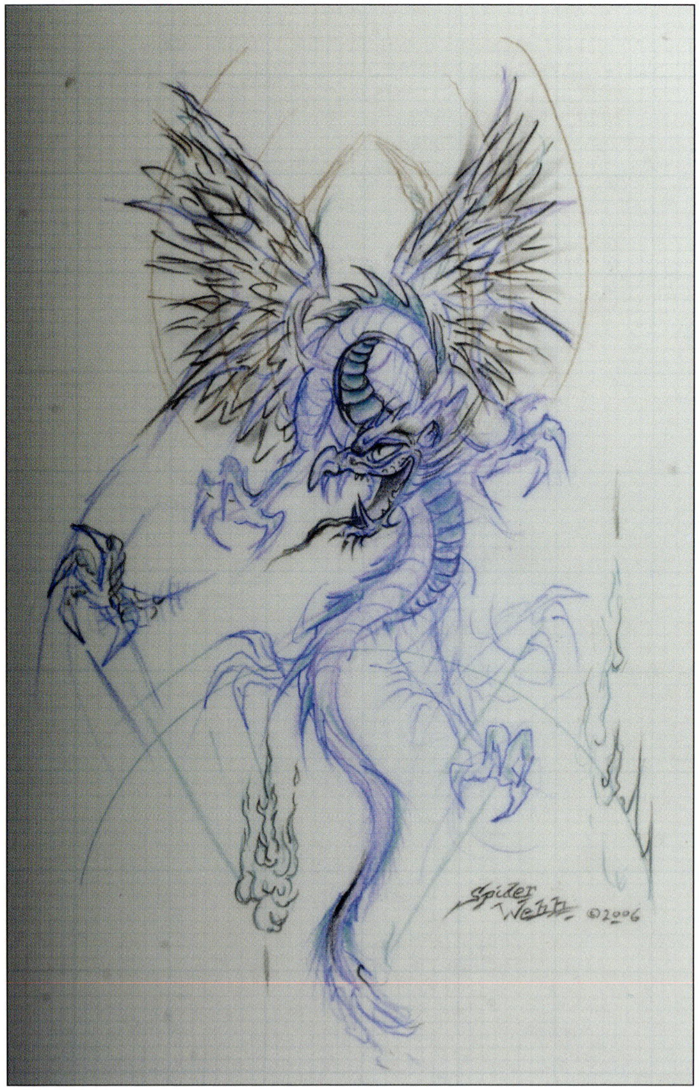

"Planet of Peril." Pencil on Vellum paper, 11" x 17". 2006.

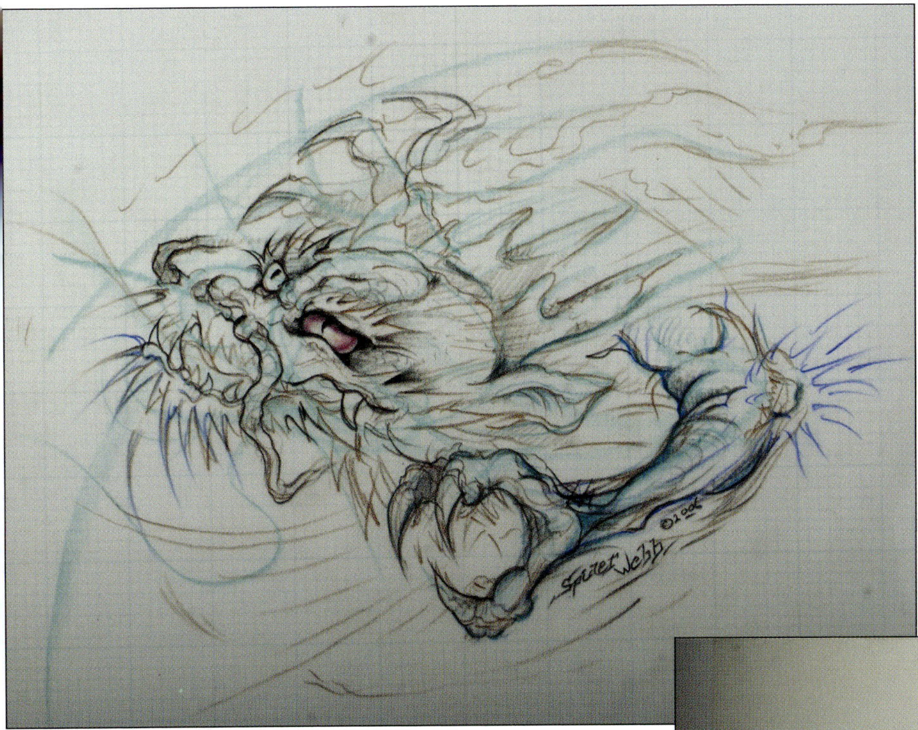

"Tunnel of Terror." Pencil on Vellum paper, 11" x 17". 2006.

"Shattering Doom." Pencil on Vellum paper, 8 1/2" x 11". 1979.

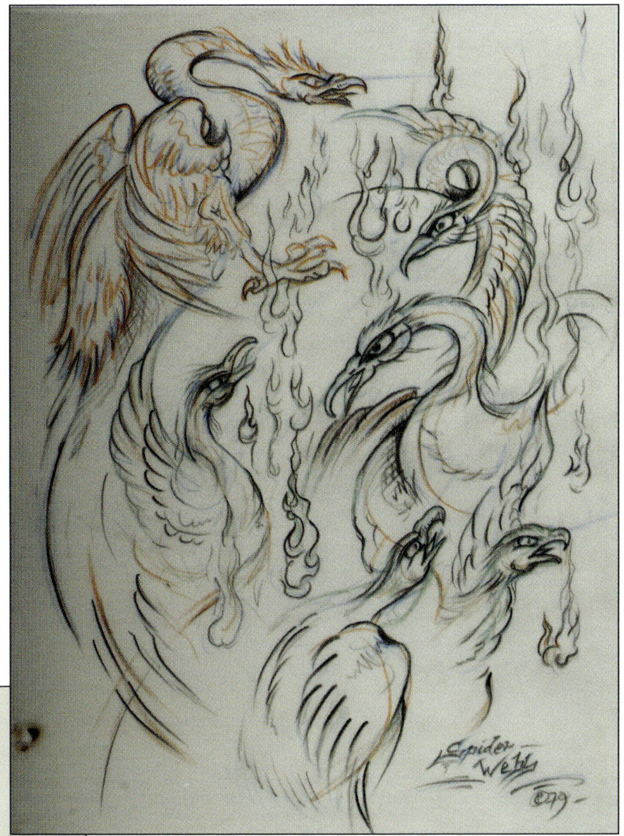

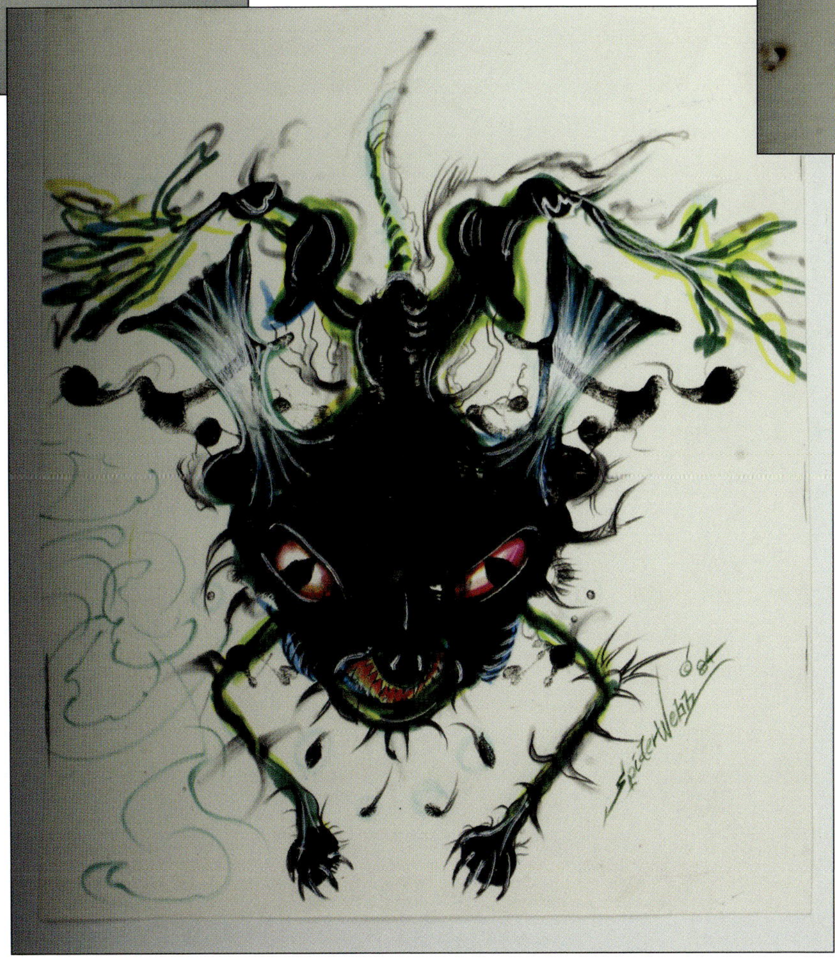

"Flaming Torture." Mixed media on paper, 8 1/2" x 11". 1984.

I'll be dead soon and you'll still be alive. So stop complaining.
—*S.W.*

All repairs, like a broken heart, are short term.
—*S.W.*

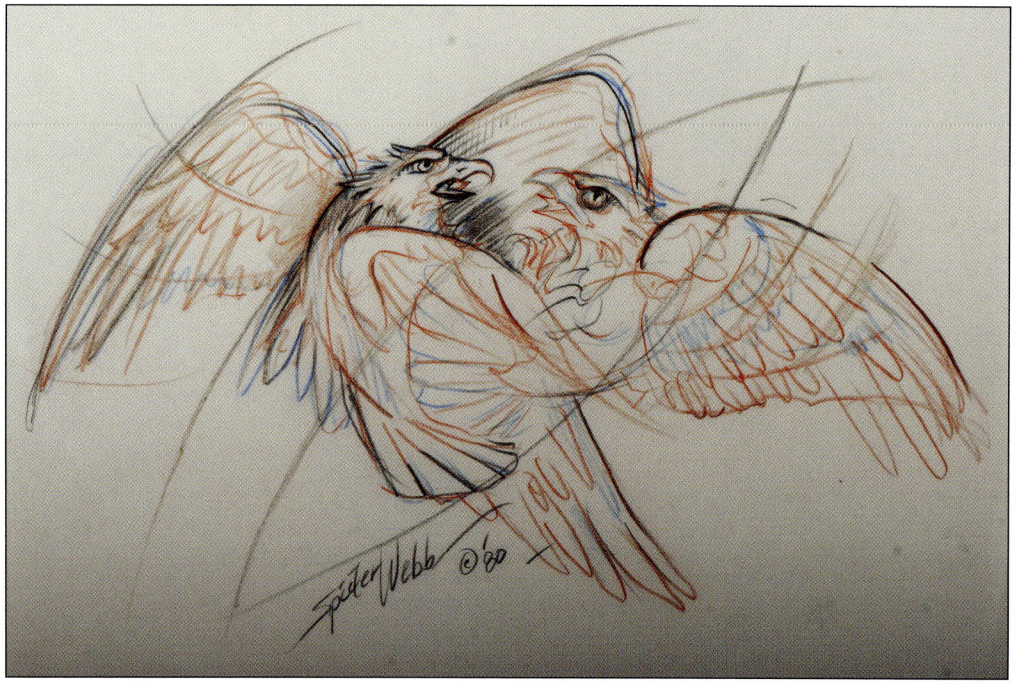

"Tournament of Death." Pencil on Vellum paper, 11" x 17". 1980.

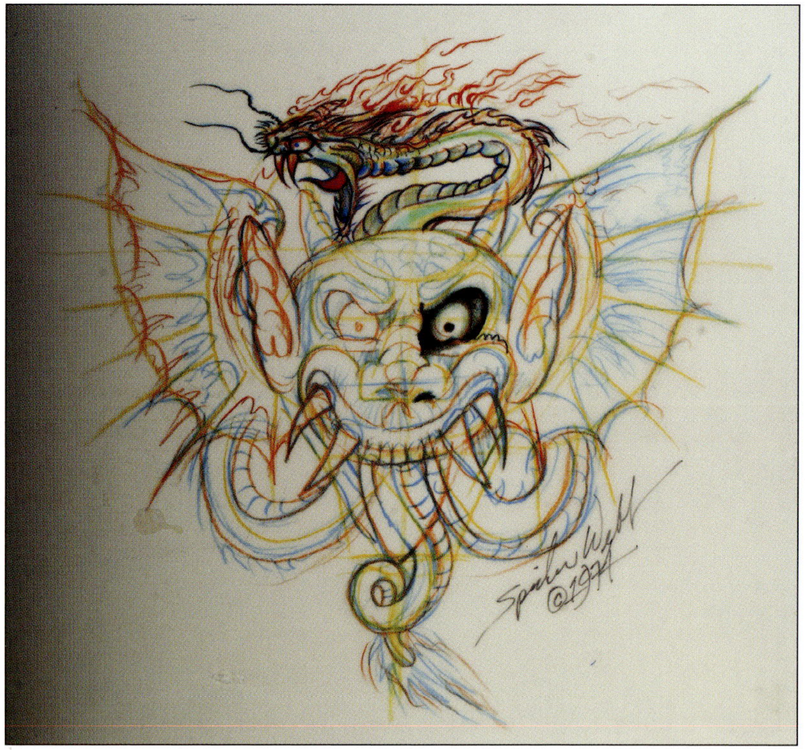

"Unseen Peril." Pencil on Vellum paper, 10" x 12". 1974.

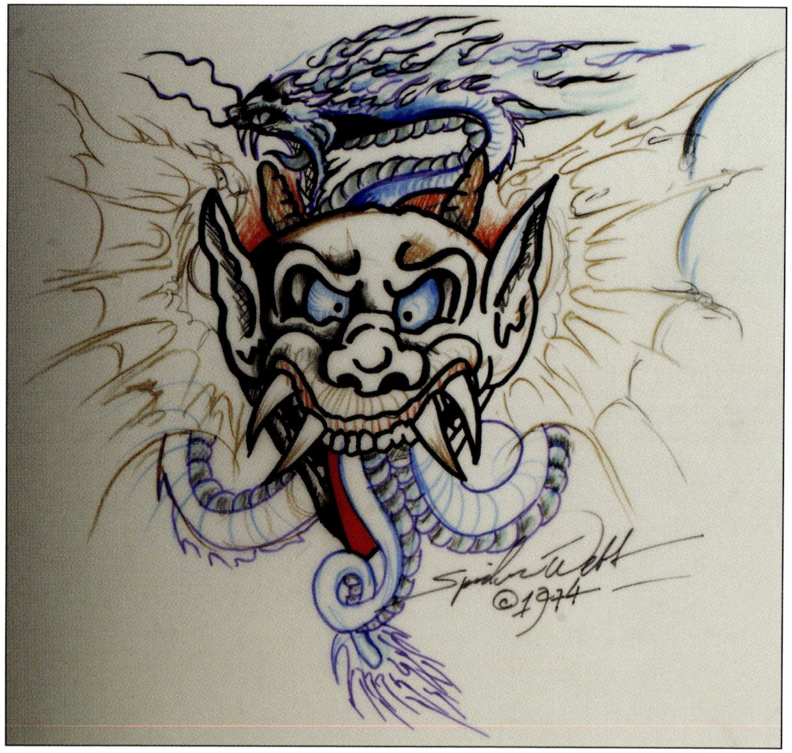

"Tears on a Statue." Pencil on Vellum paper, 10" x 12". 1974.

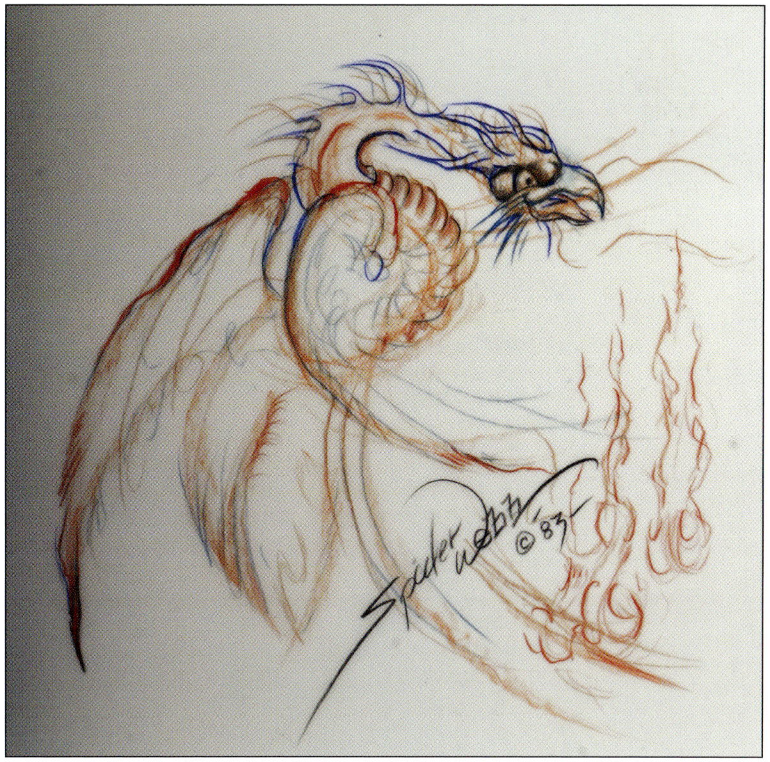


"Butcher Bill Poole." Pencil on Vellum paper, 10" x 12". 1983.

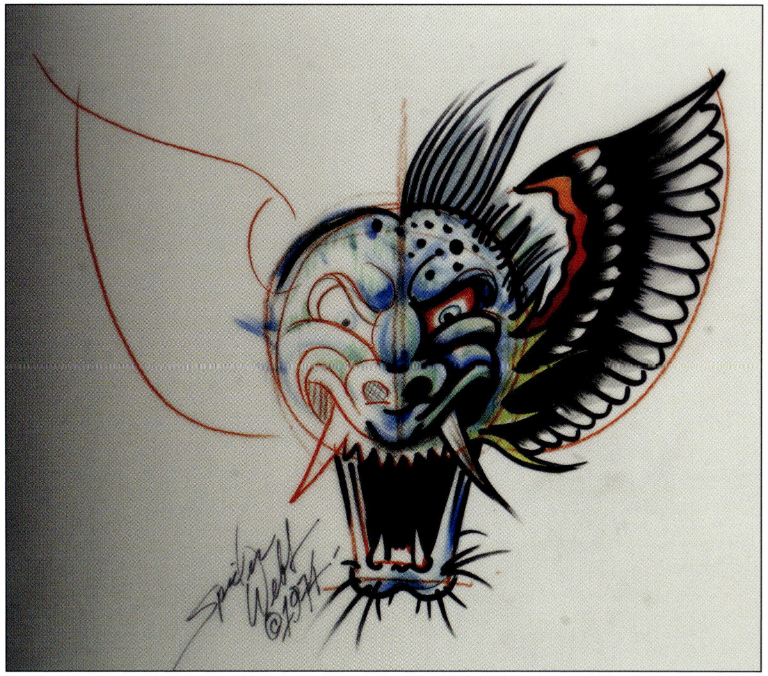


"Hold Fast." Pencil on Vellum paper, 10" x 12". 1974.

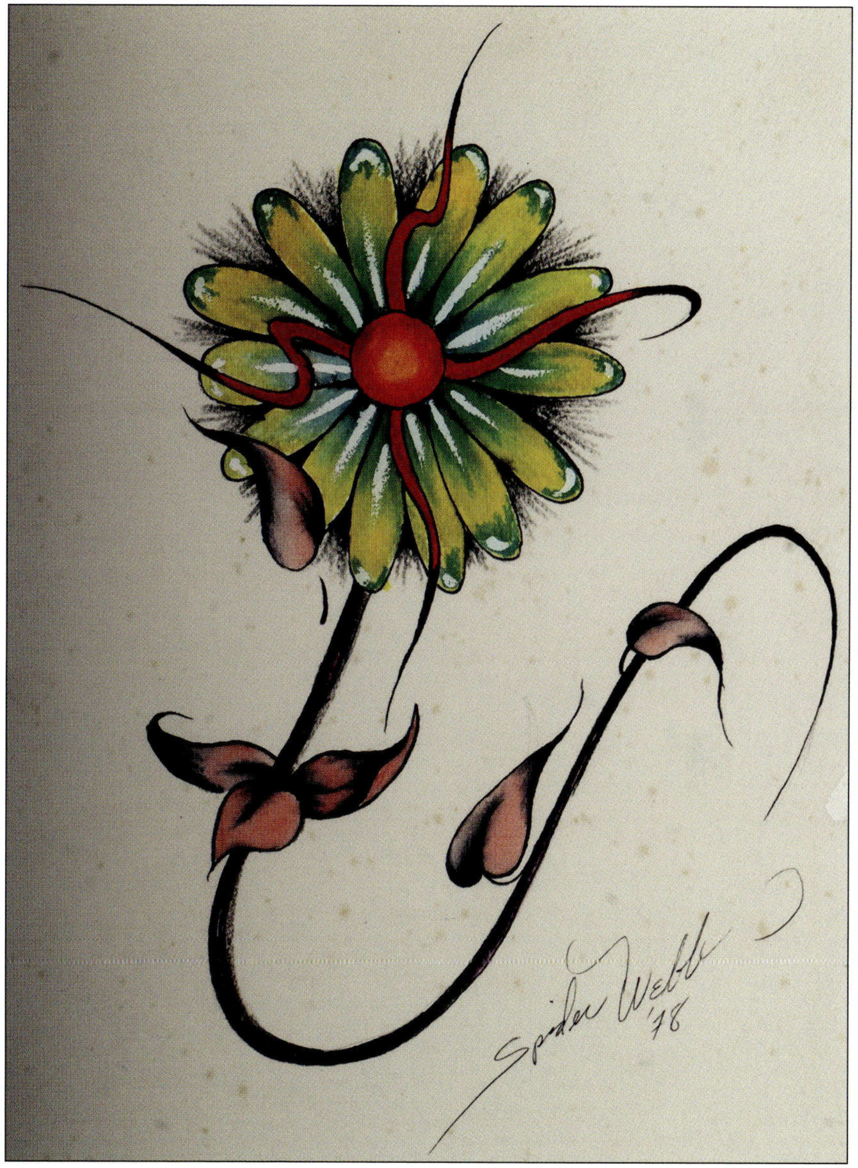


"Hold De Butt." Ink and watercolor on Archer paper, 9" x 12". 1978.

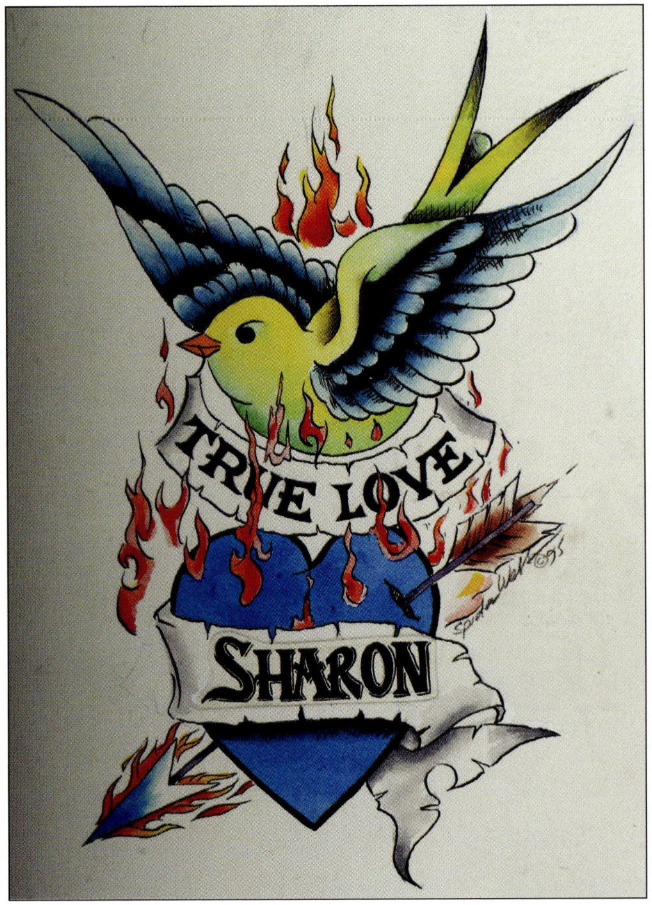


"Big Sue (the Turtle)." Ink and water color on Archer paper, 9" x 12". 1995.

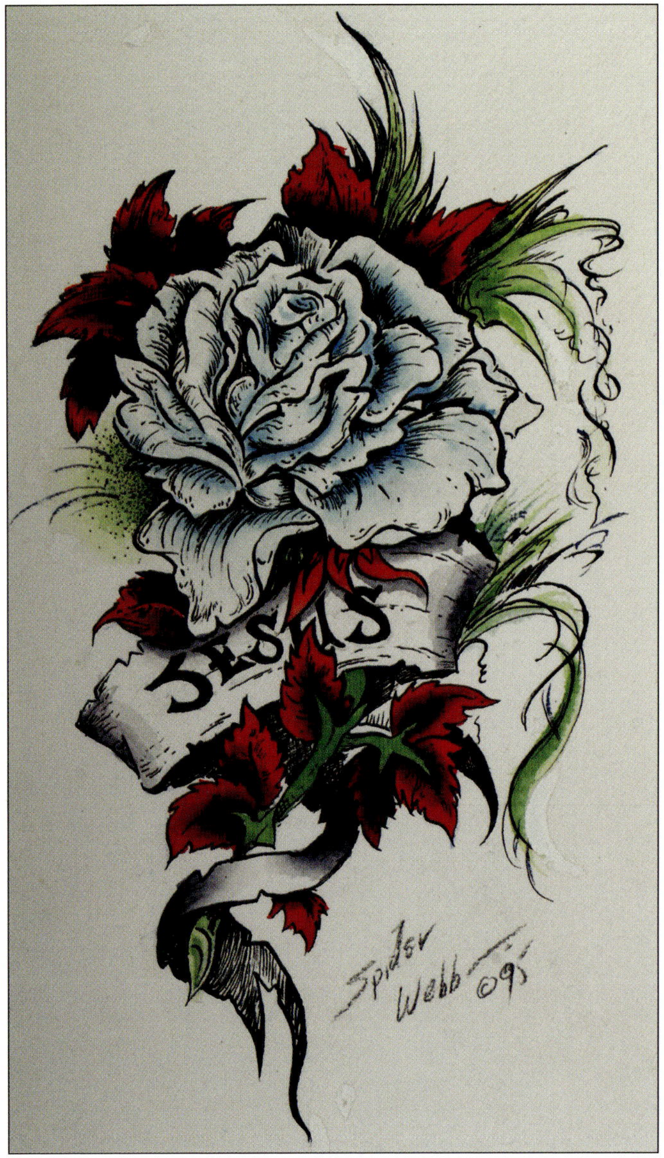


"Swamp Angels." Ink and watercolor on Archers paper, 9" x 12". 1995.

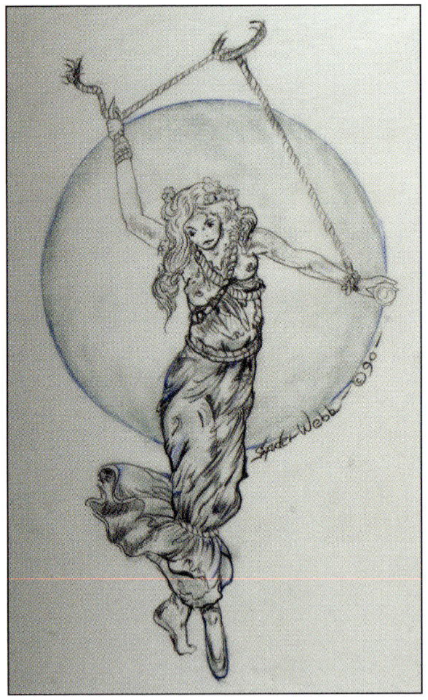

"Daybreak Boys." Pencil on Vellum paper, 9" x 12". 1990.

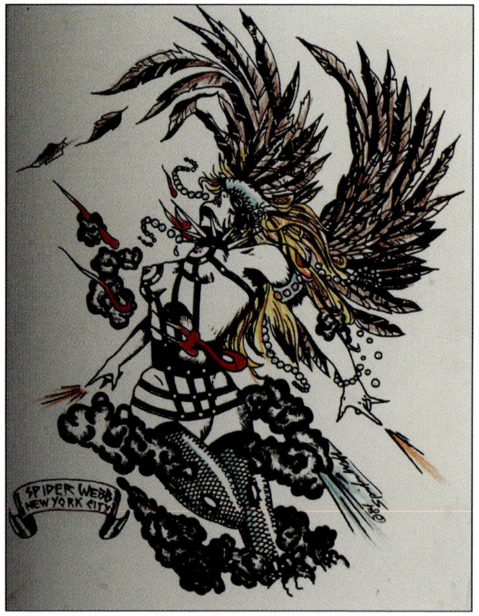


"Whyos." Ink and watercolor on Archers paper, 9" x 12". 1984.

I couldn't help myself or anyone else, all was lost.
It was yesterday's rainbow and not a dream.

—*S.W.*

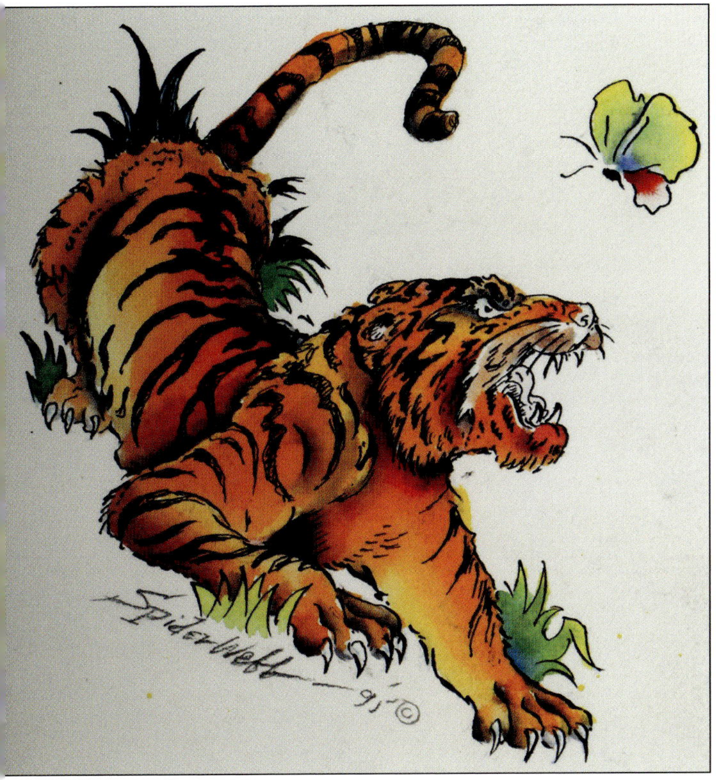

"Kate Flannery." Ink and watercolor on Archers paper, 9" x 12". 1995.

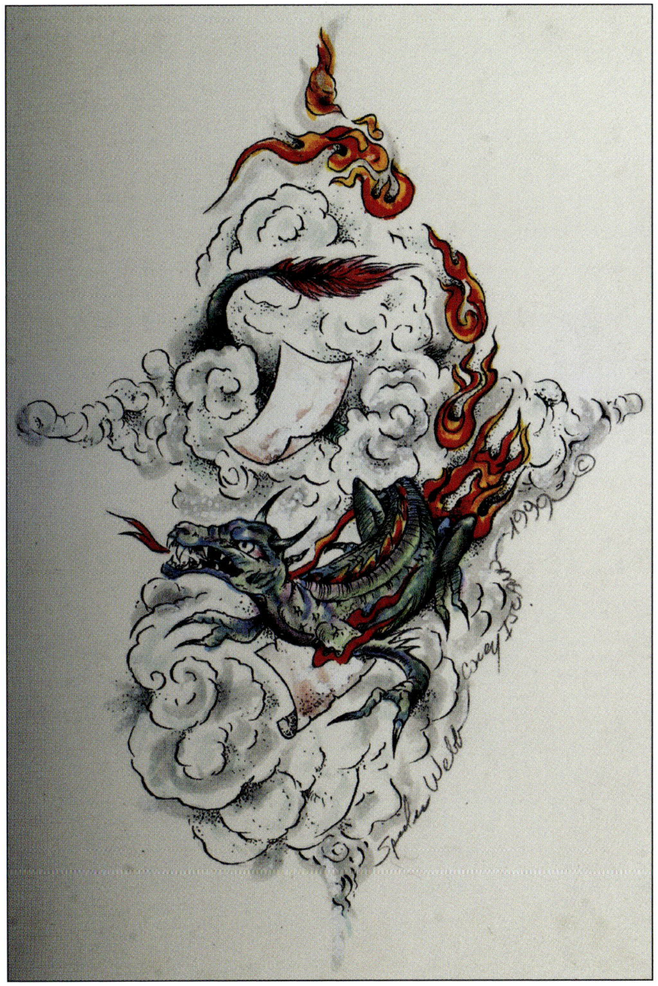

"Hudson Dusters." Ink and watercolor on Archers paper, 9" x 12". 1999.

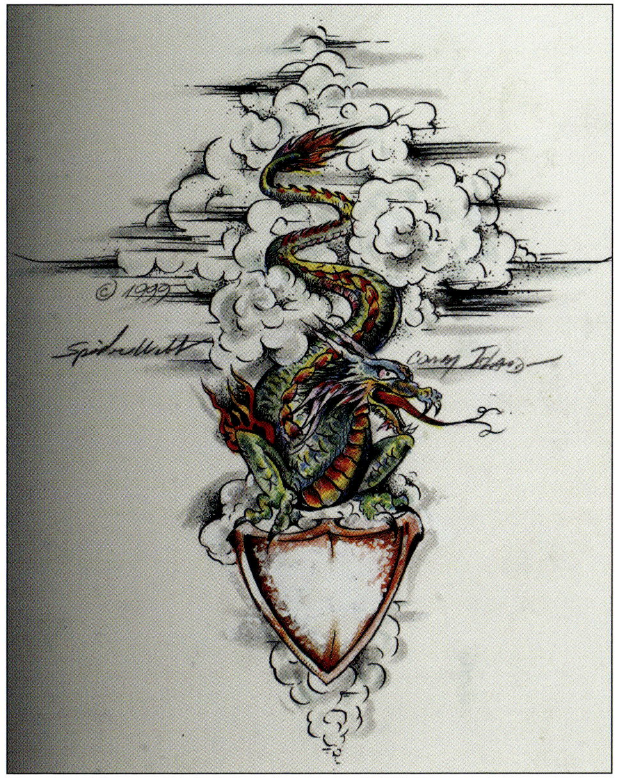

"Your House is Built on Babies' Skulls." Ink and watercolor on Archers paper, 9" x 12". 1999.

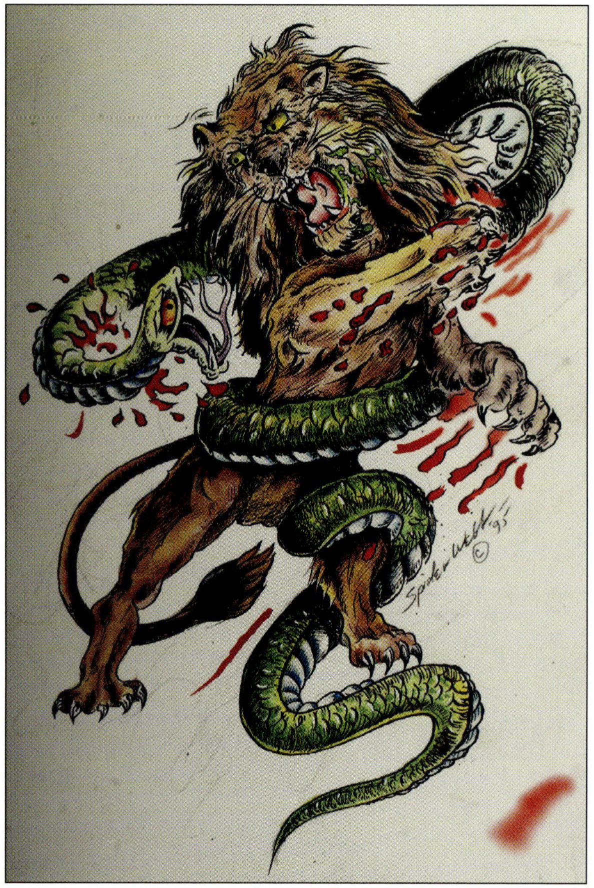

"Red Light Lizzie." Ink and watercolor on Archers paper, 9" x 12". 1995.

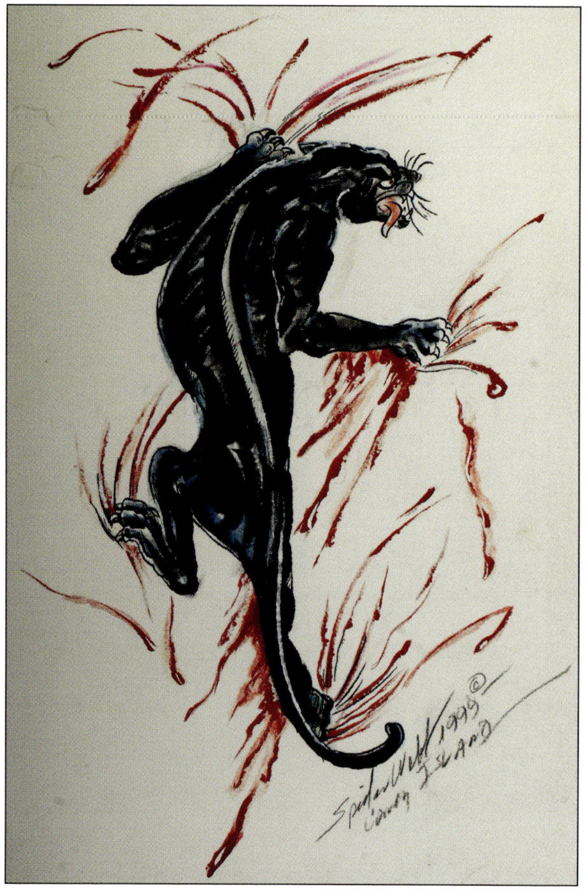

"Jane the Grabber." Mixed media on Archers paper, 9" x 12". 1999.

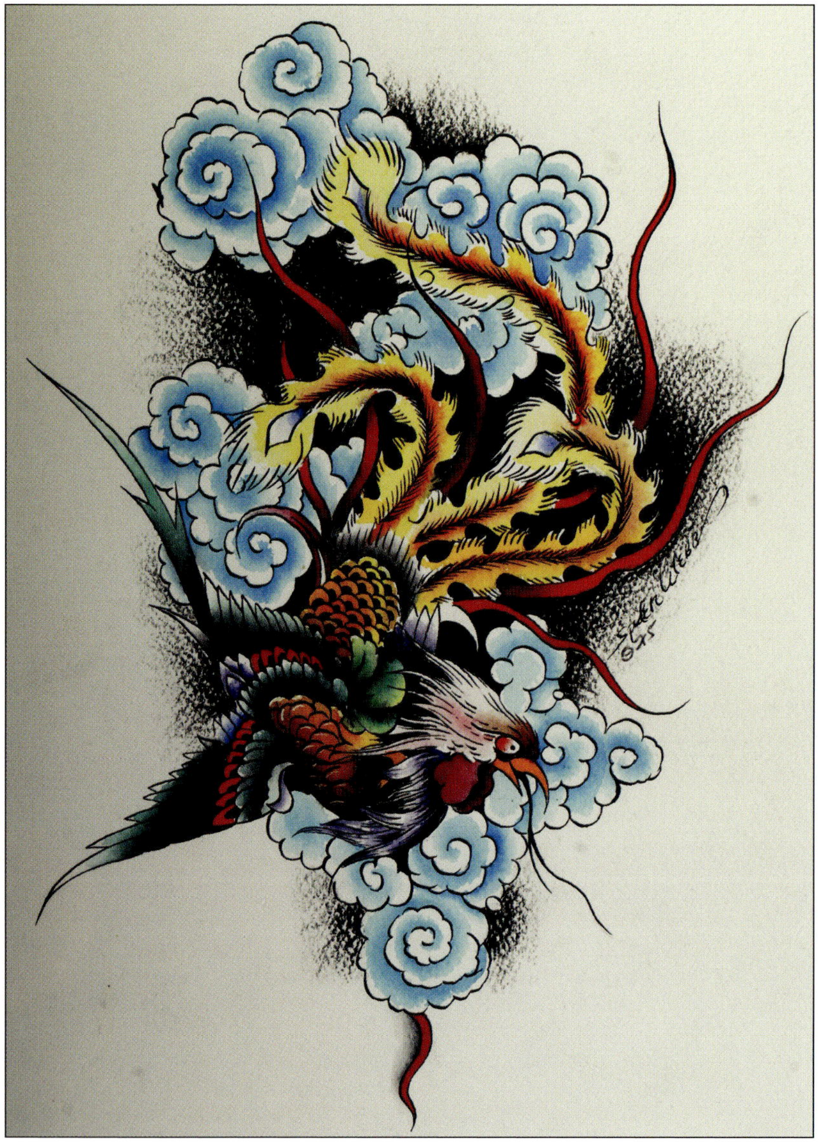

"Satan's Circus." Ink and watercolor on Archers paper, 9" x 12". 1975.

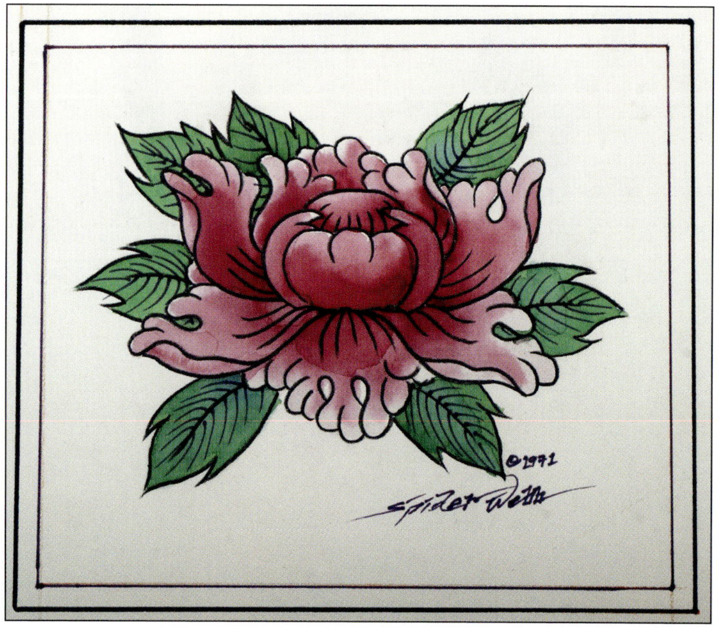

"Poverty Row." Ink and watercolor on paper, 8" x 10". 1971.

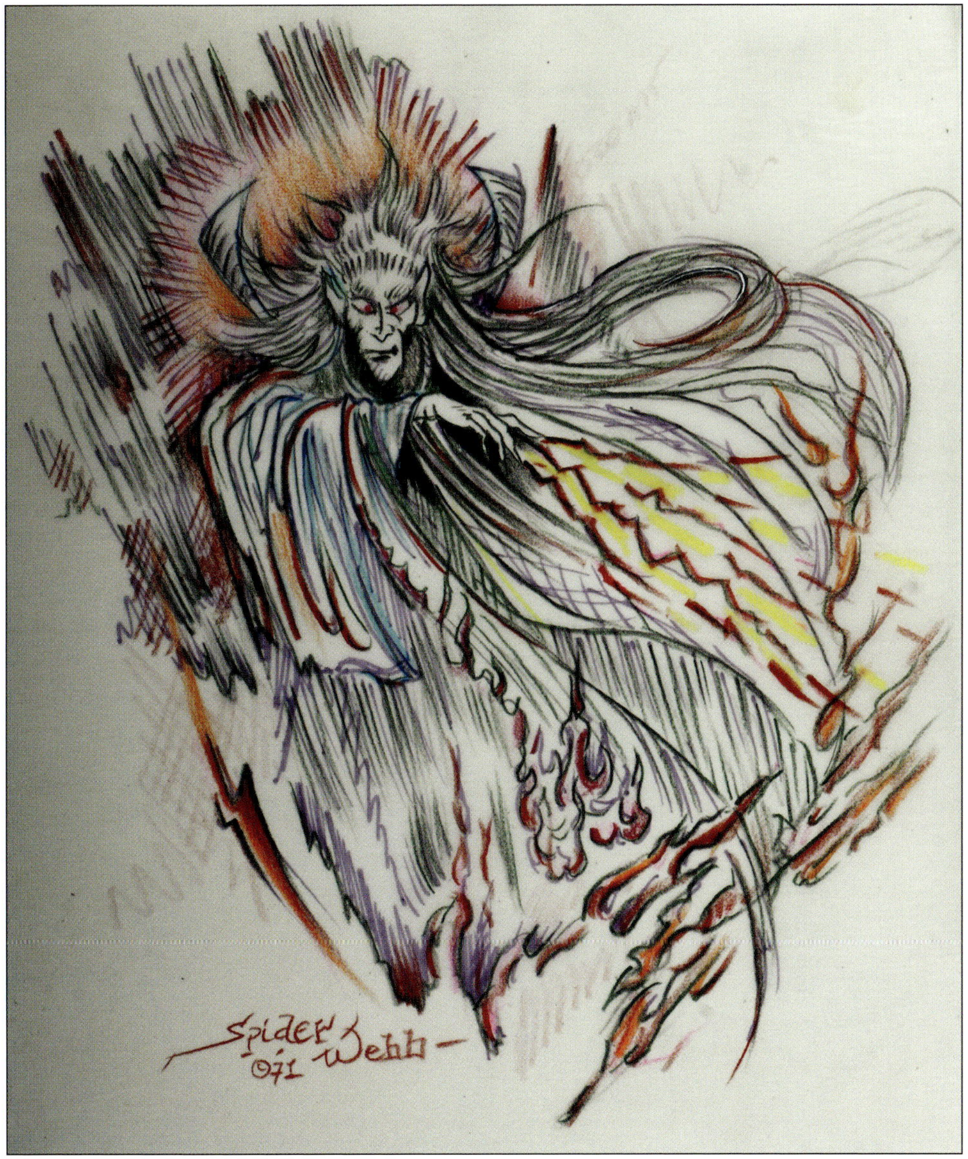


"Apples from Strangers." Pencil on Vellum paper, 8" x 10". 1971.

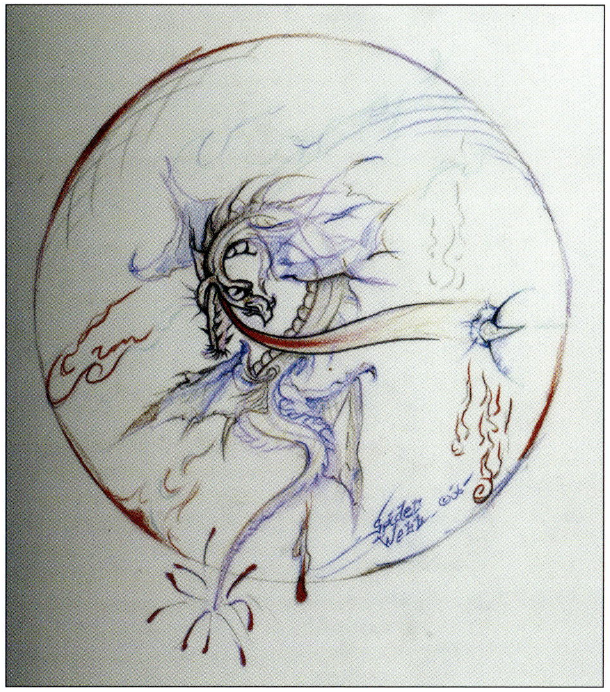

"MSG for Don." Pencil on Vellum paper, 8" x 10". 2006.

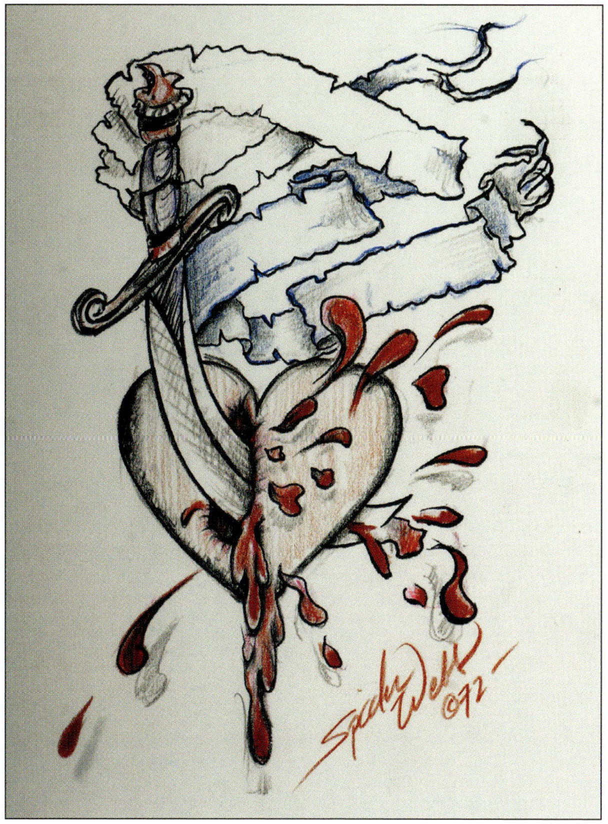

"NYC Bin Ching Union." Pencil on Vellum paper, 9" x 12". 1972.

From AOL news (Oct. 29): "An inmate accused of forcibly tattooing a slain ten year old girl's name onto her killers forehead in an Indiana prison, was the victim's cousin, a family friend said." And I say, "Just another very good reason for tattoo starter kits."

—*S.W.*

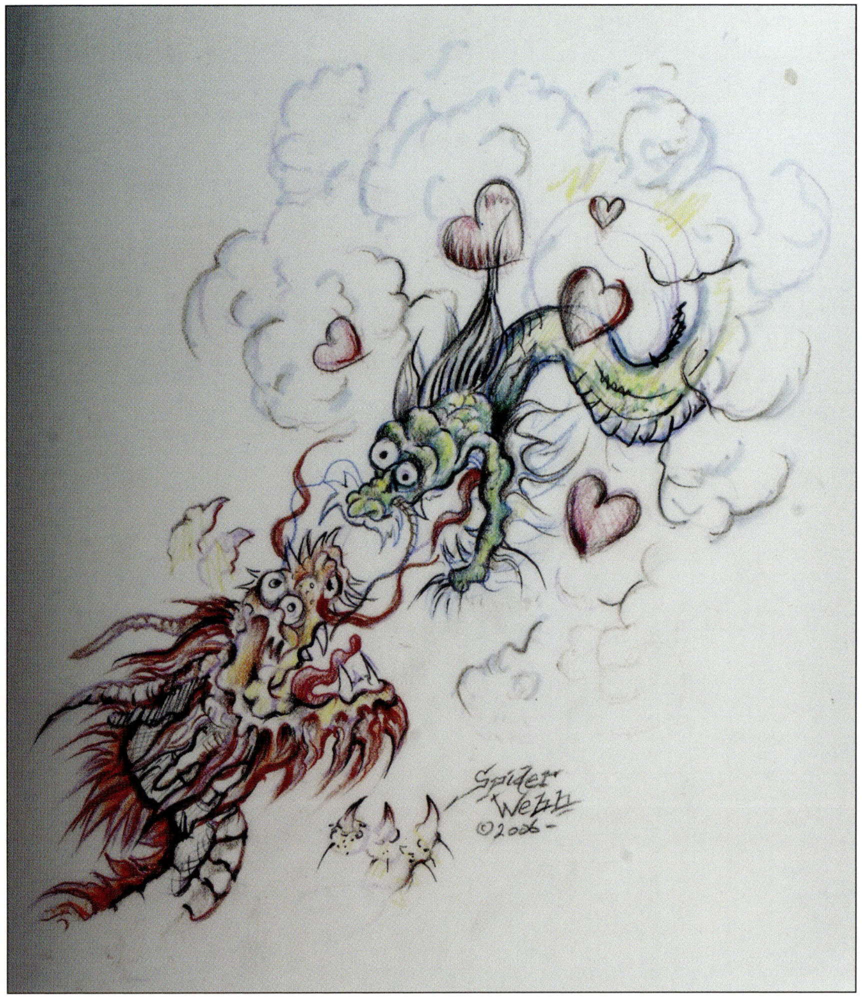


"Hooch-Goochy Mary." Pencil on Vellum paper, 8 1/2" x 10". 2006.

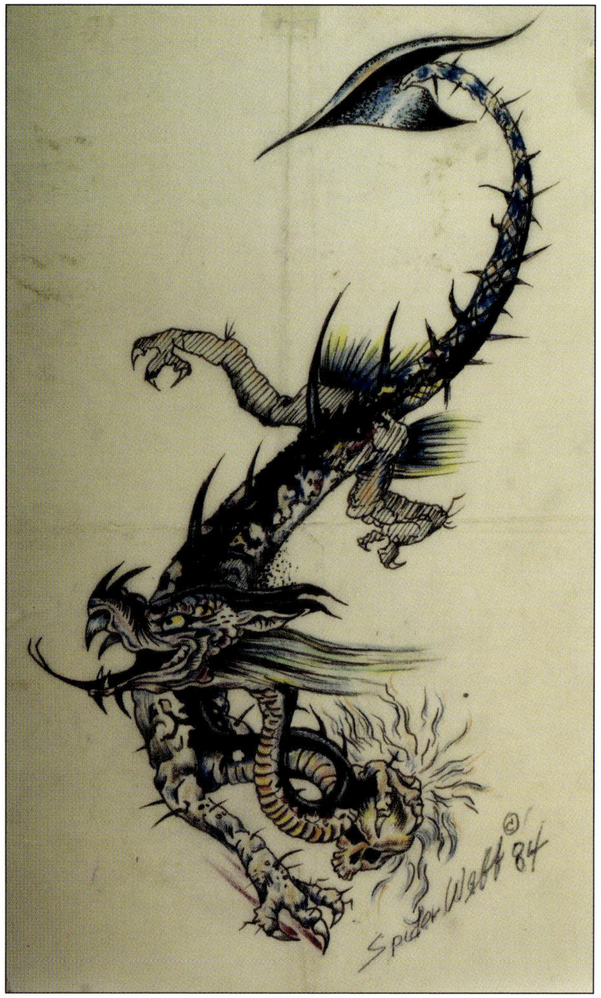


"Ice Cream Eaters." Mixed media on paper, 8" x 11". 1984.

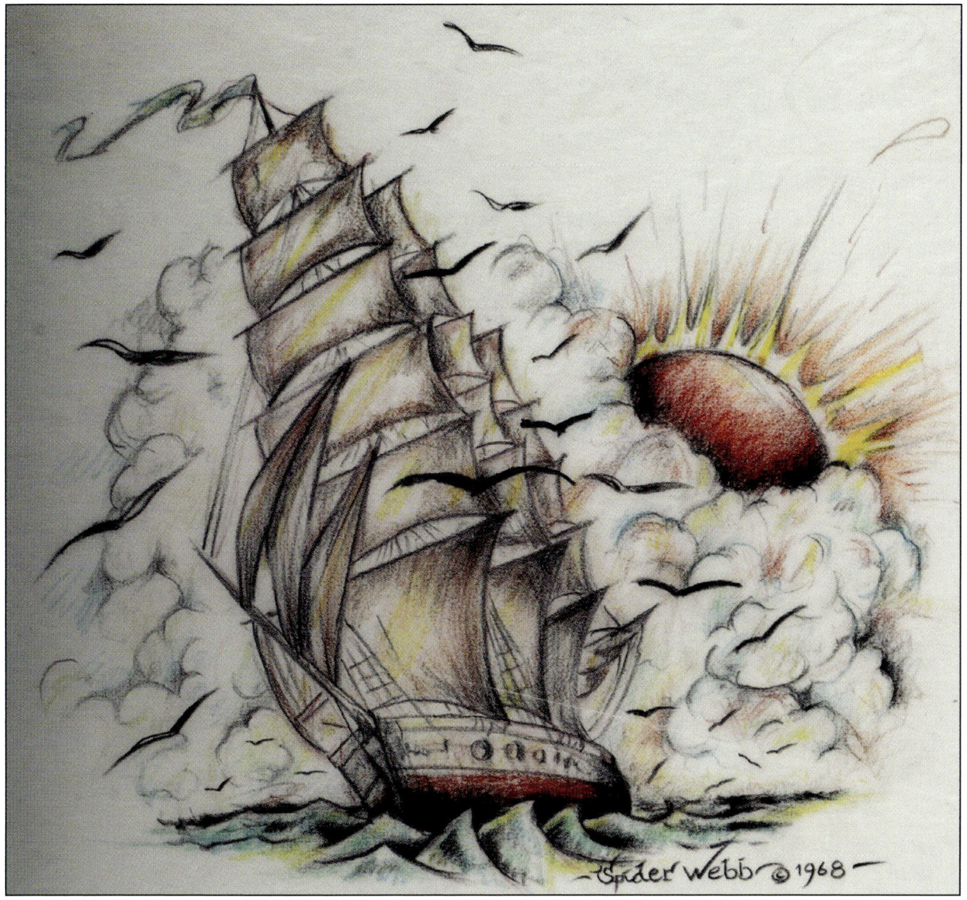


"Fagin's Kiddies." Pencil on paper, 9" x 12". 1968.

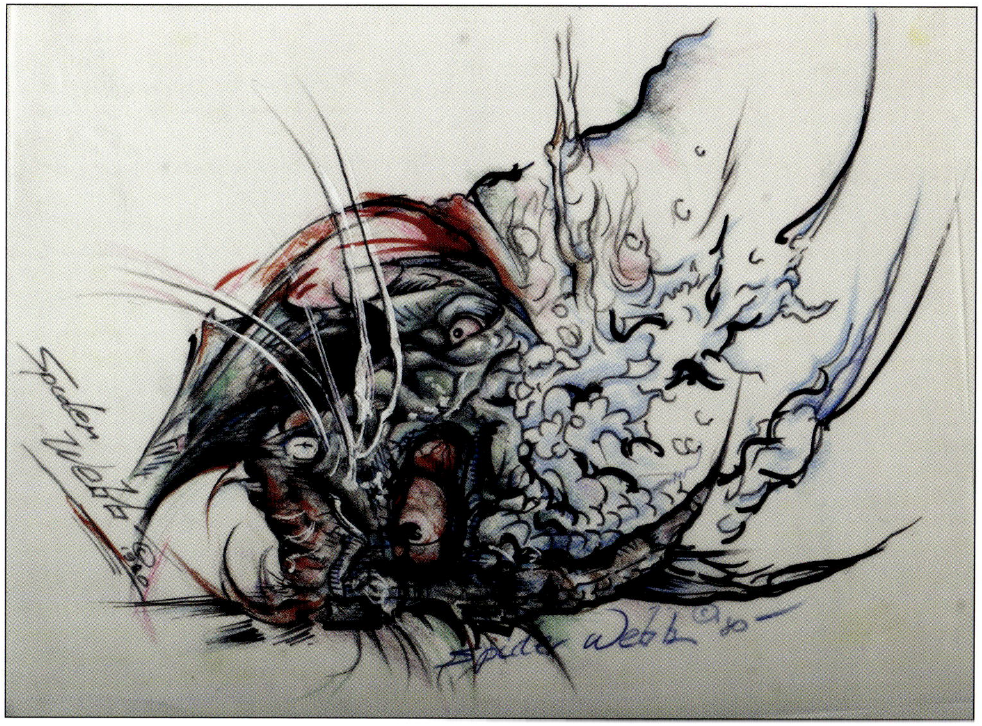


"Slung-Shot." Pencil on Vellum paper, 9" x 12". 1980.

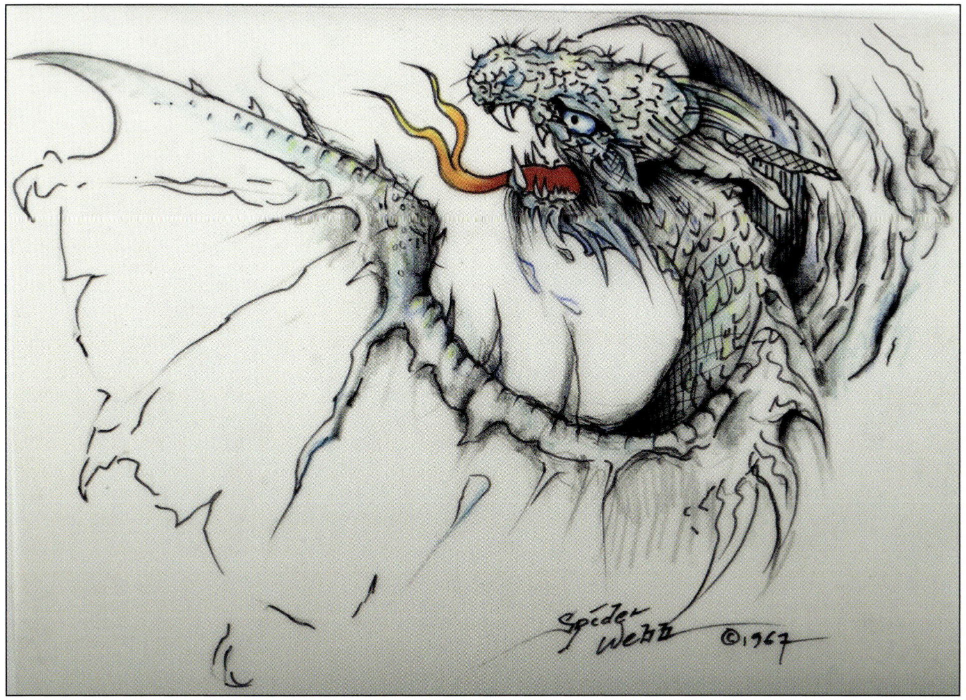


"From Hell to Breakfast." Pencil on Vellum paper, 9" x 12". 1967.

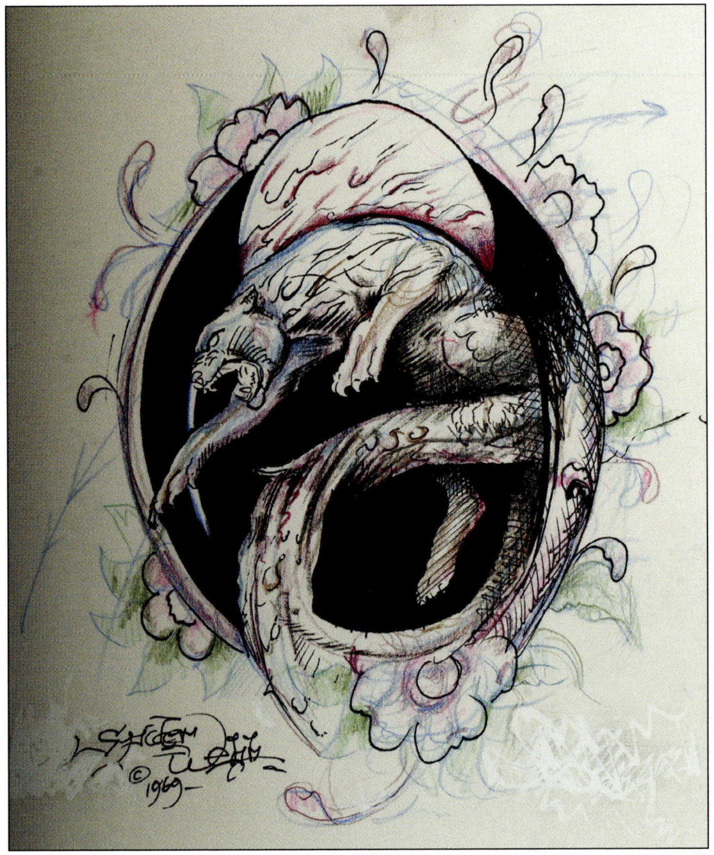

"Barrel Fever." Pencil on Vellum paper, 9" x 12". 1969.

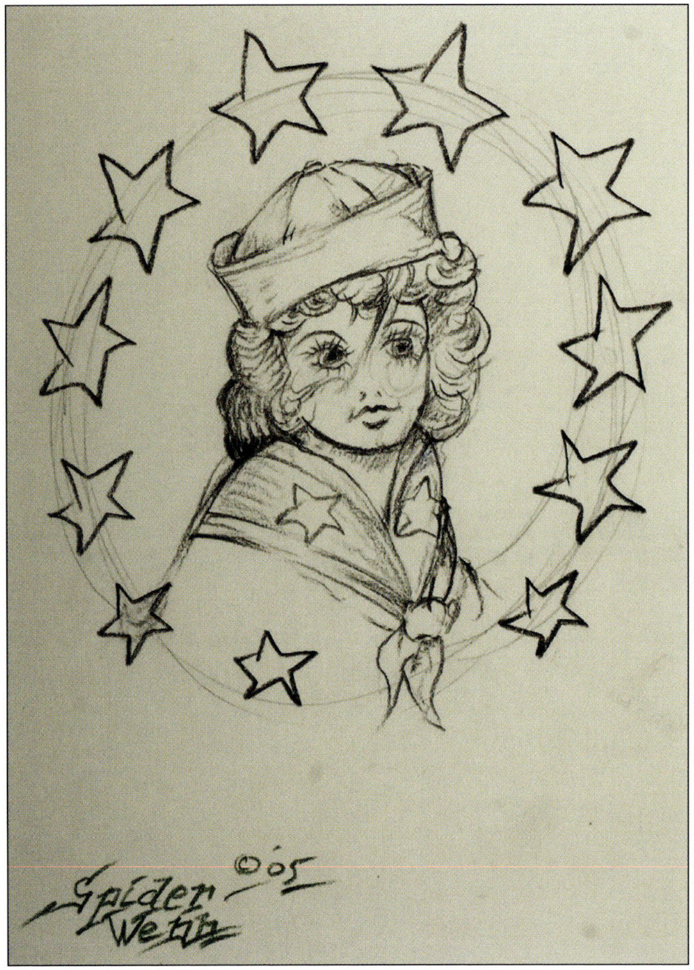


"The Tombs." Pencil on Vellum paper, 8" x 10". 2005.

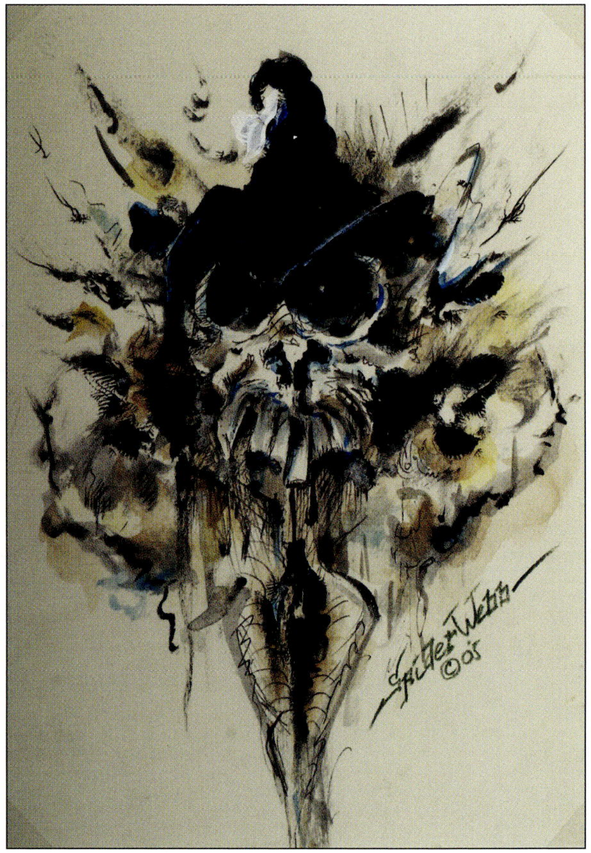

"Cows and Kisses." Pencil on Vellum paper, 8" x 10". 2005.

I was just trying to show the little girl scout some affection when her mum yelled at us...

—*S.W.*

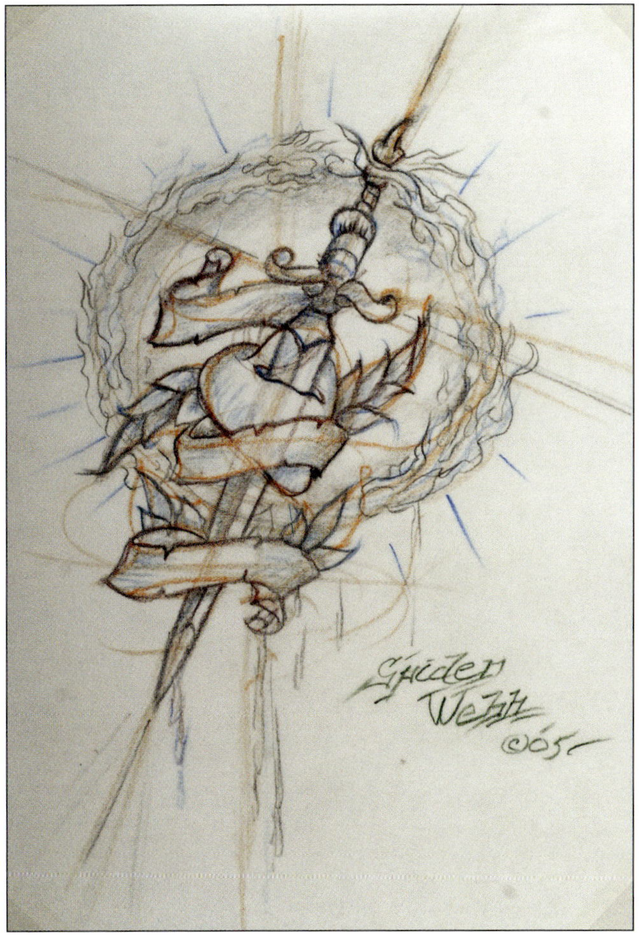

"Flash Panny." Pencil on Vellum paper, 4" x 8". 2005.

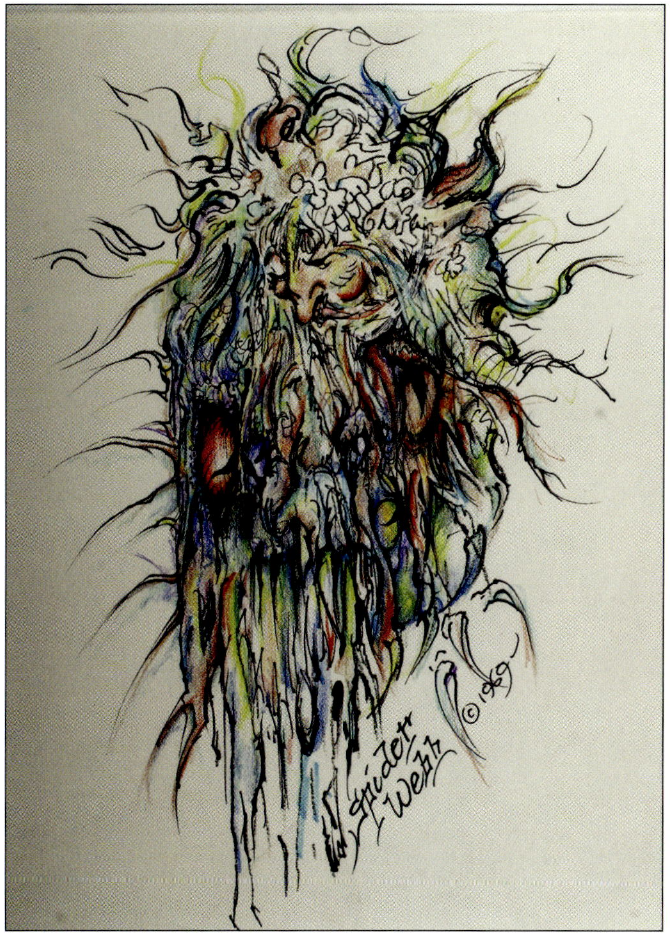

"Frog and Pudding, NYC." Pencil on Vellum paper, 9" x 12". 1969.

People, incapable of pure love, always have to mix love and hate.

—*S.W.*

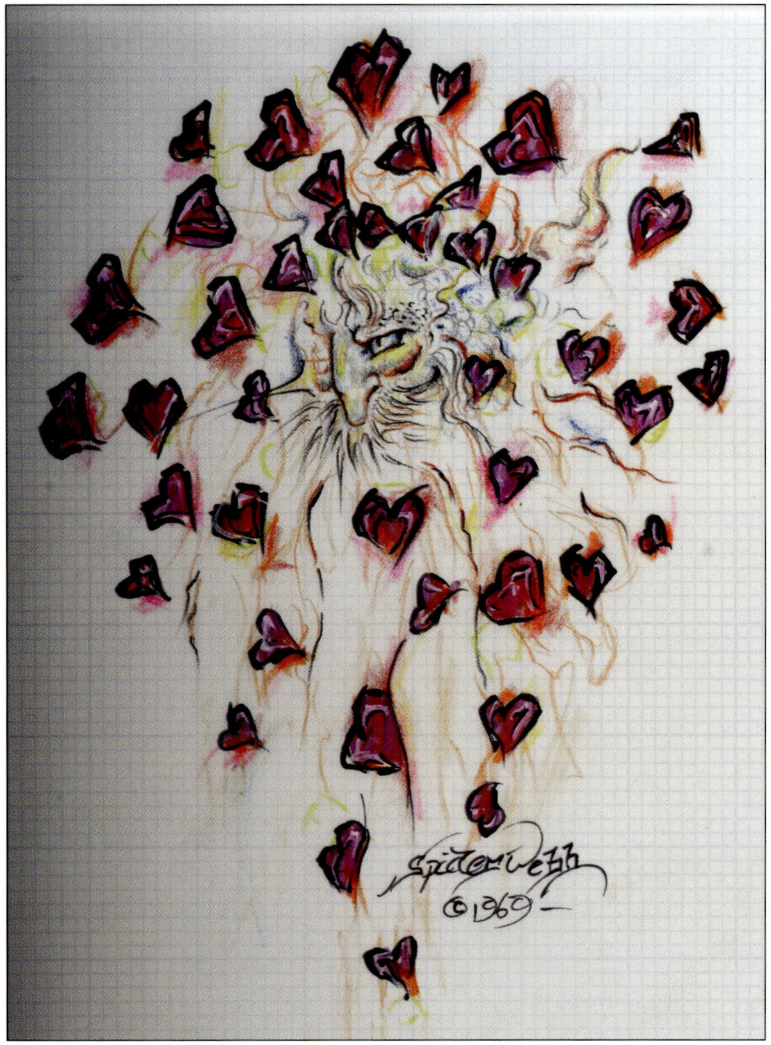


"Left Handed Wife." Pencil on Vellum paper, 9" x 12". 1969.

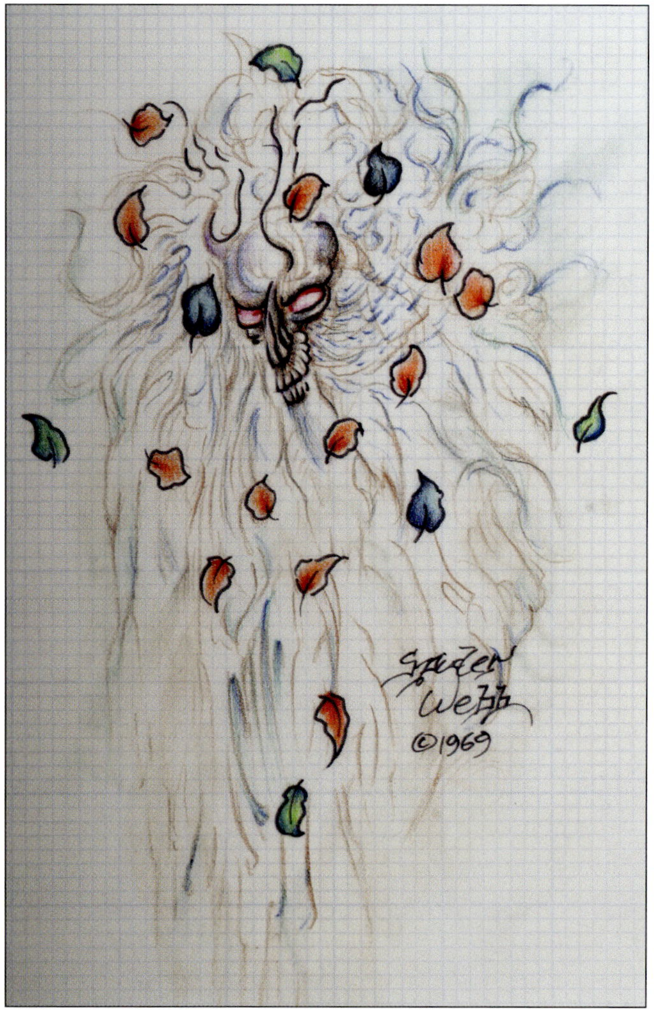


"Tombstone Smile." Pencil on Vellum paper, 9" x 12". 1969.

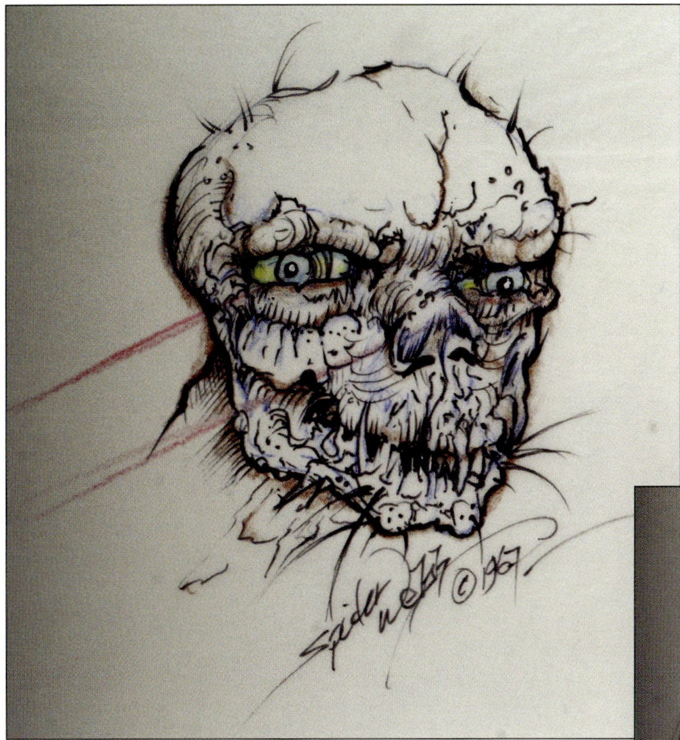

"Venus' Curse." Pencil on Vellum paper, 11" x 17". 1967.

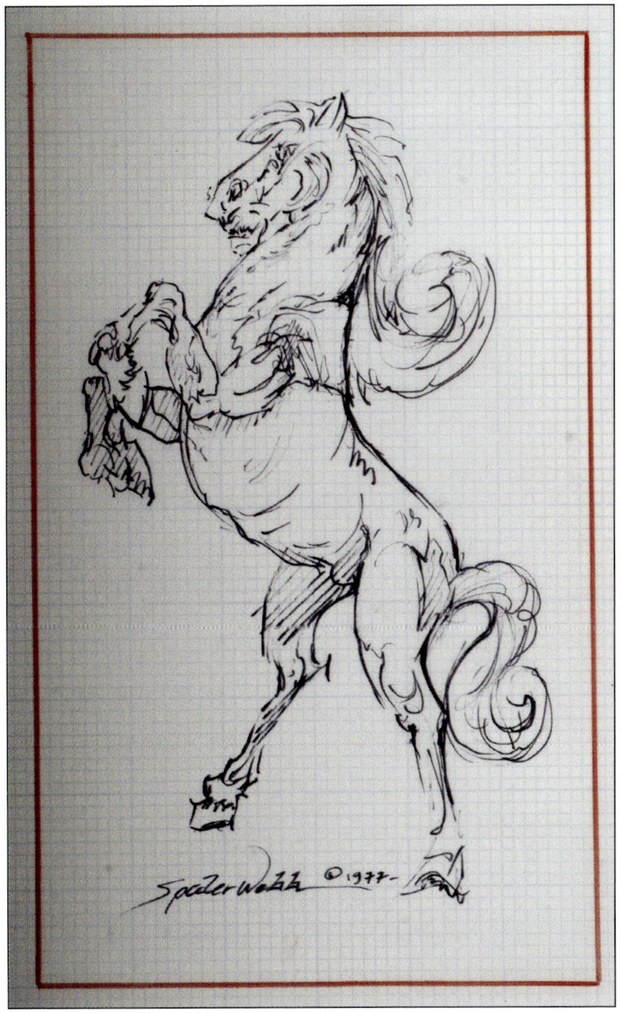

"Drifting Toward Unparalleled Catastrophe." Pencil on Vellum paper, 11" x 14". 1977.

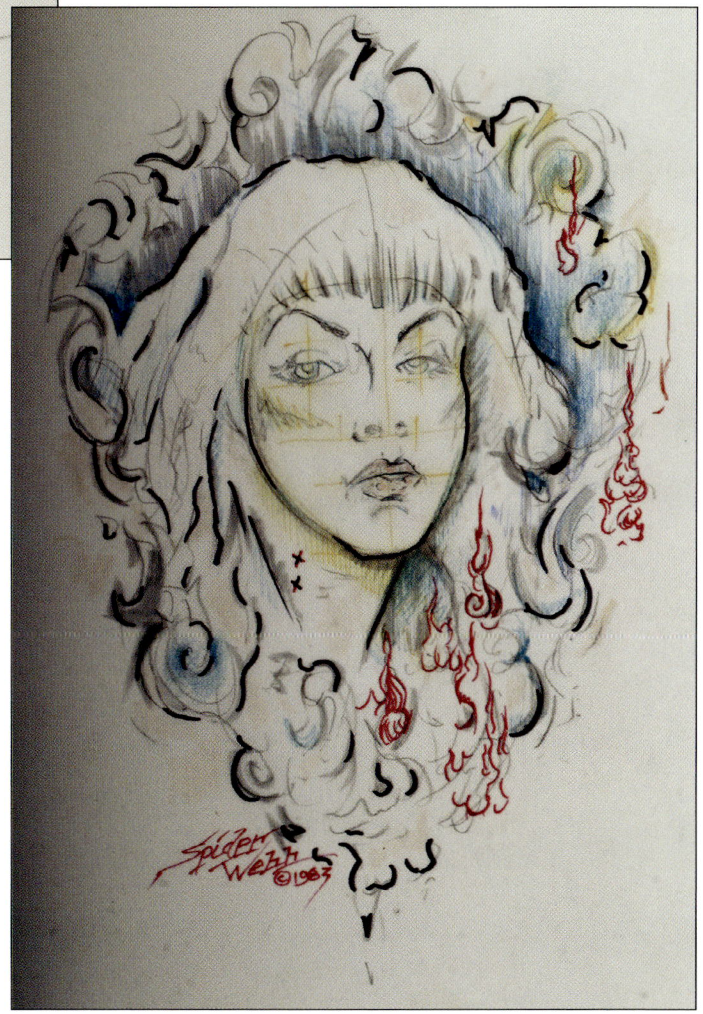

"Autonomous Reality." Pencil on Vellum paper, 11" x 17". 1983.

Because of high buildings in New York City, there is always people to look down on.
—*S.W.*

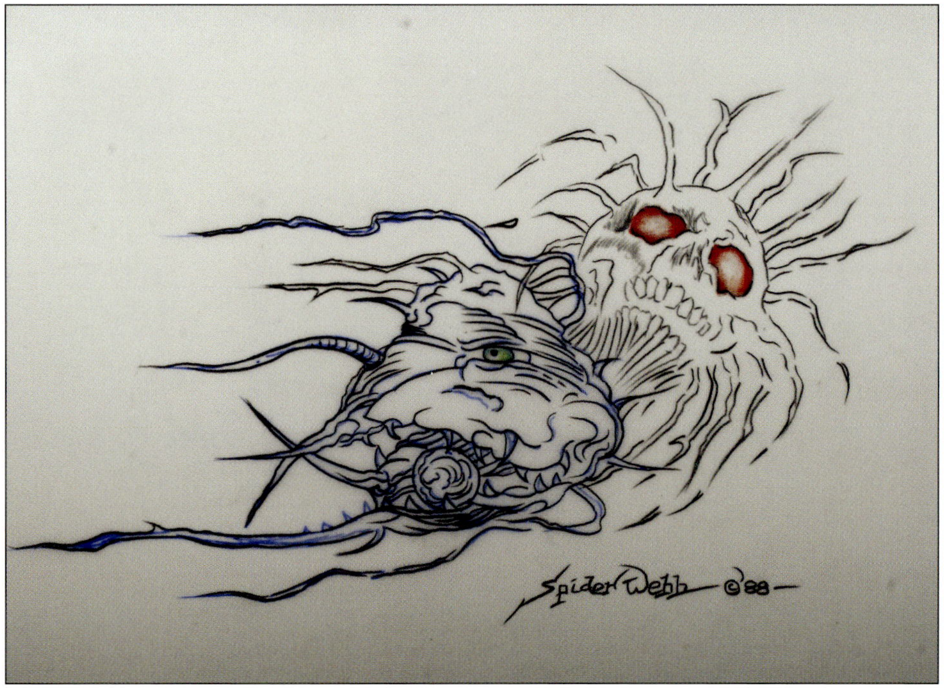

"External Flow of Time." Pencil on Vellum paper, 11" x 17". 1988.

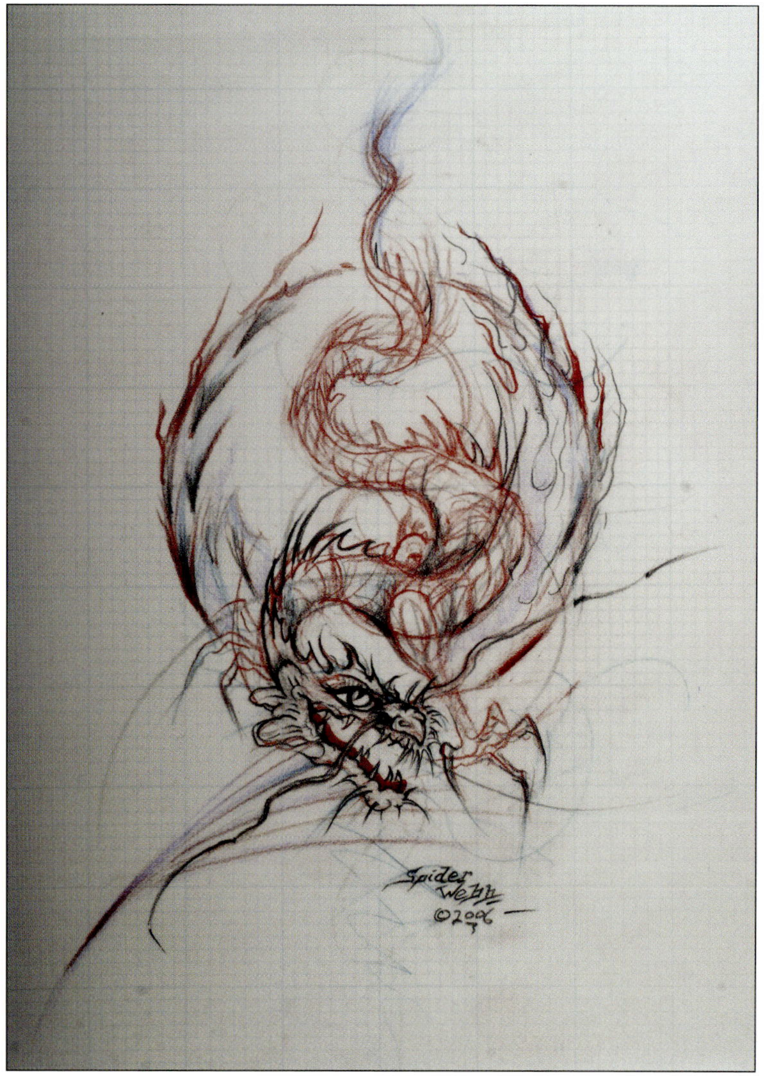

"Job Best Teach." Pencil on Vellum paper, 11" x 17". 2006.

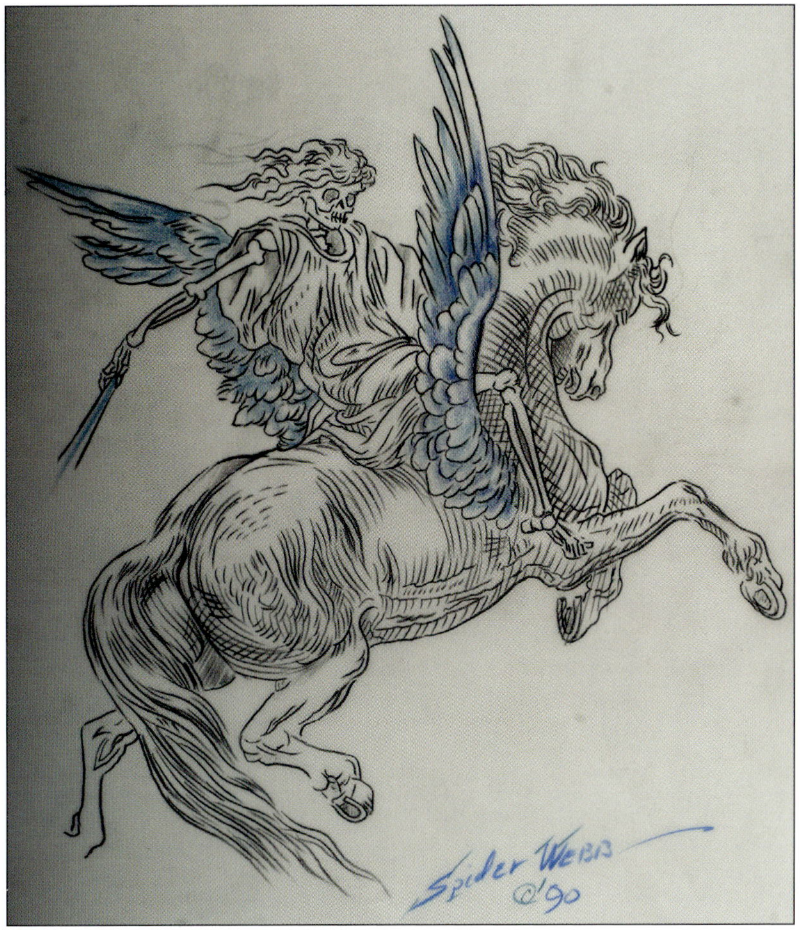


"Smooth as a Prom Queen's Thighs, Just as Dangerous." Pencil on Vellum paper, 9" x 12". 1990.

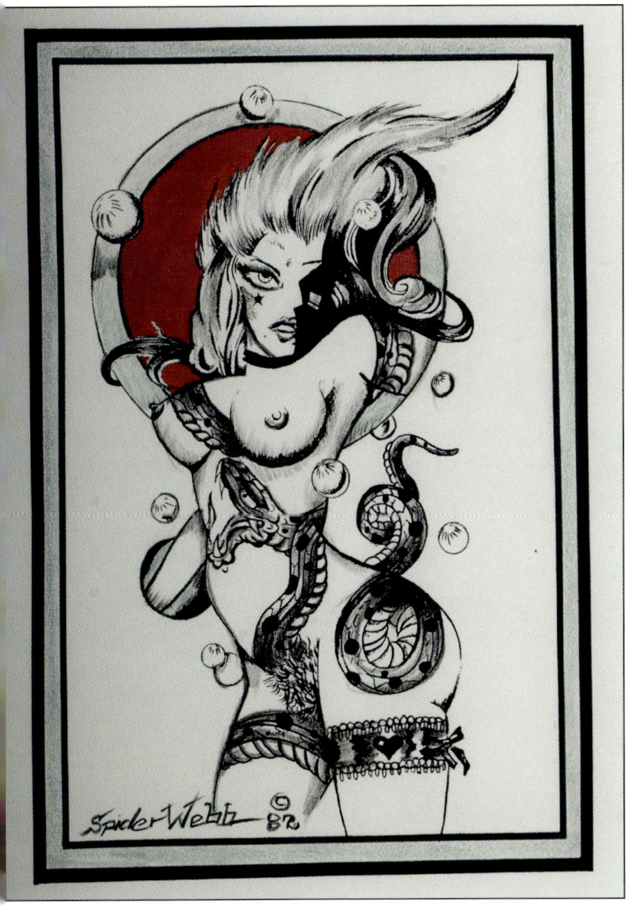


"She Lies Like Most People Breathe." Pencil on paper, 9" x 12". 1987.

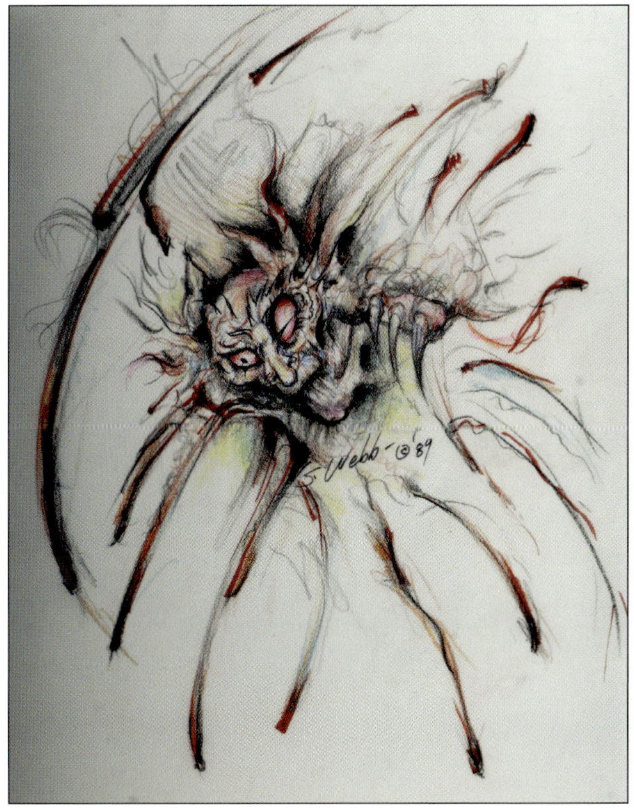


"Sleeplng wlth Impossible Memories." Pencil on Vellum paper, 8 1/2" x 11". 1989.

The secret to commercial success
is always mediocrity.

—*S.W.*

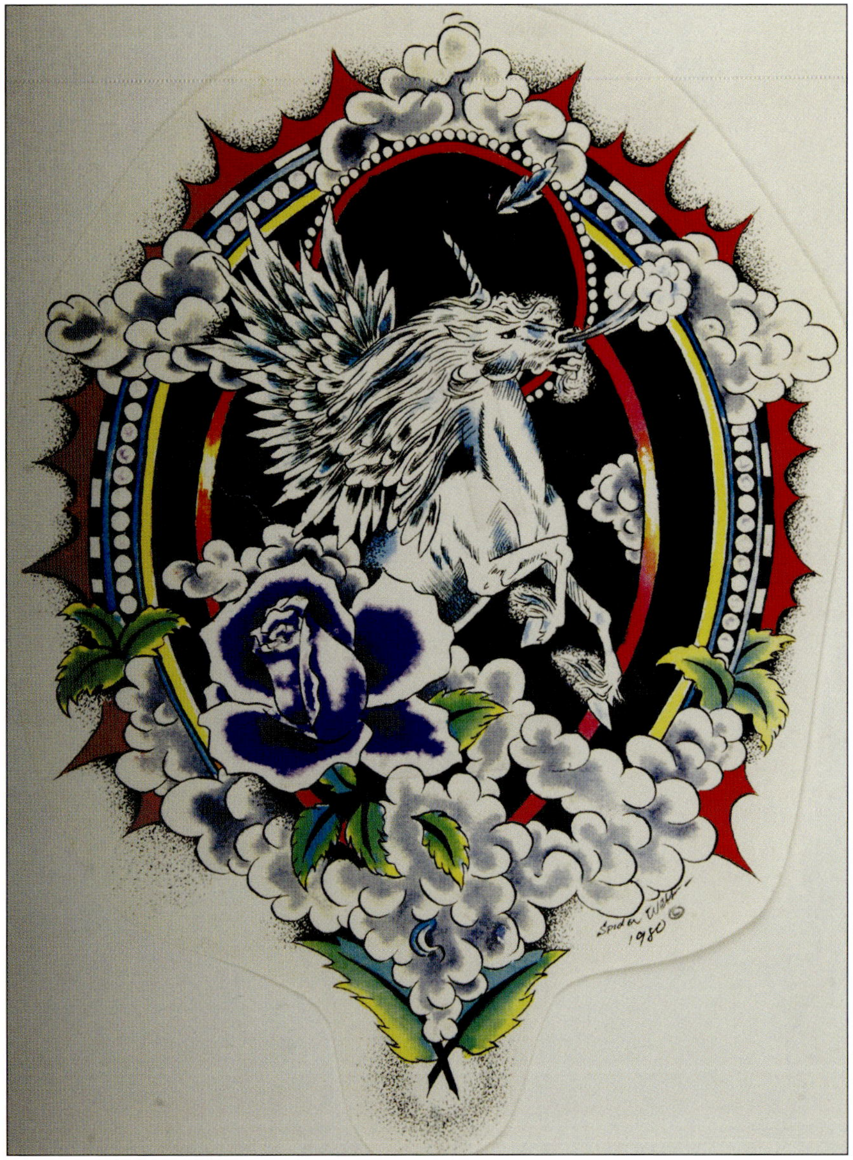

"Living Life Backwards." Mixed media on paper, 11" x 14". 1980.

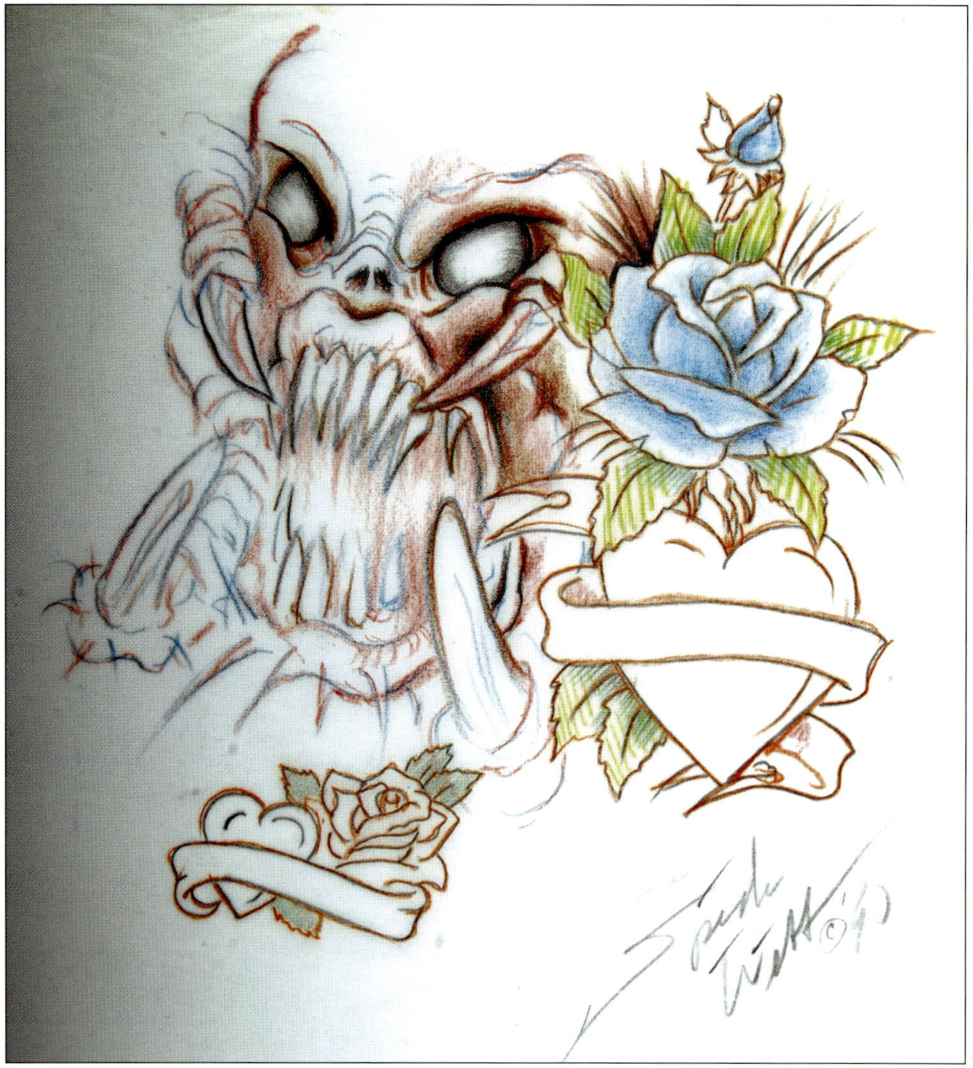

"Winning Wars, Losing Battles." Pencil on Vellum paper, 9" x 12". 1990.

I have five passports. How else can one get around and smoke good cigars?

—*S.W.*

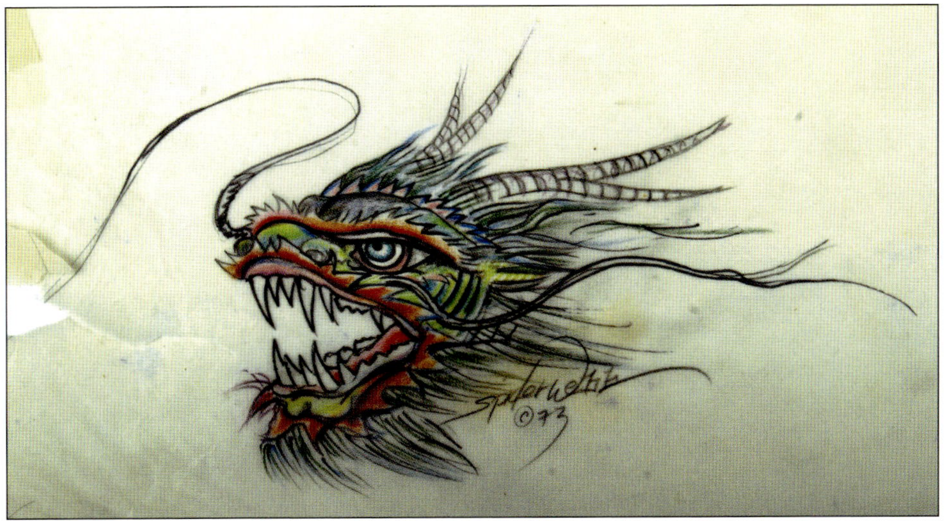

"Boo-hooing for the Past." Pencil on Vellum paper, 11" x 17". 1973.

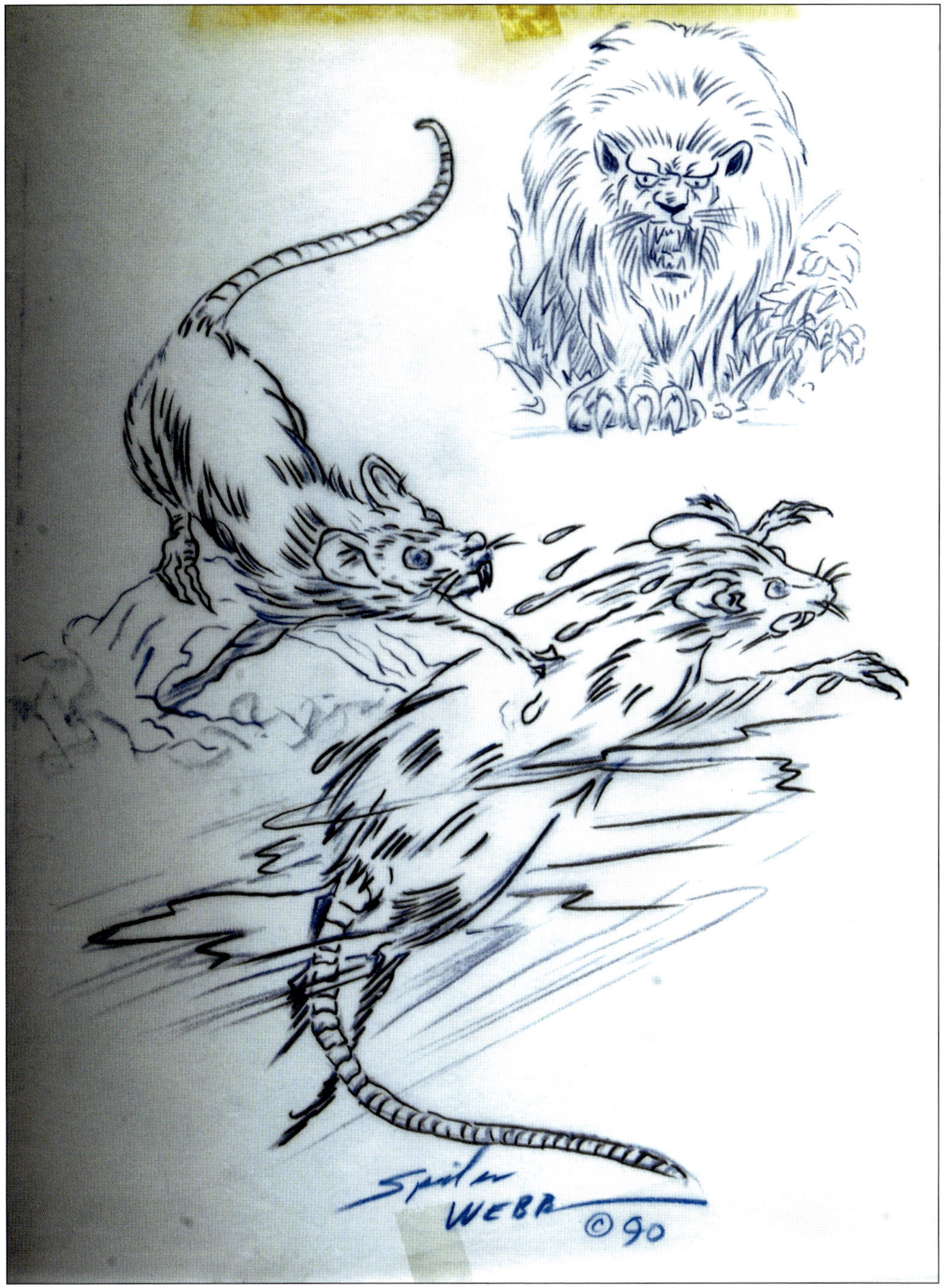


"You Only Die a Few Times." Pencil on Vellum paper, 11" x 14". 1990.

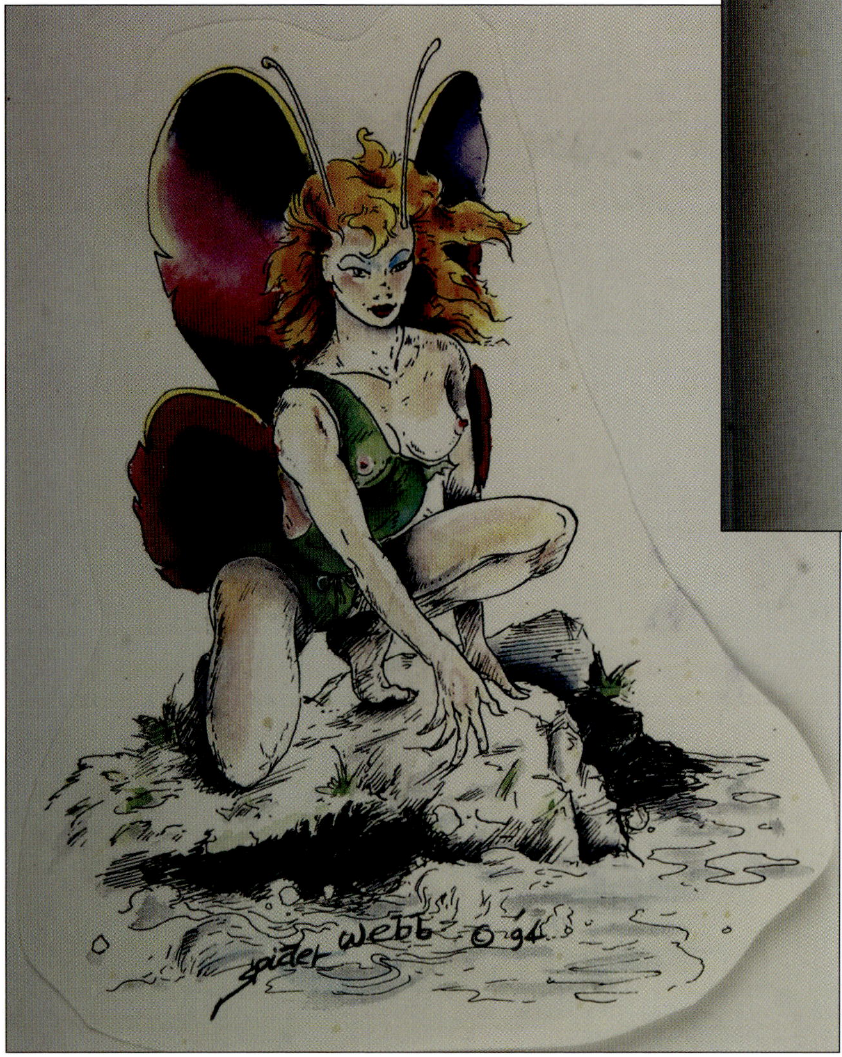

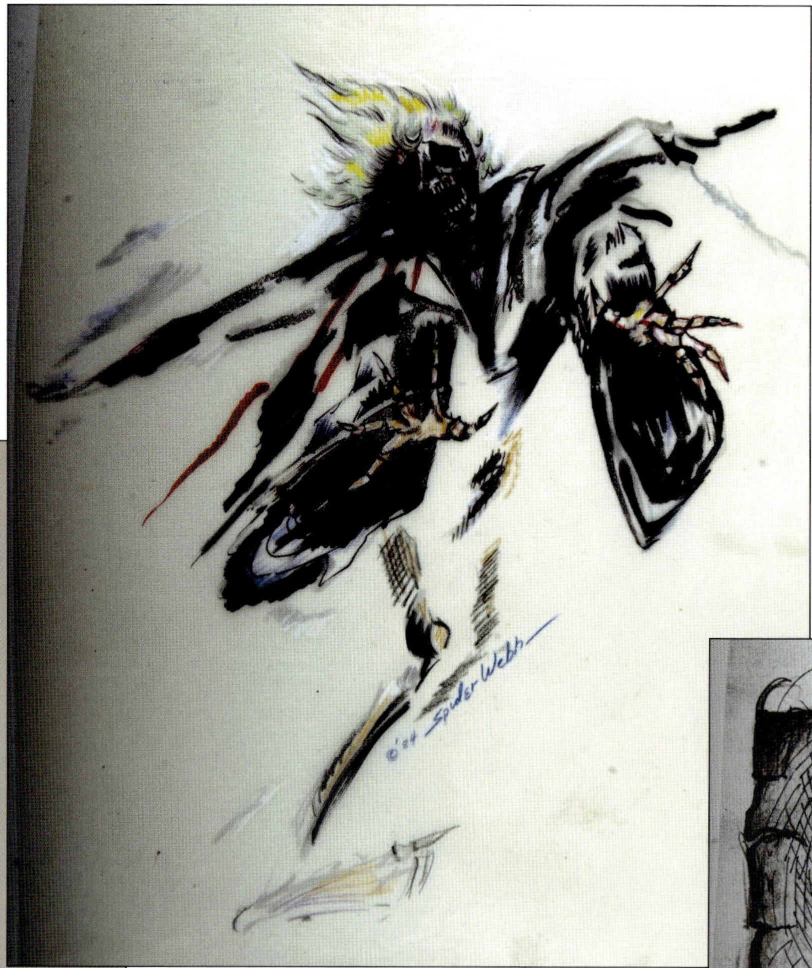

"Angel Dogs." Mixed media on paper, 9" x 12". 1984.

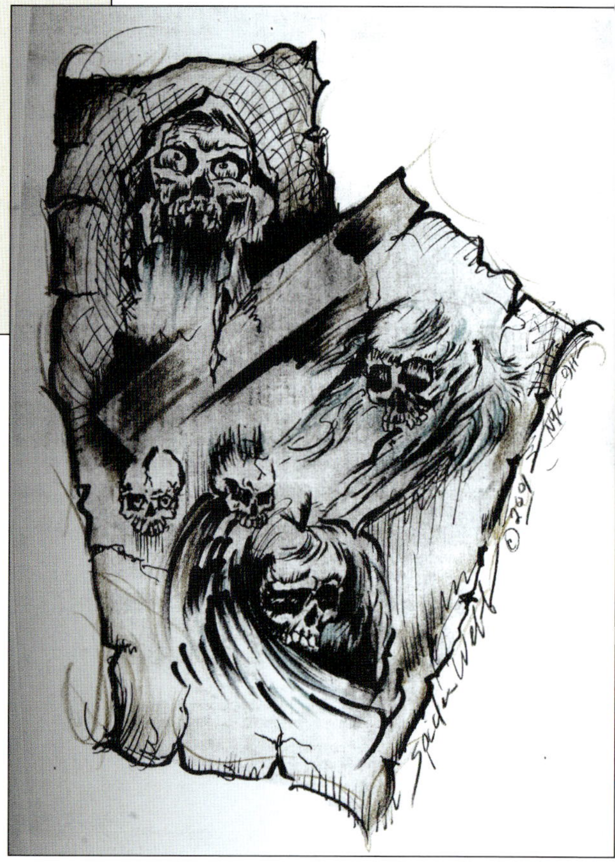

"New York City Sorrow III." Pencil on paper, 9" x 12". 2001.

"Give It Away to Keep It All." Ink and watercolor on Archers paper, 9" x 12". 1994.

Come into my dreams for they are without tears and I'll see you happy.
—*S.W.*

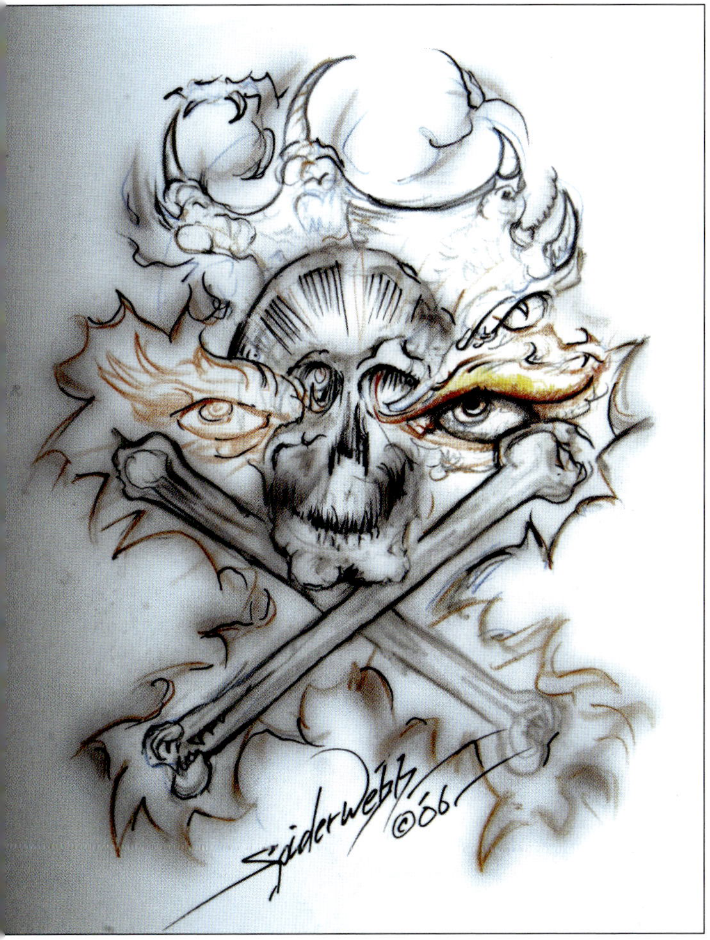


"Hear the Fish Scream." Pencil on Vellum paper, 11" x 17". 2006.

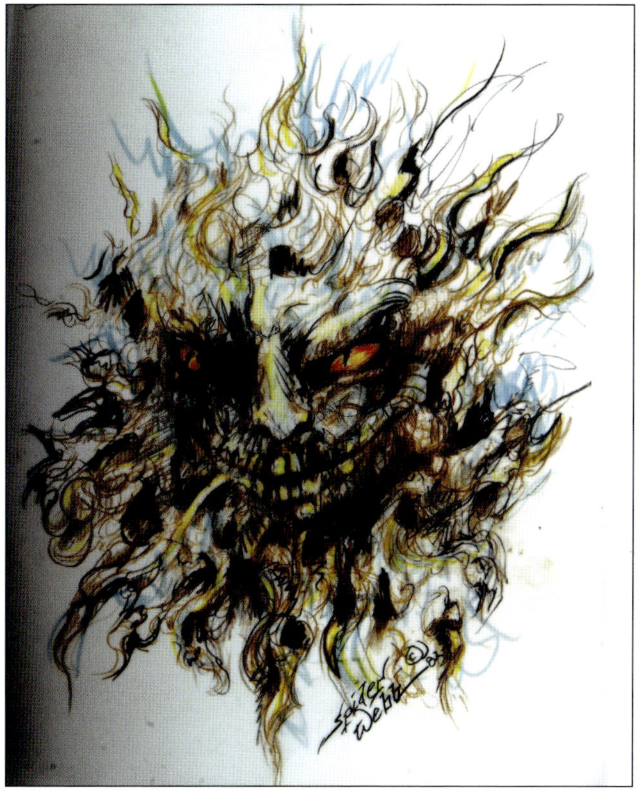

"Here Today, Gone Yesterday." Pencil on Vellum paper, 11" x 17". 1982.

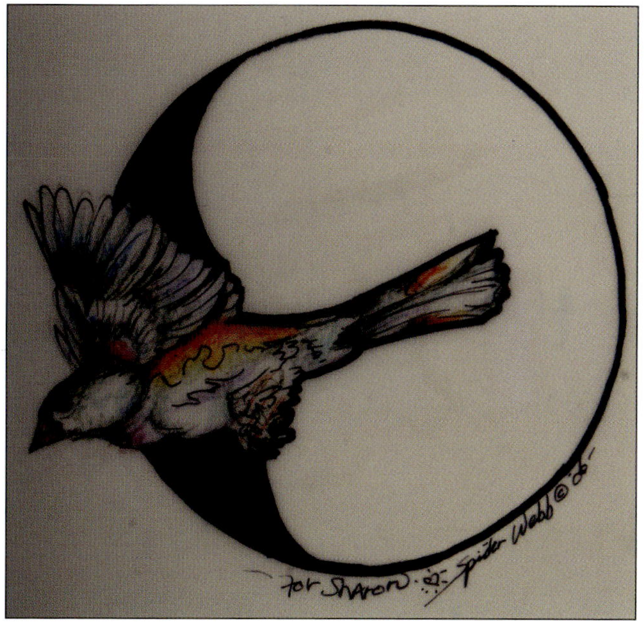


"If Only I Had Your Brains." Pencil on Vellum paper, 9" x 12". 2006.

Never ponder your existence or be aware of it. Just be.
—*S.W.*

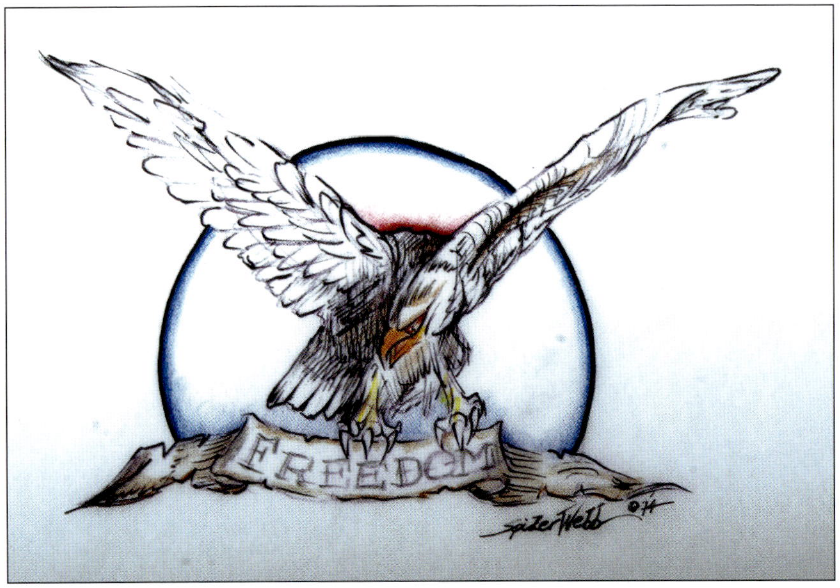


"Mass Destruction, The Hallmark of Terrorism." Pencil on Vellum paper, 11" x 17". 1974.

"Riding Out a Four-Hour Erection." Ink on Archers paper, 9" x 12". 1989.

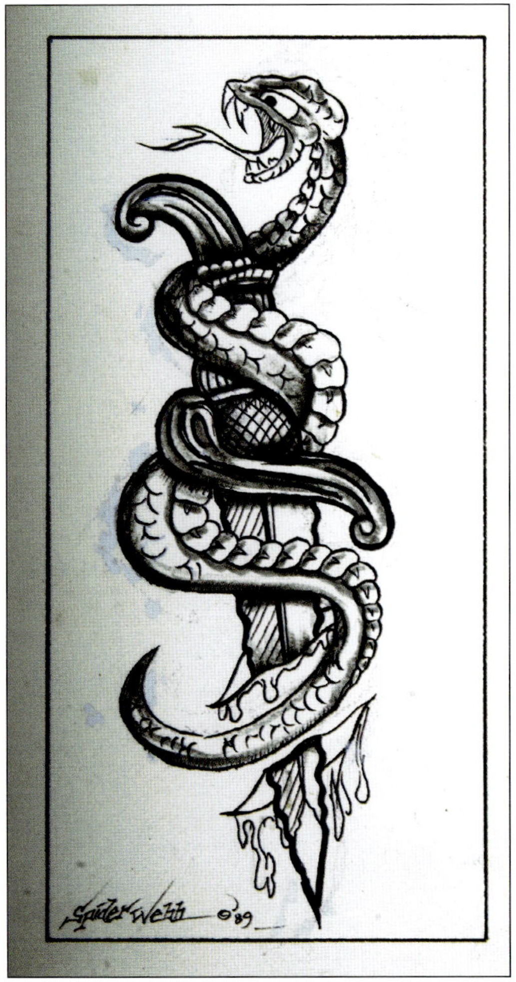

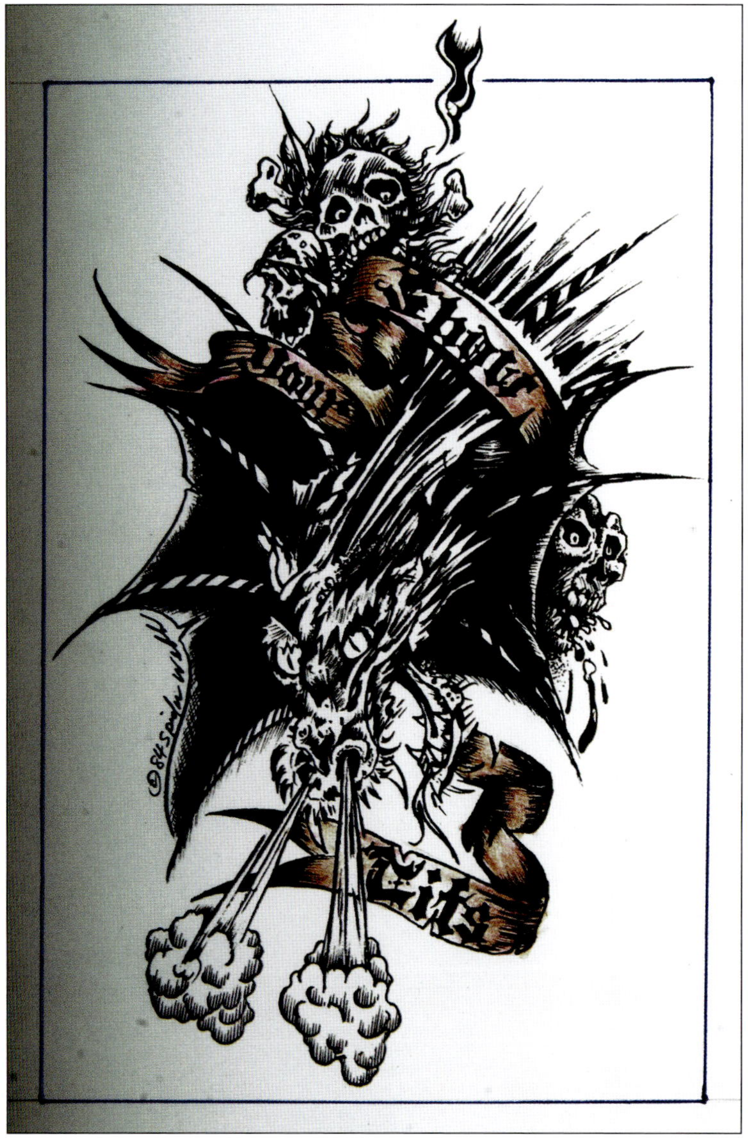

"Intense Silence Making Ears Ring." Ink on Archers paper, 9" x 12". 1984.

"Juice in the Old Coconut." Pencil on Vellum paper, 11" x 17". 1979.

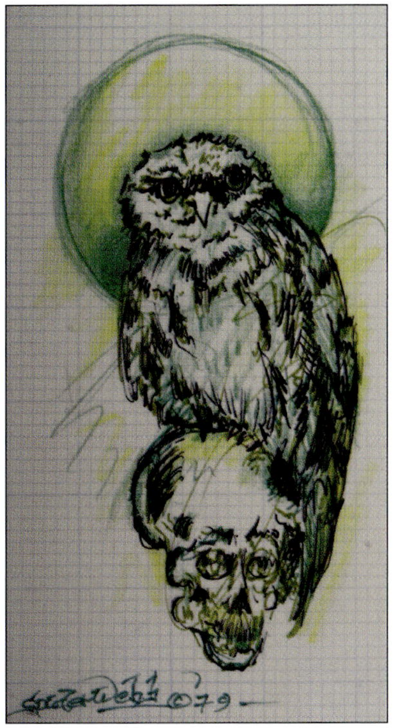

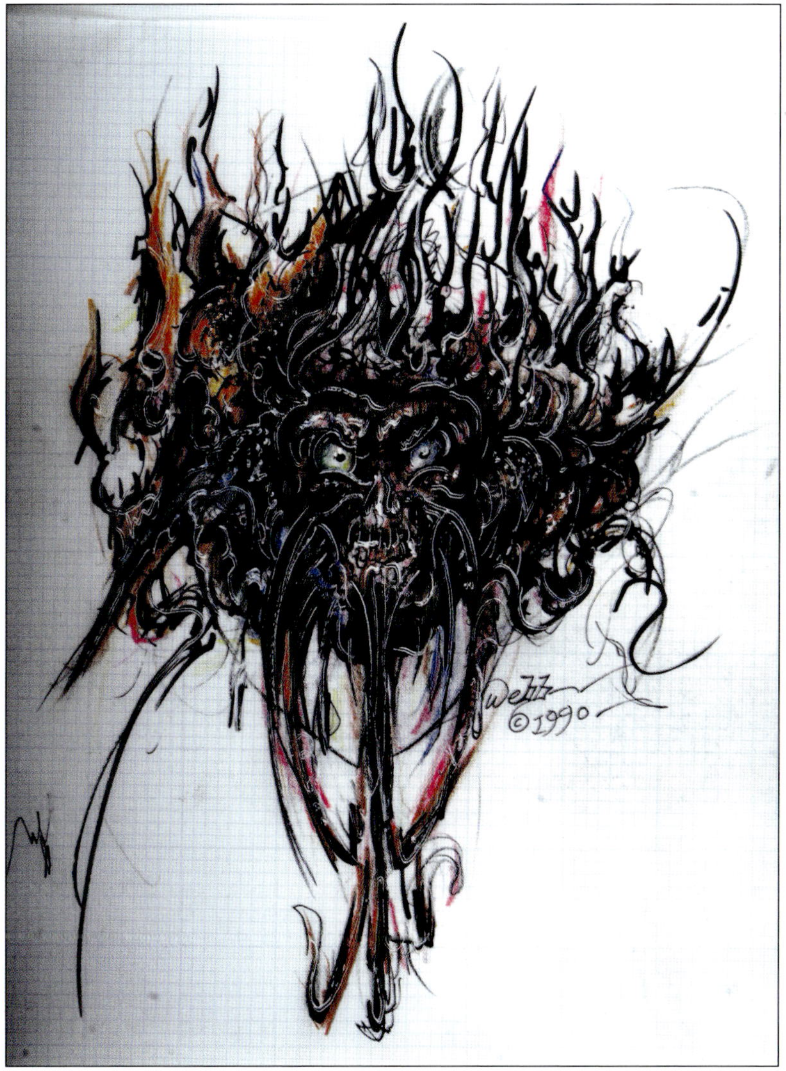

"My Nanny's Unmentionables." Pencil on Vellum paper, 11" x 17". 1990.

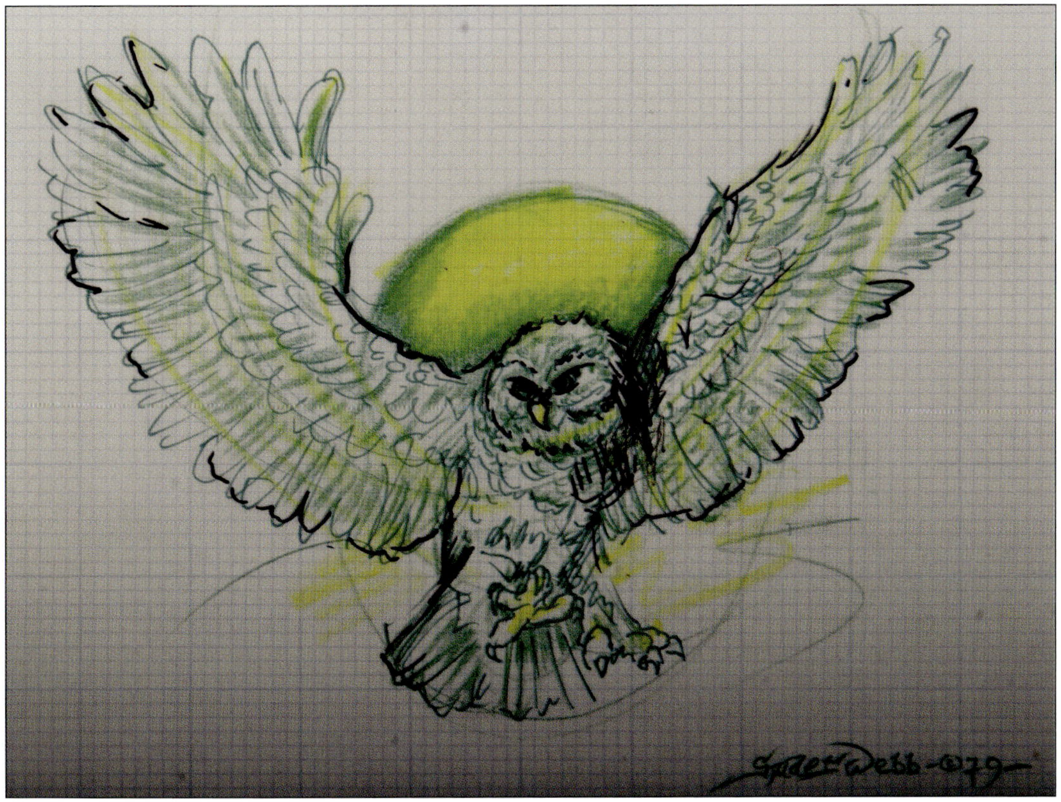

"Living a Dream – Pissing Up Rope." Pencil on Vellum paper, 11" x 17". 1979.

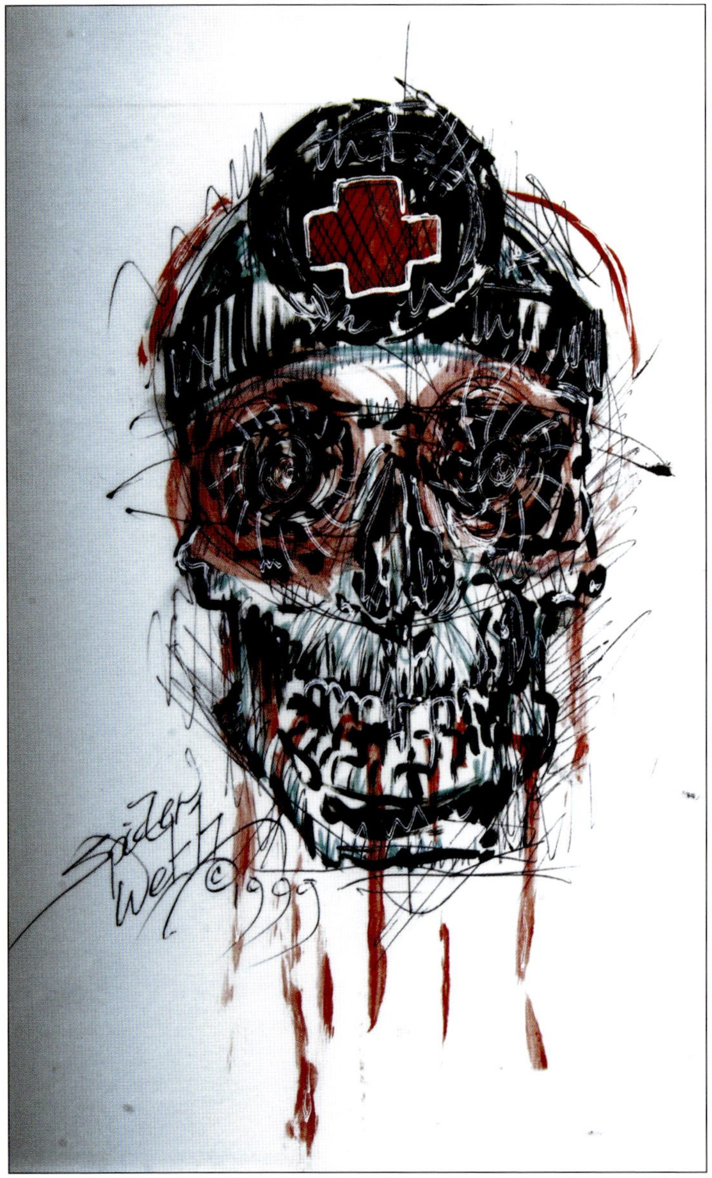

“Lighting Tampon Fuses II.” Pencil on Vellum paper, 9" x 12". 1999.

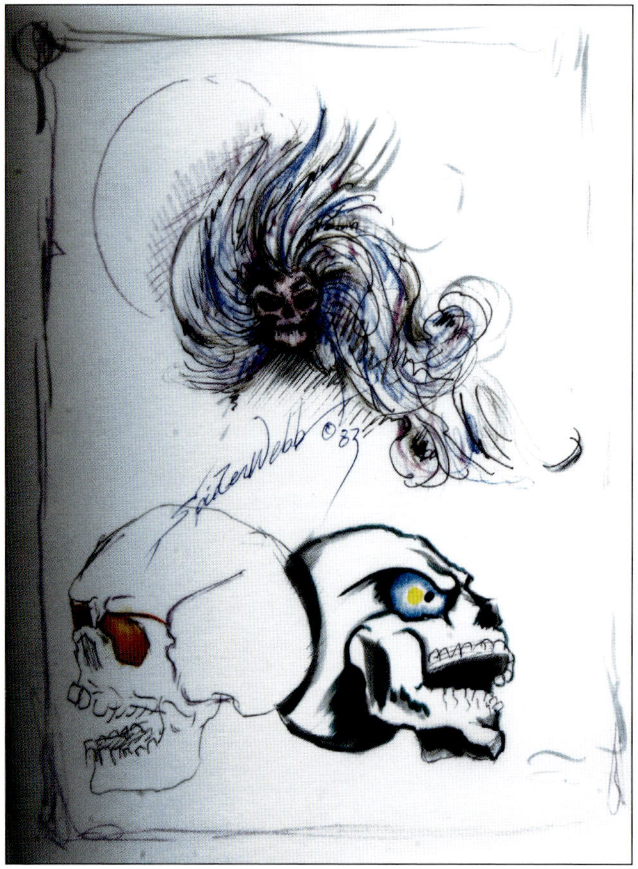

“Little Minds Afraid of Big Images.” Pencil on Vellum paper, 11" x 17". 1983.

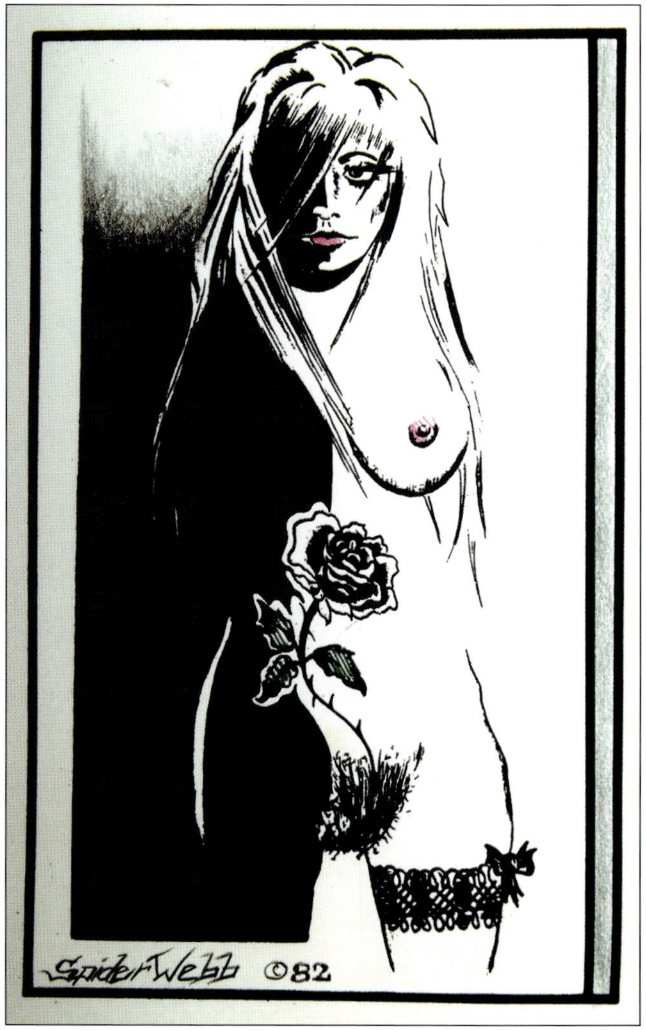


“Common Decency Makes Me Blush.” Pencil on board, 8" x 10". 1982.

What was done to me created me.
—*S.W.*

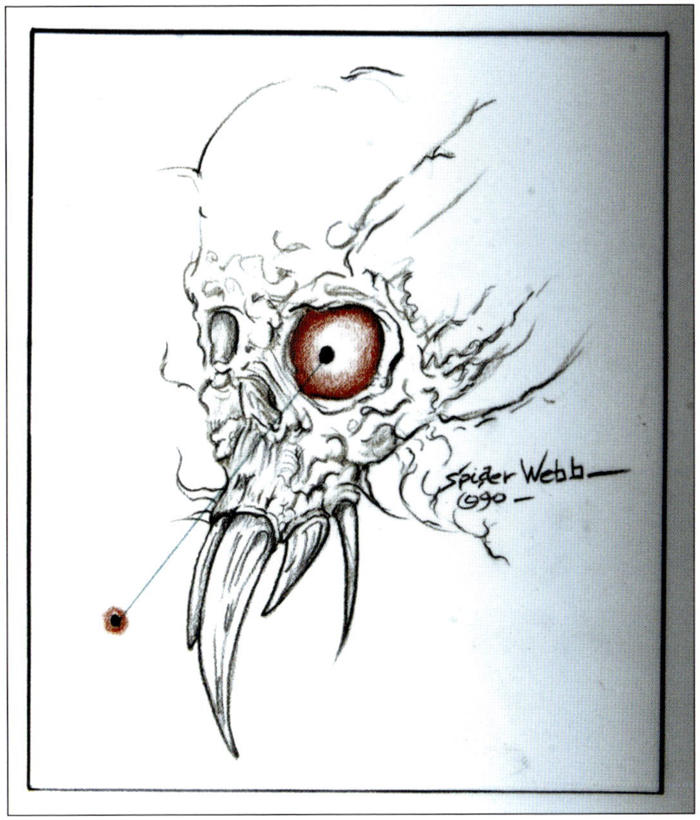

"Without a Purpose – All Is Lost." Pencil on Vellum paper, 9" x 12". 1990.

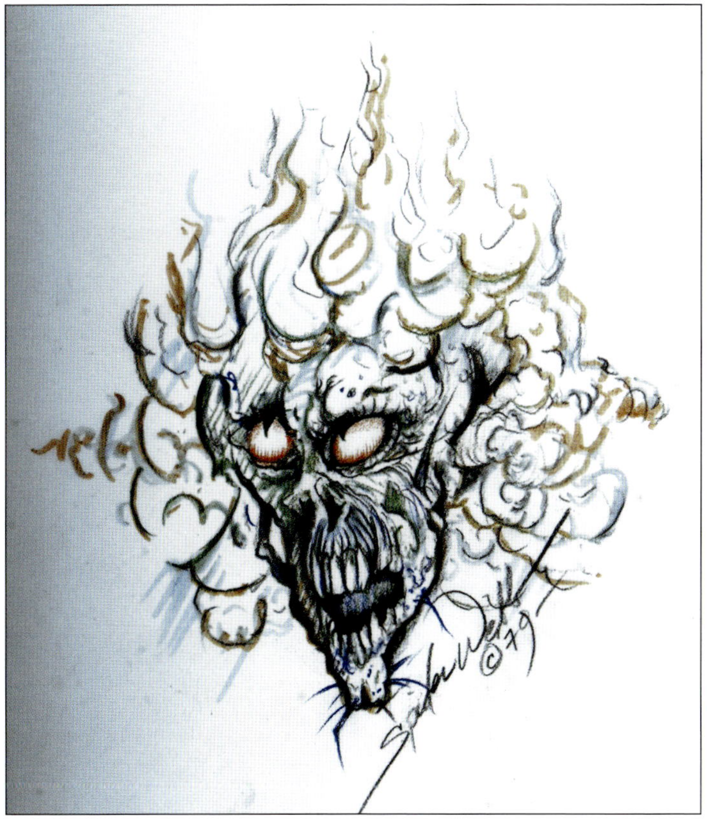

"Selling Tickets for Your Good Times." Pencil on Vellum paper, 9" x 12". 1979.

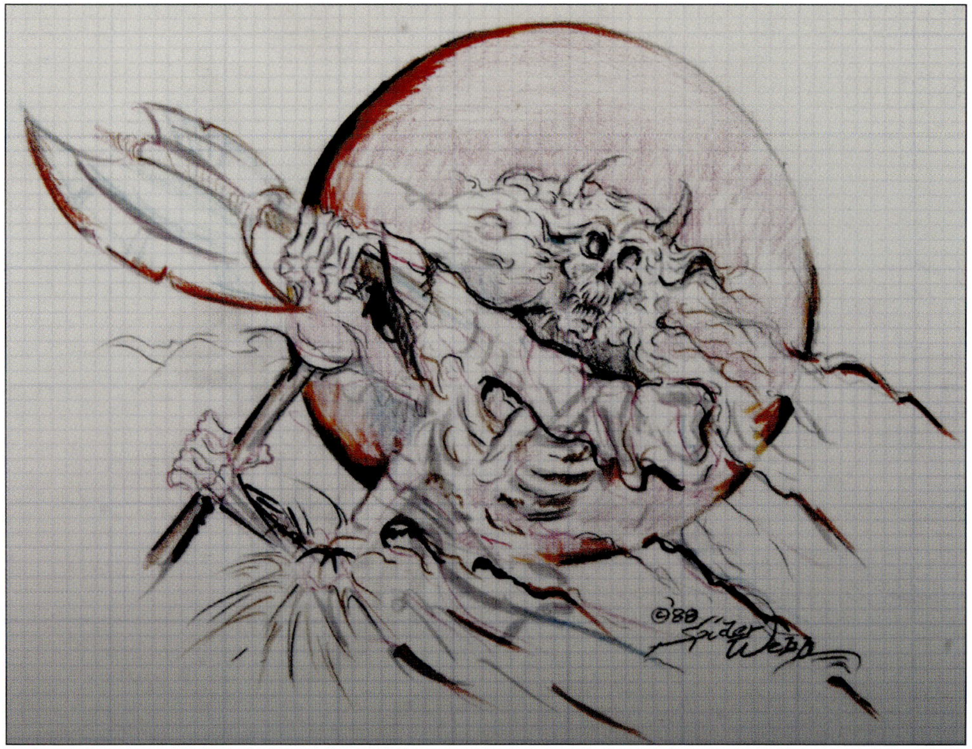

"The Great Illusion of Life: Reality and Dreams." Pencil on Vellum paper, 11" x 17". 1988.

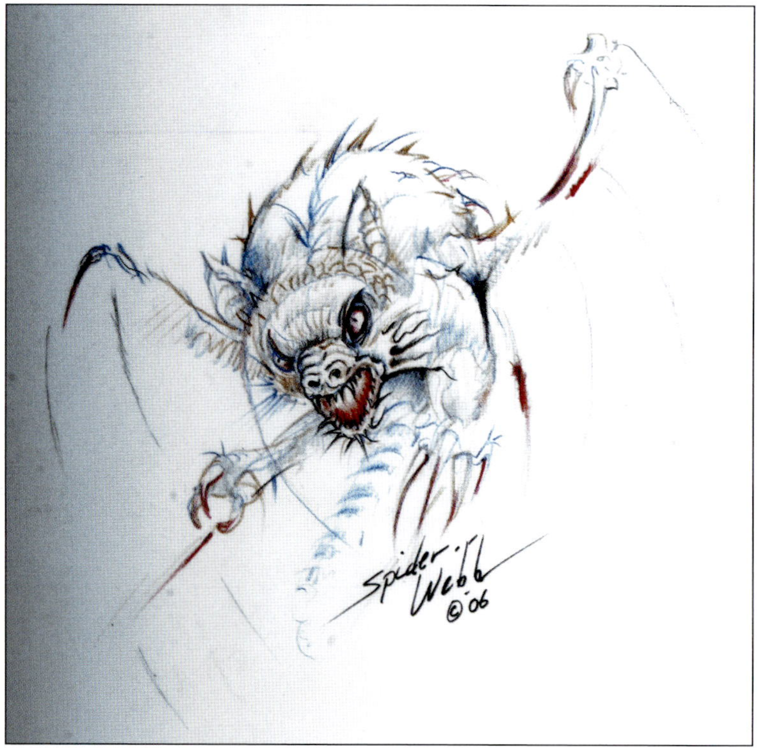

"Learning Humility From Failure." Pencil on Vellum paper, 9" x 12". 2006.

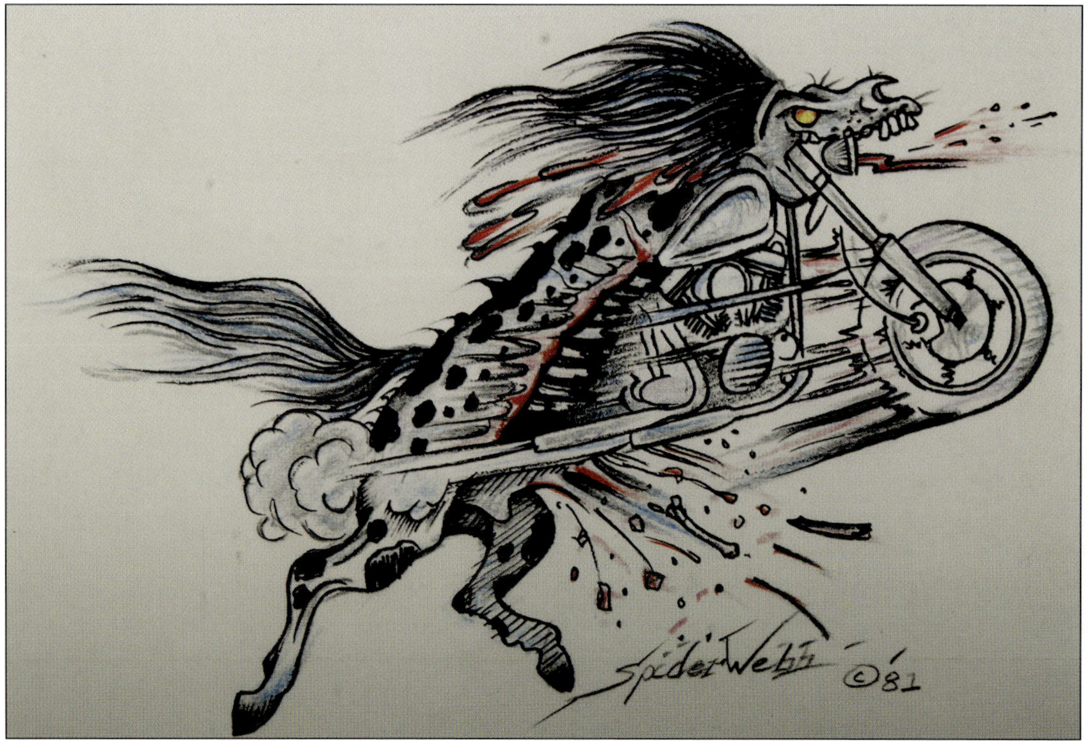

"Dreams Without Tears."
Pencil on Vellum paper,
11" x 17". 1981.

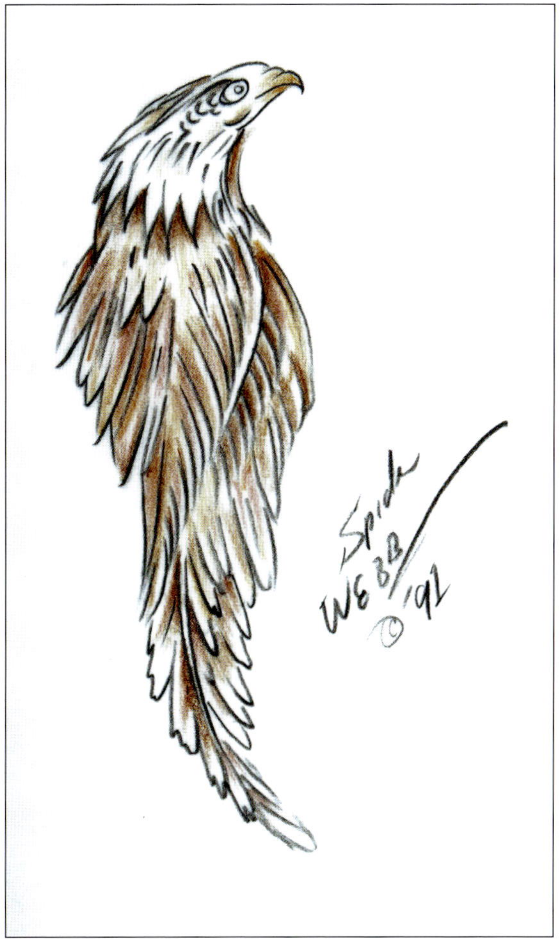

"Never Part With Your Illusions." Pencil on Vellum paper, 8" x 10". 1991.

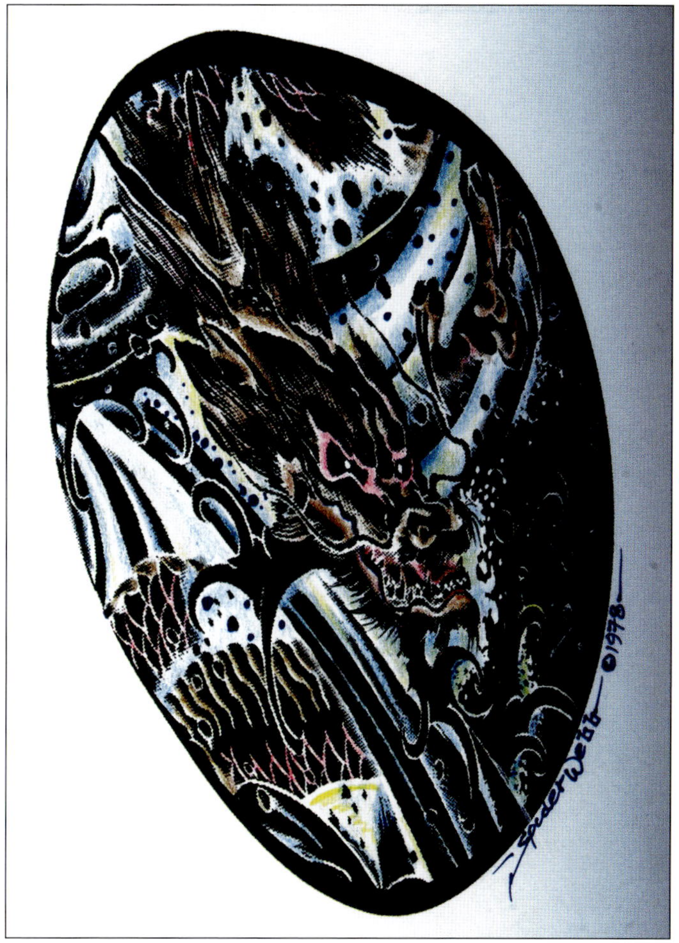

"Nothing Sounds Alive." Pencil on paper, 8" x 10". 1978.

I reached for my cell phone (to call for help) then saw my severed hand on the floor and I was reaching only with a bloody stump.

—*S.W.*

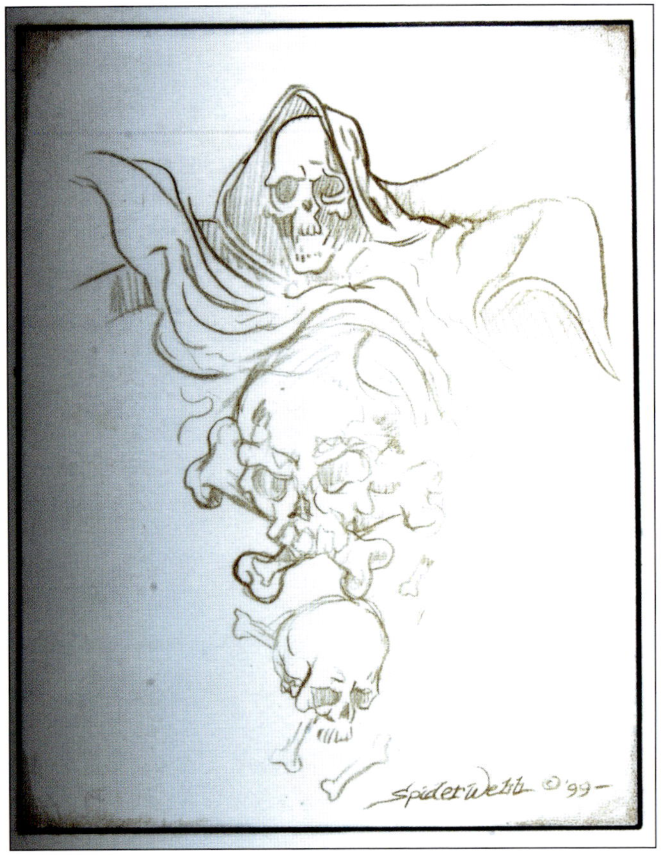

"Getting Back to the Great Times." Pencil on Vellum paper, 9" x 12". 1999.

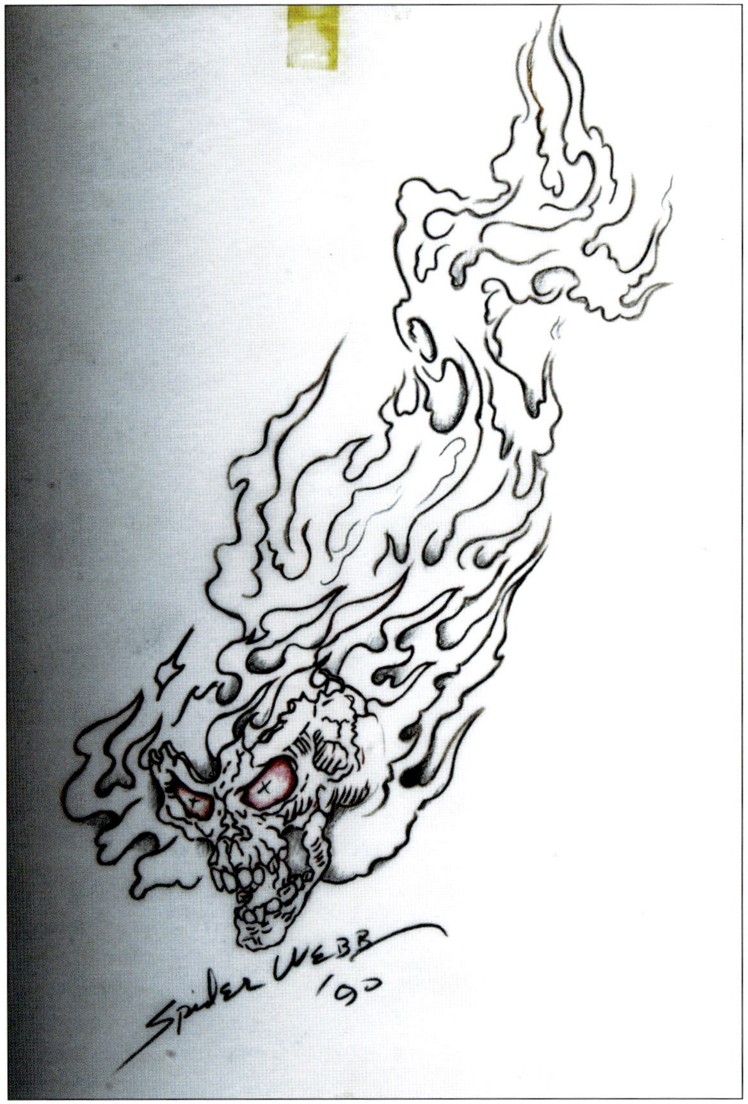


"Silence Is More Than the Absence of Noise." Pencil on Vellum paper, 9" x 12". 1990.

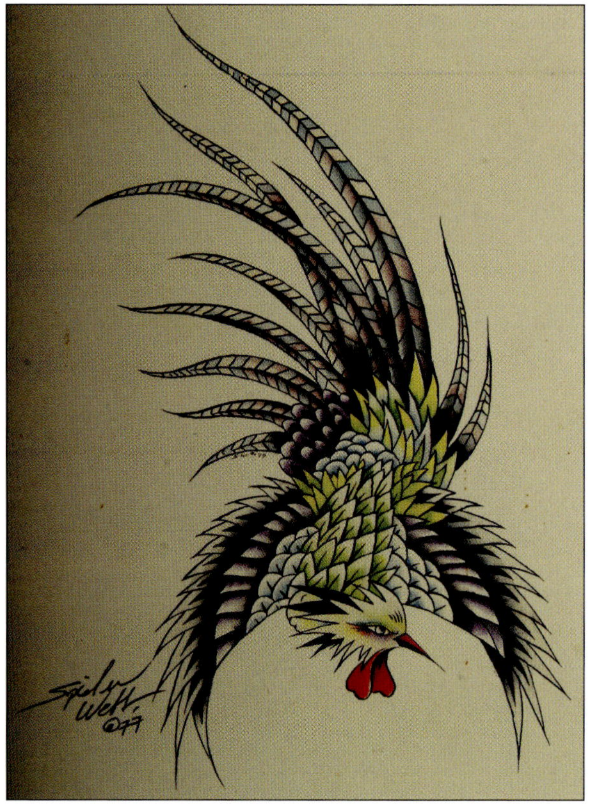

"Justifies Nor Excuses Nothing – Love." Pen and watercolor on Archers paper, 8" x 12". 1977.

Doing something different with a purpose is one of my ways.
—*S.W.*

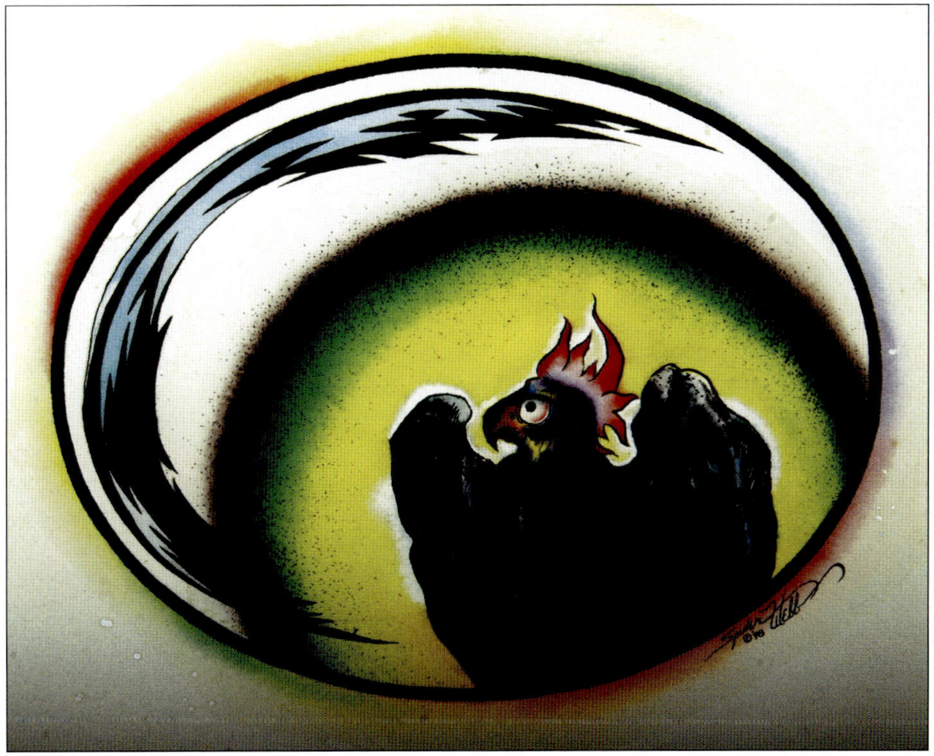

"Negativity, the Absoluteness of Death." Pen and watercolor on Archers paper, 8" x 12". 1978.

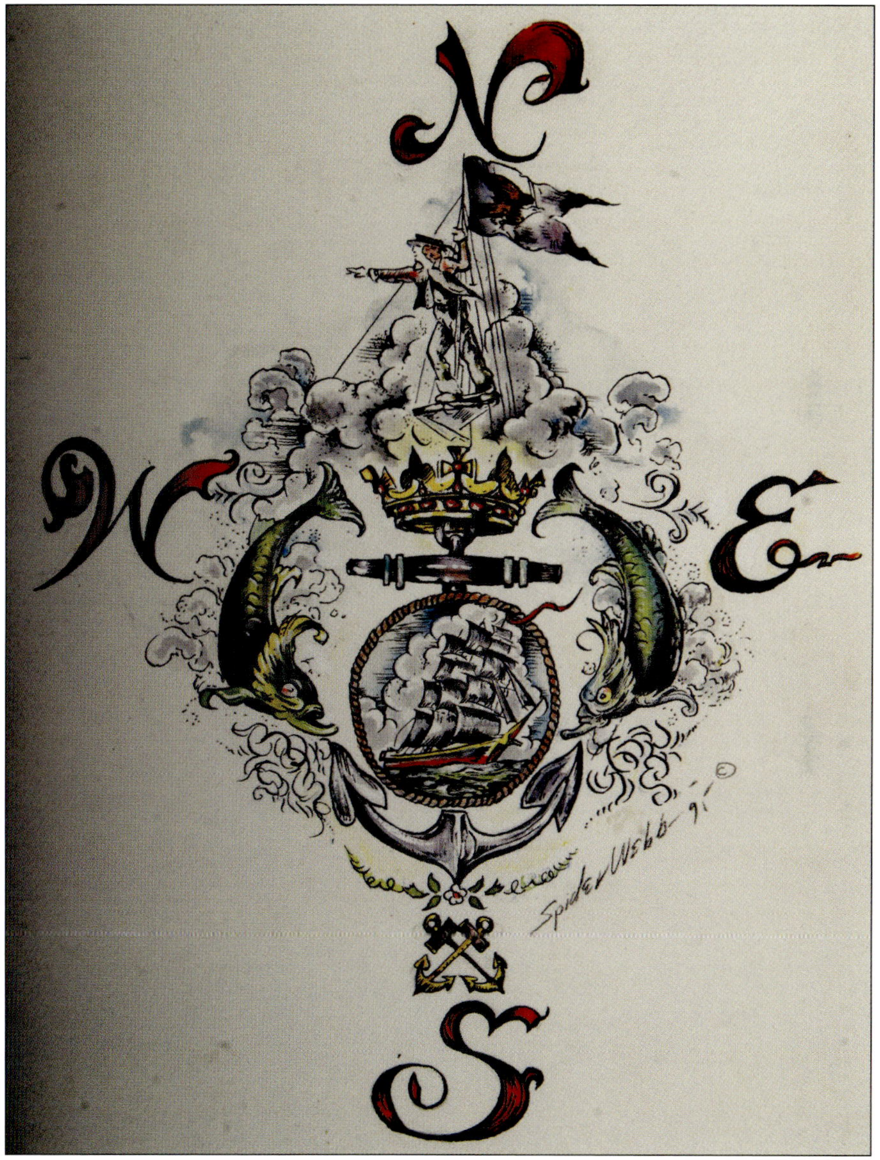


"Lousy Values...My Kind of Girl." Pen and watercolor on Archers paper, 8" x 12". 1995.

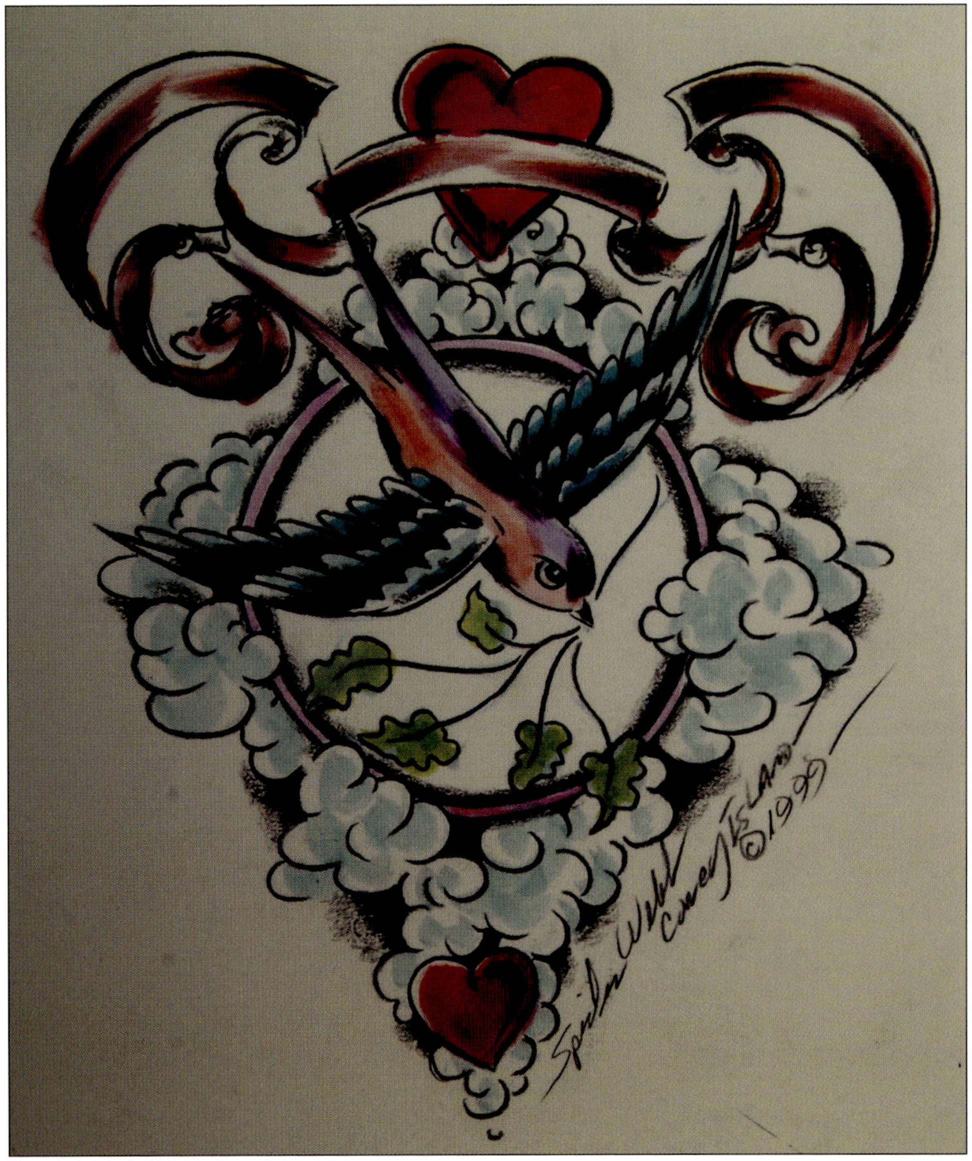

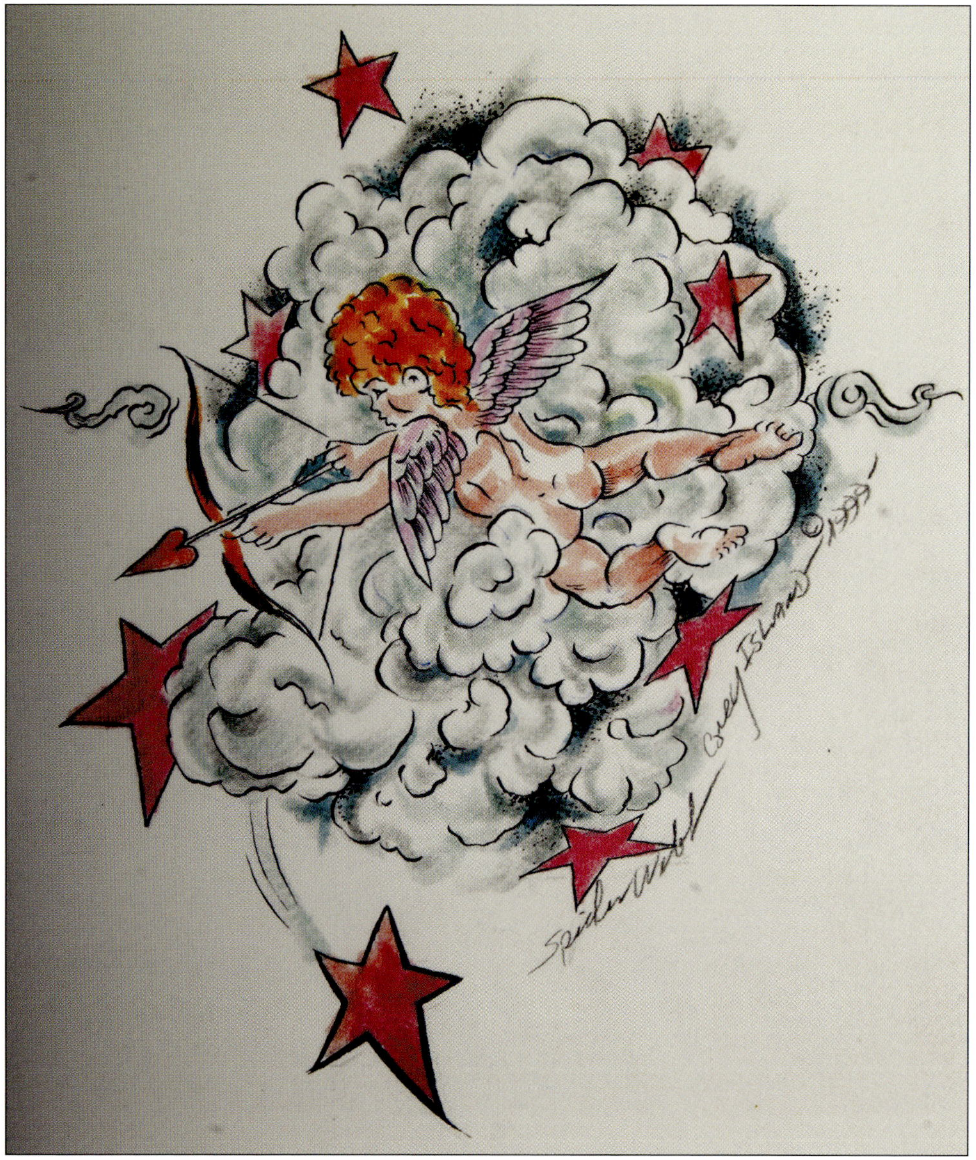

"I'm Not Lazy. It's Just That I Don't Care." Ink and watercolor on Archers paper, 9" x 12". 1999.

"If You See a Restroom – Use It."
Pencil on paper, 8" x 10". 1999.

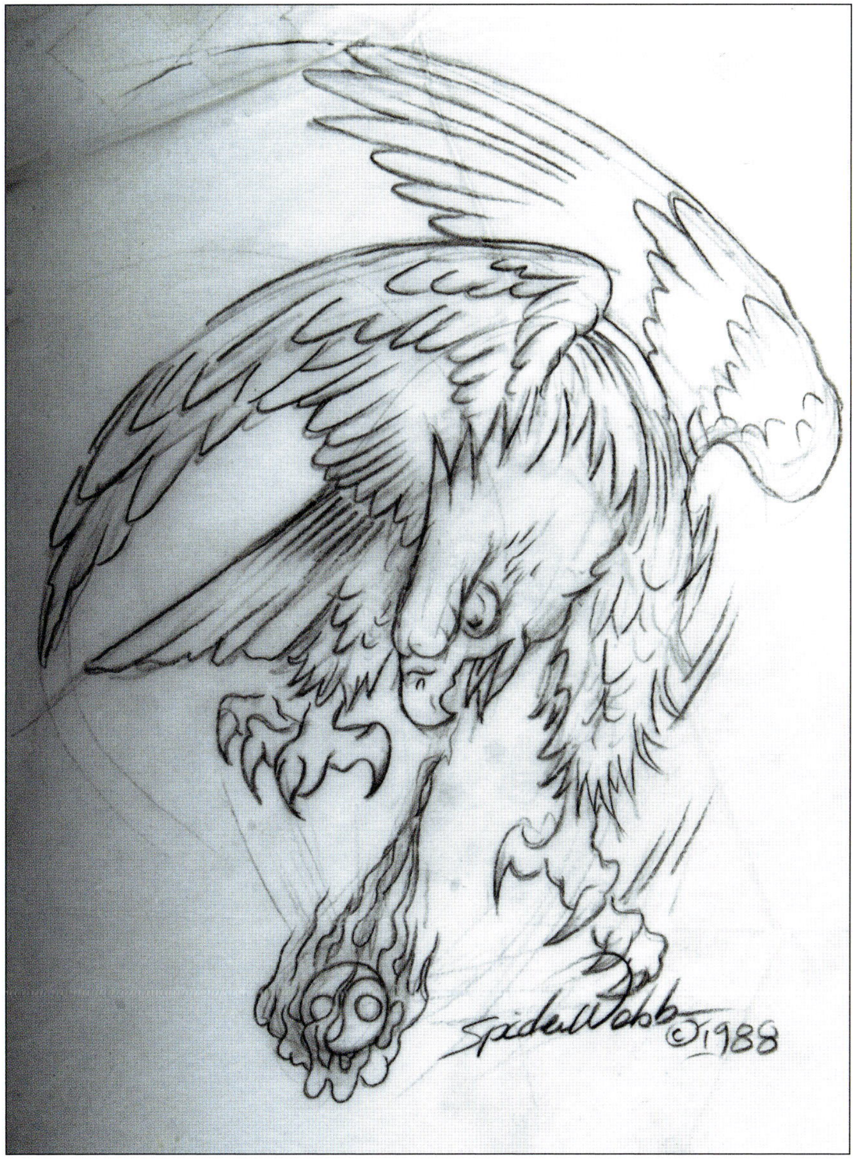


"Death Spoke To Me." Ink and watercolor on Archers paper, 9" x 12". 1988.

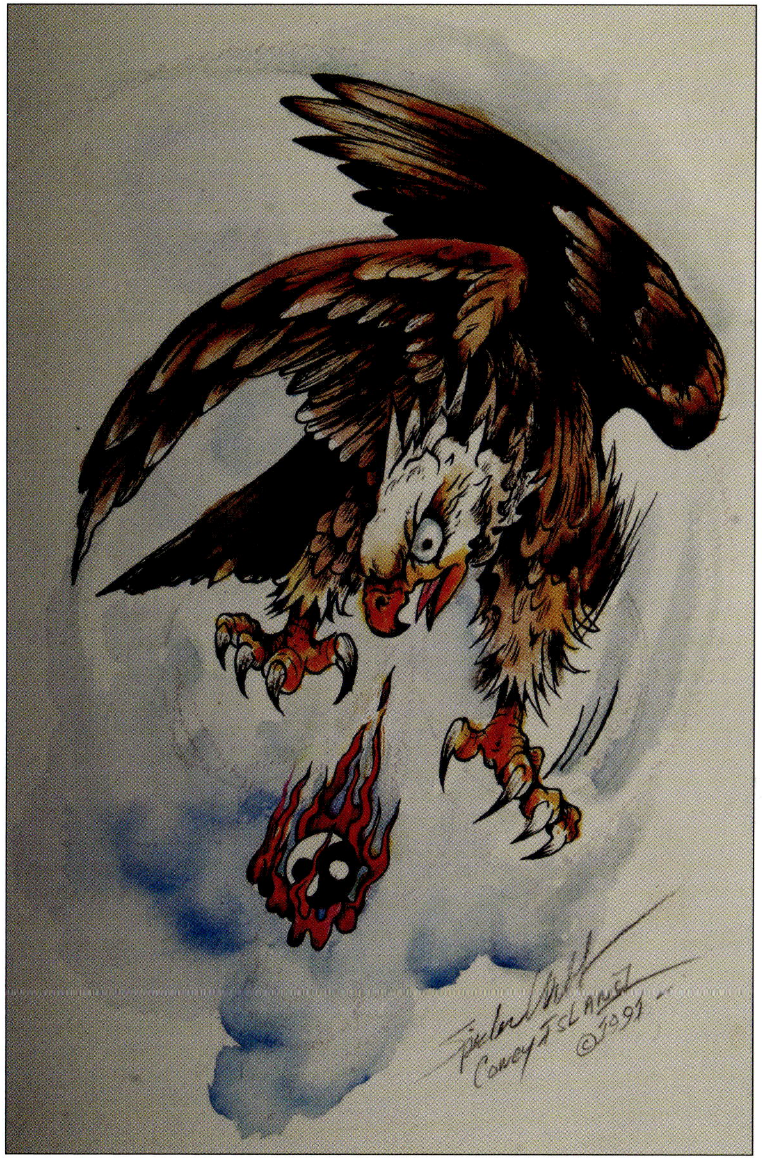

"Dancing with Death." Ink and watercolor on Archers paper, 9" x 12". 1991.

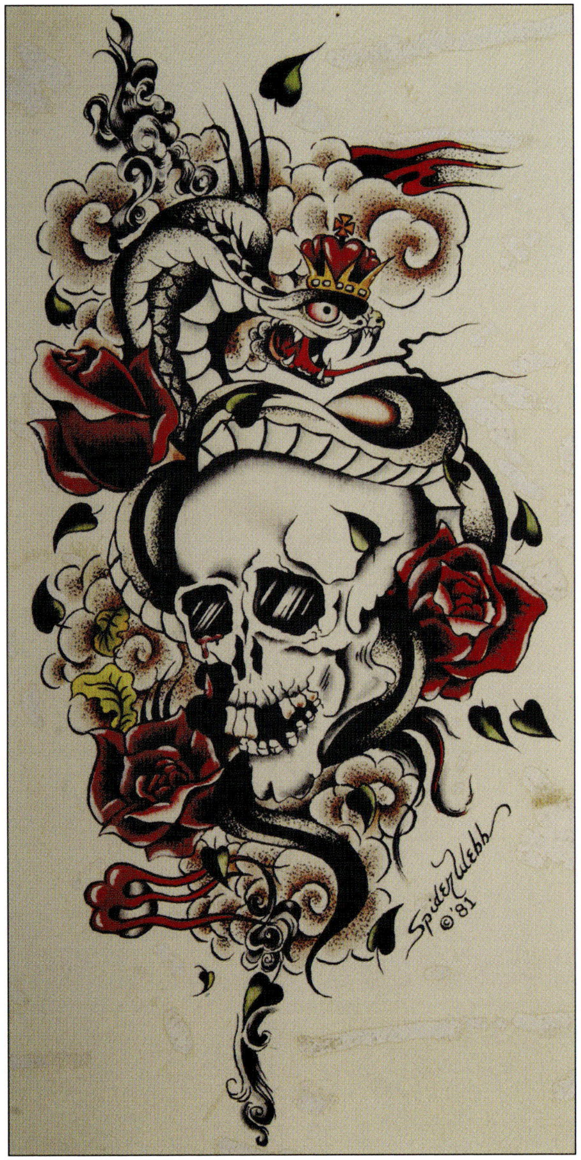


"Somebody Please Stop Me." Ink and watercolor on Archers paper, 9" x 12". 1981.

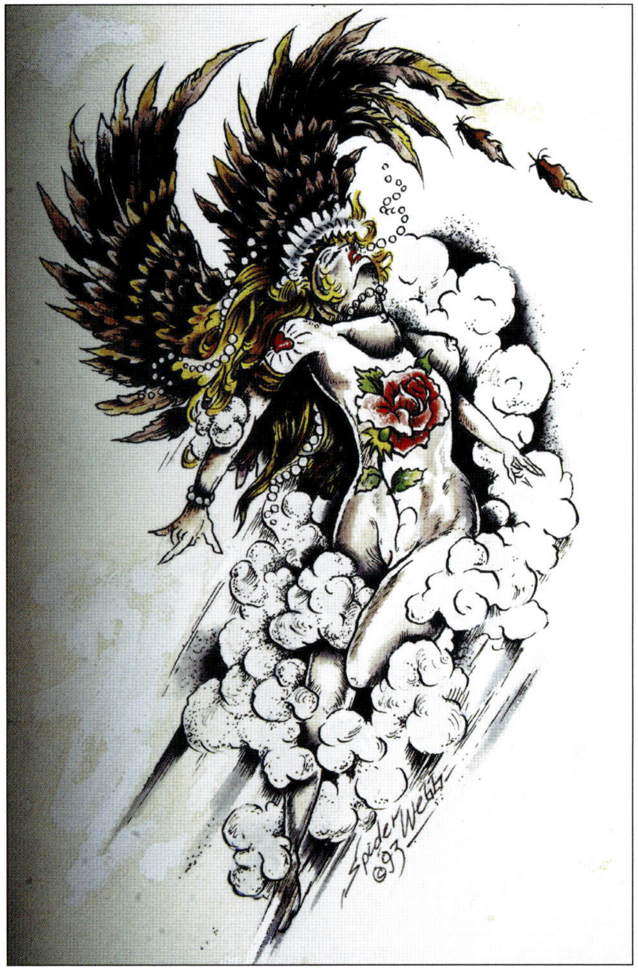


"Go Peddle Your Little Trinkets." Ink and watercolor on Archers papers, 9" x 12". 1993.

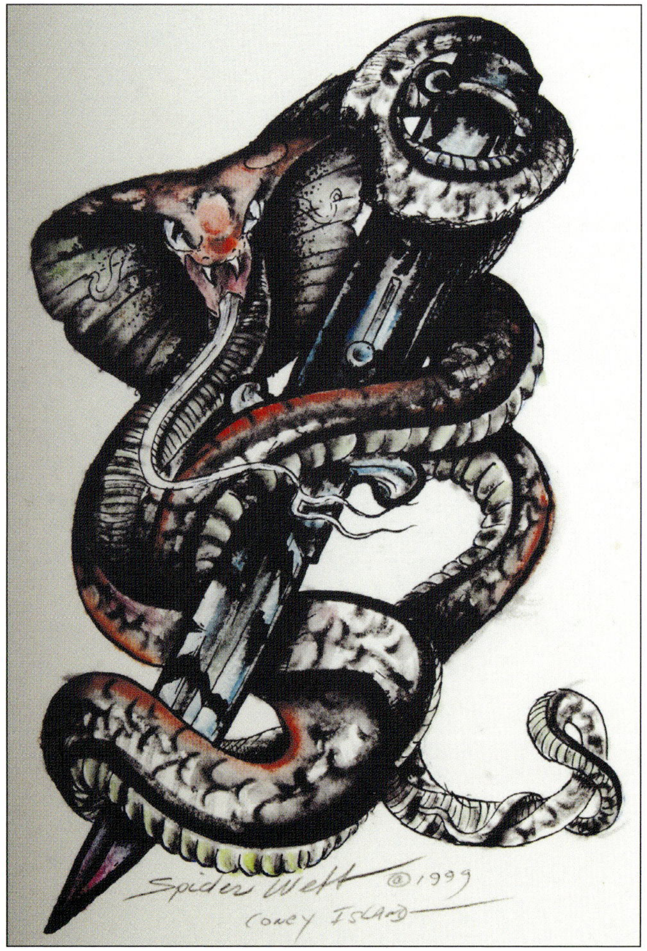


"A Permanent Temporary Arrangement." Ink and watercolor on Archers paper, 9" x 12". 1999.

To truly enjoy a good cigar you must be in a still environment so all your senses can absorb the smoke. The only breeze should be her young firm body swaying to your puffs, and the love in her eyes for you and everything you stand for.

*—S.W.*

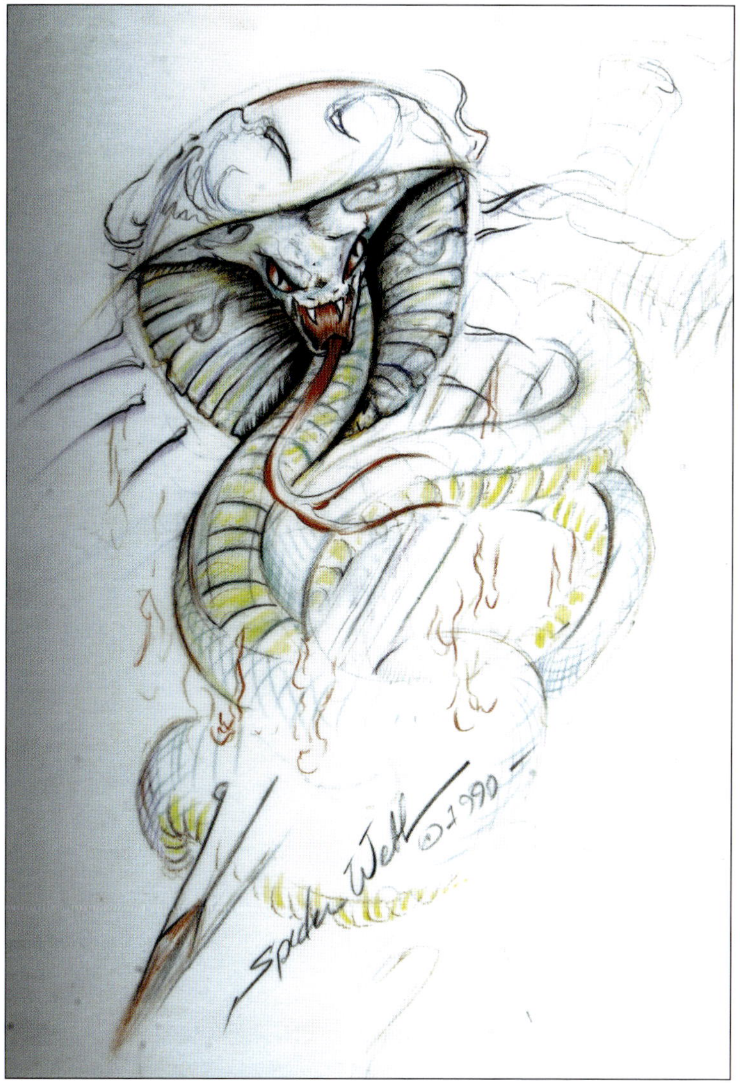

"It's All About All Of Us Together." Pencil on Vellum paper, 9" x 12". 1990.

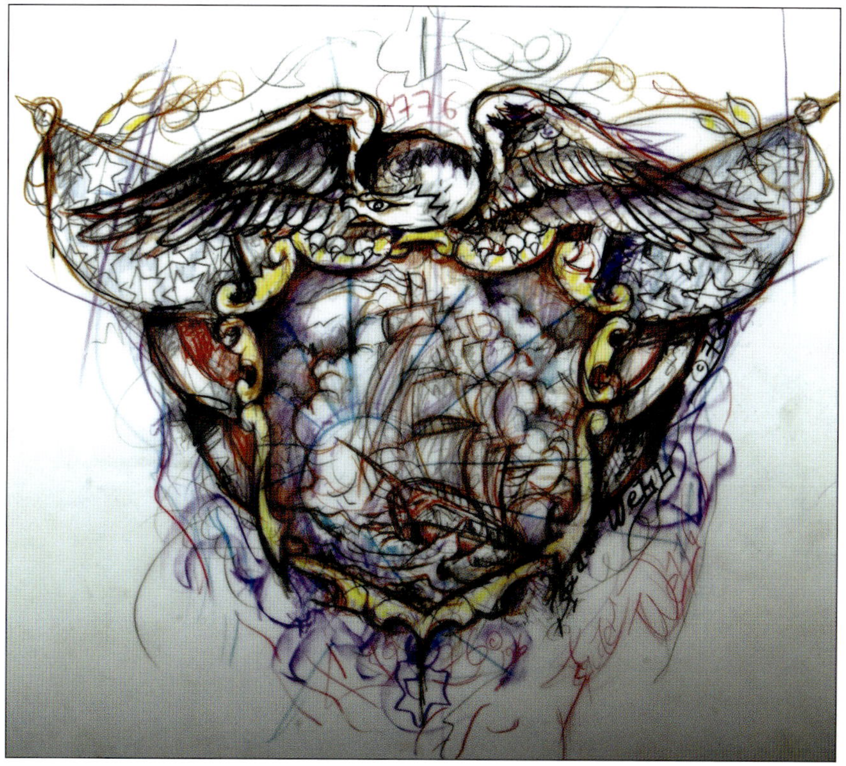

"Words, Faster Than Life." Pencil on Vellum paper, 12" x 14". 1976.

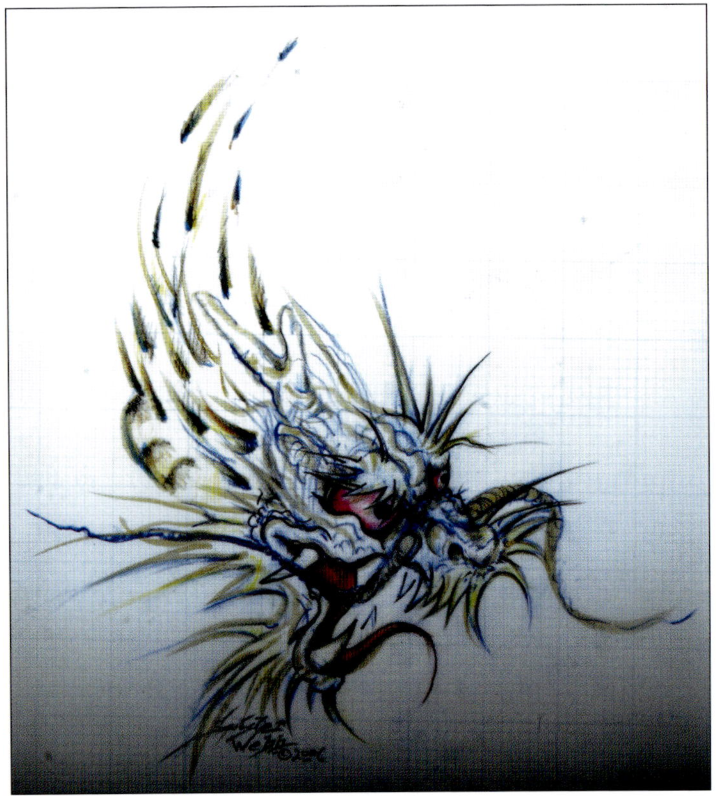

"Fucken 'A' Strychnin in the Beer." Pencil on Vellum paper, 12" x 14". 2006.

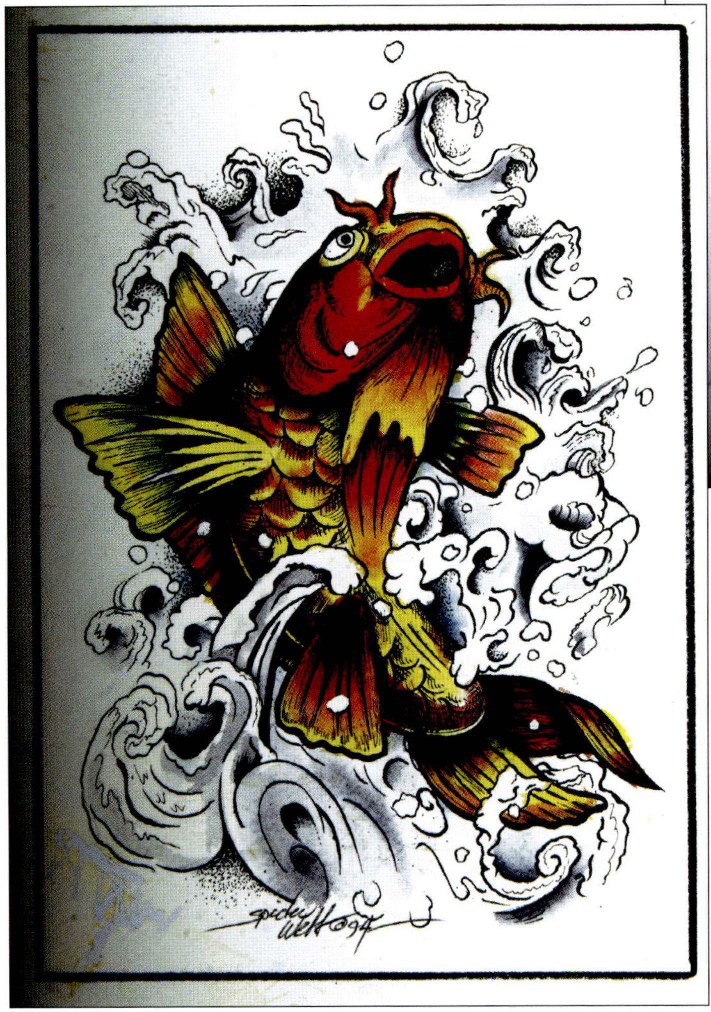

"What We Believe Shapes What We See." Ink and watercolor on Archers paper, 9" x 12". 1994.

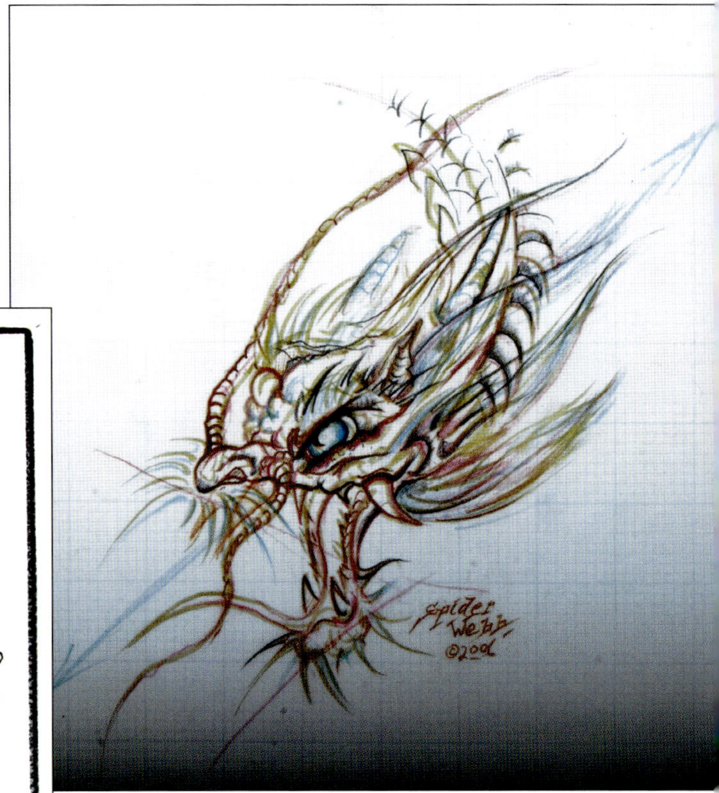

"You Are, We Are. It's All Confection." Pencil on Vellum paper, 9" x 12". 2006.

You can't get what I got – Nobody can buy what I have.

—*S.W.*

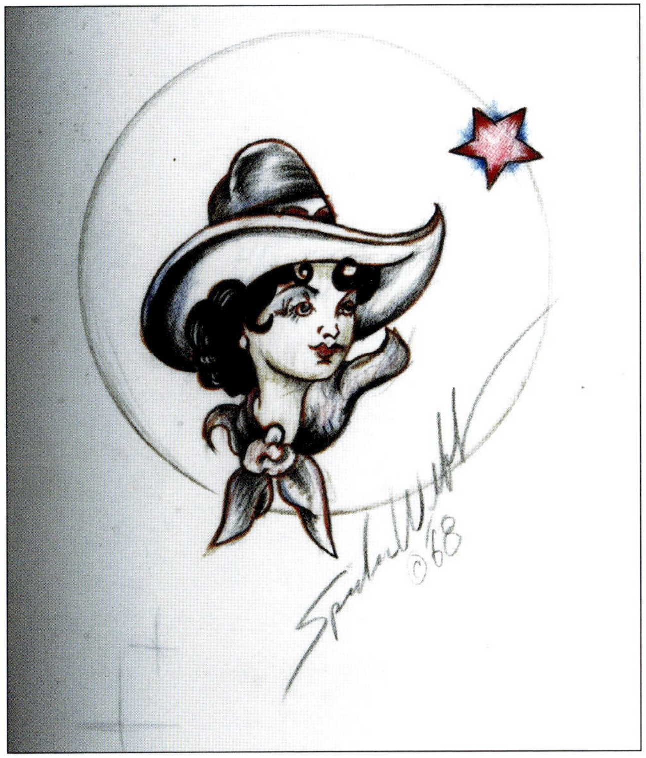

"Chaos/God, Understanding Religion." Pencil on Vellum paper, 8 1/2" x 10". 1968.

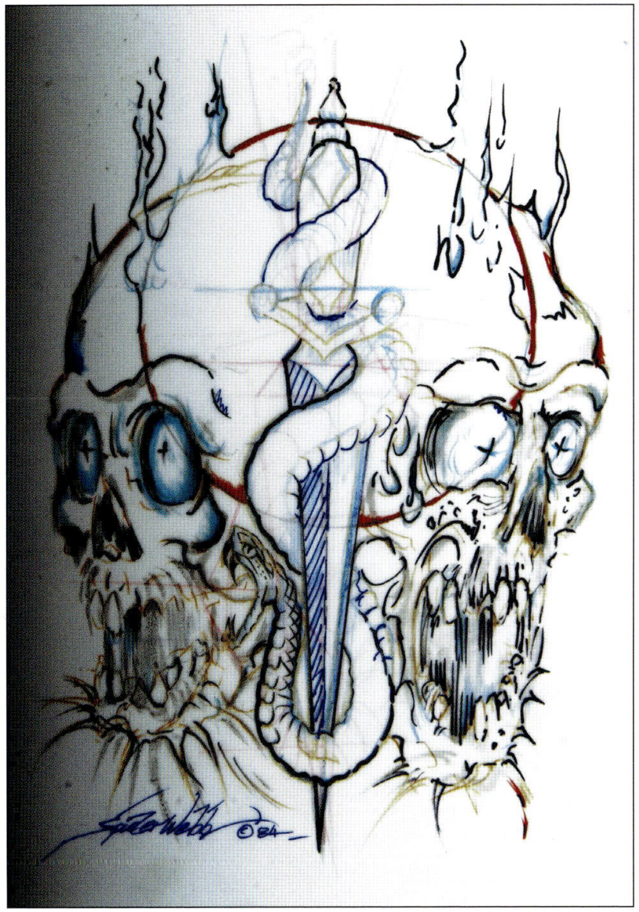

"Creating Information or Hypothesis?" Pencil on Vellum paper, 9" x 12". 1984.

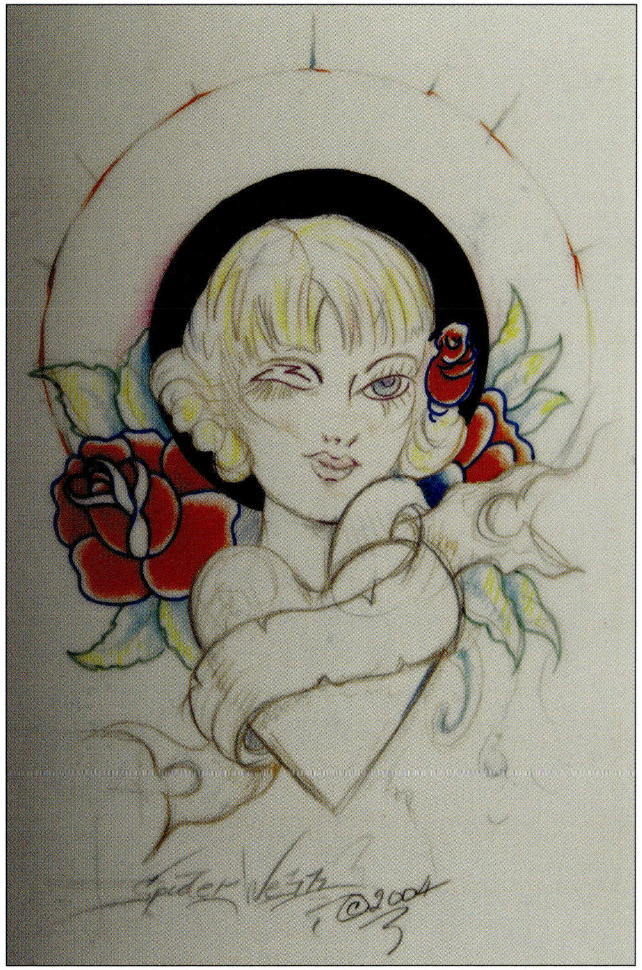

"Death's Desire, the Best of Everything." Pencil on Vellum paper, 9" x 12". 2004.

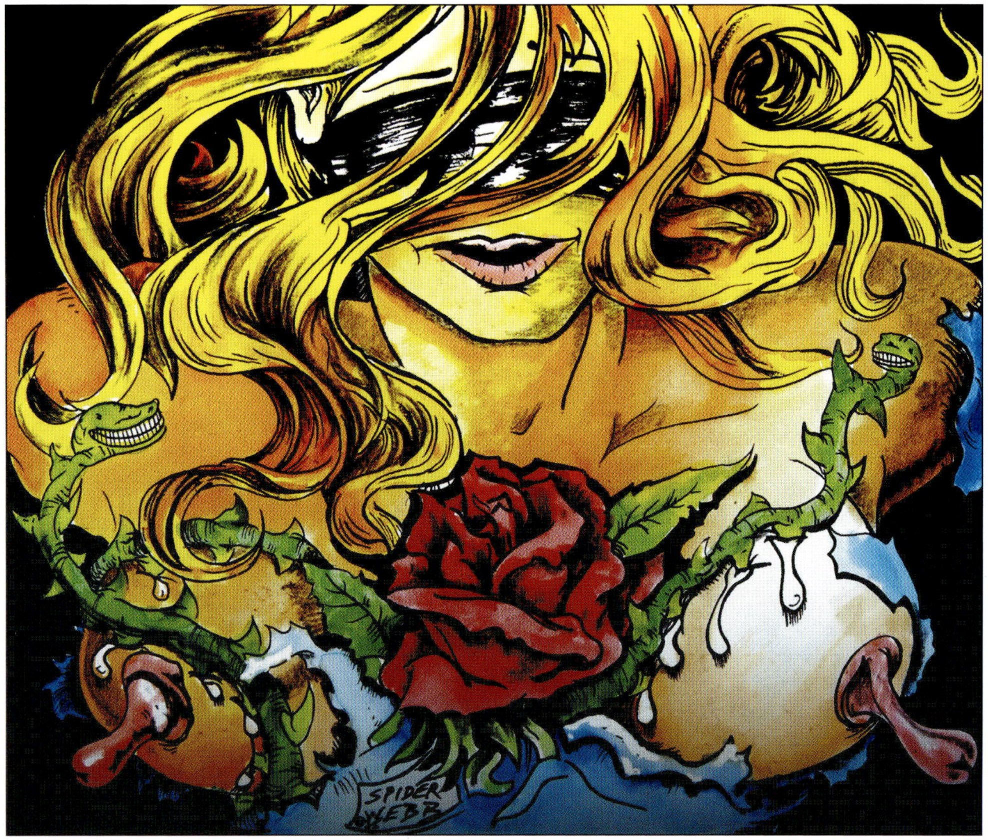

"Disappointed High Standards." Ink and watercolor on Archers paper, 9" x 12". 1975.

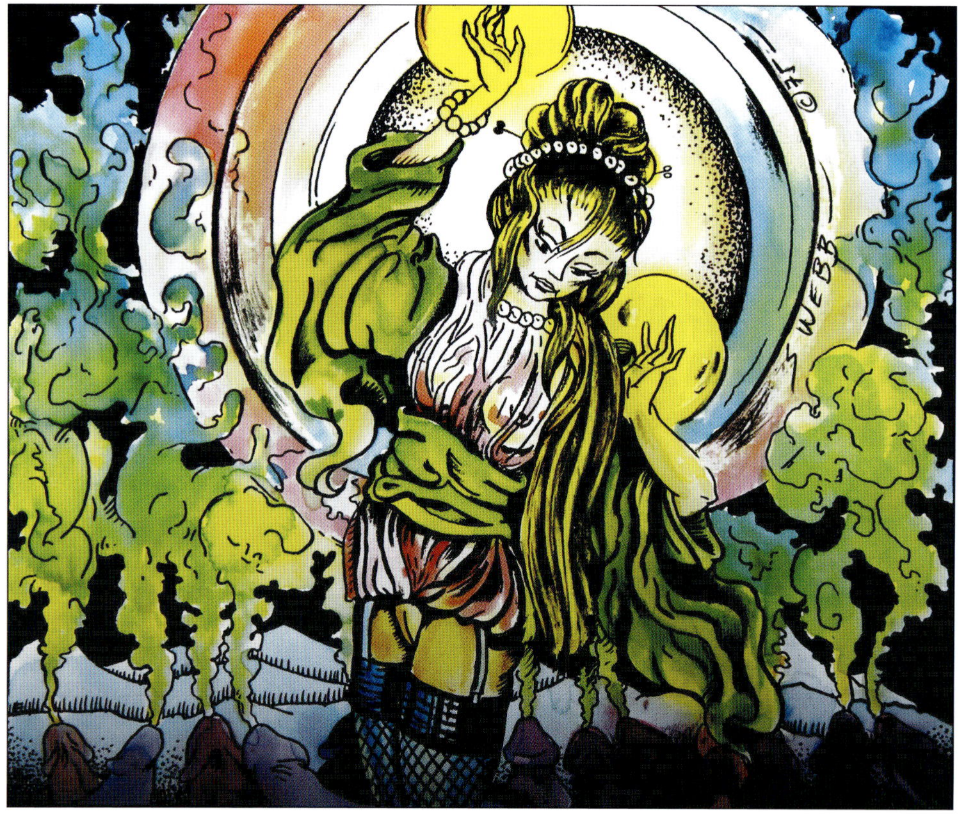

"Dwelling on Dreams and Impure Thoughts." Ink and watercolor on Archers paper, 9" x 12". 1975.

We're all looking at the same thing, but everybody sees something different. Take for example that teenage girl across the street...

*—S.W.*

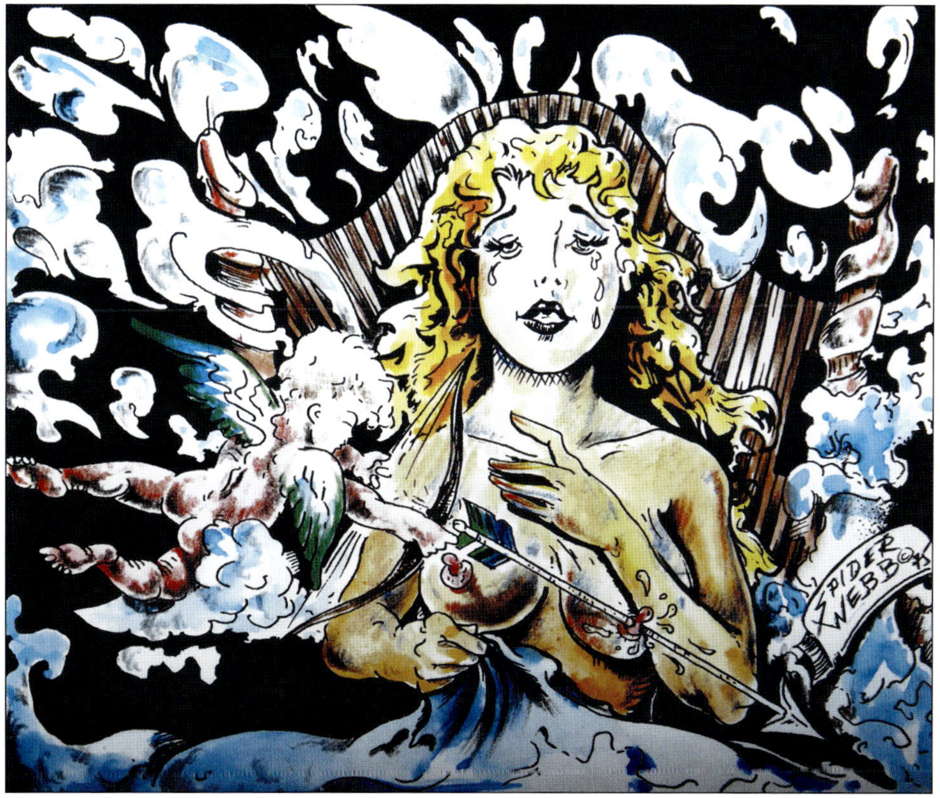


"If You Can't Do – Criticize." Ink and watercolor on Archers paper, 9" x 12". 1975.

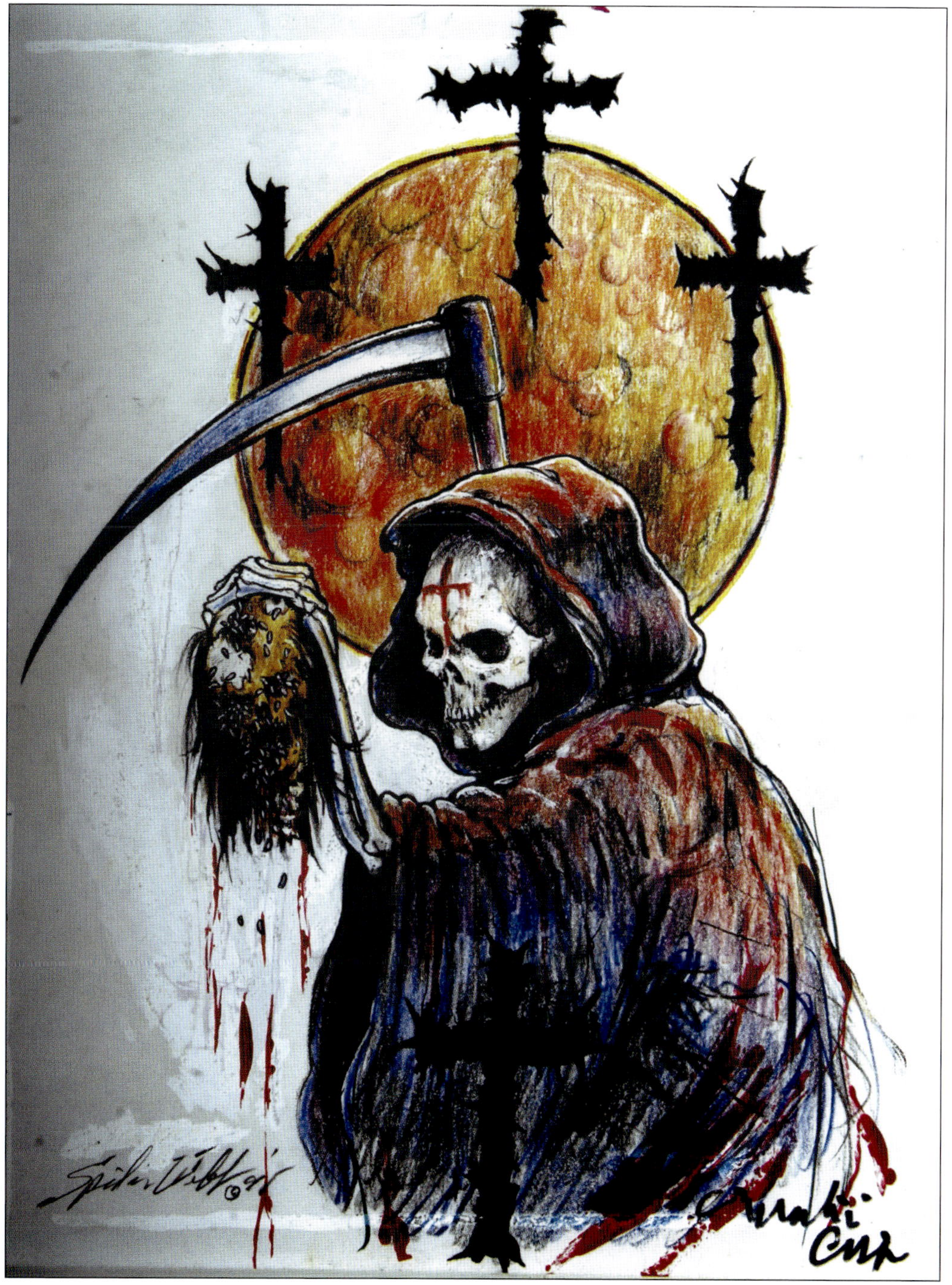

"Money No, It's Ideas and Dreams." Mixed media on paper, 9" x 12". 1995.
*Signed Spider Webb – Quentin Crisp.*

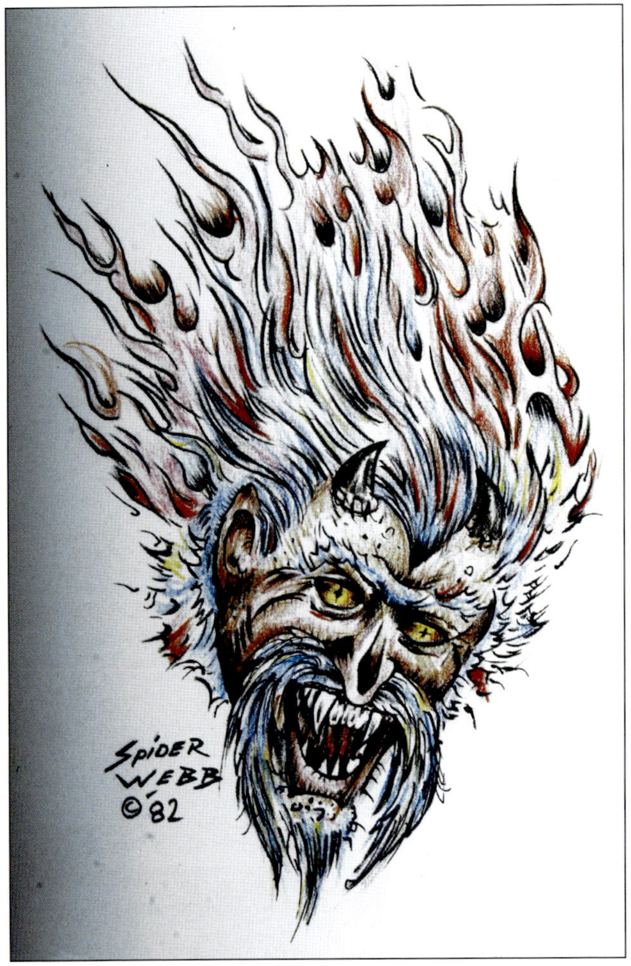


"Be Prepared to Be Amazed." Pencil on Vellum paper, 9" x 12". 1982.

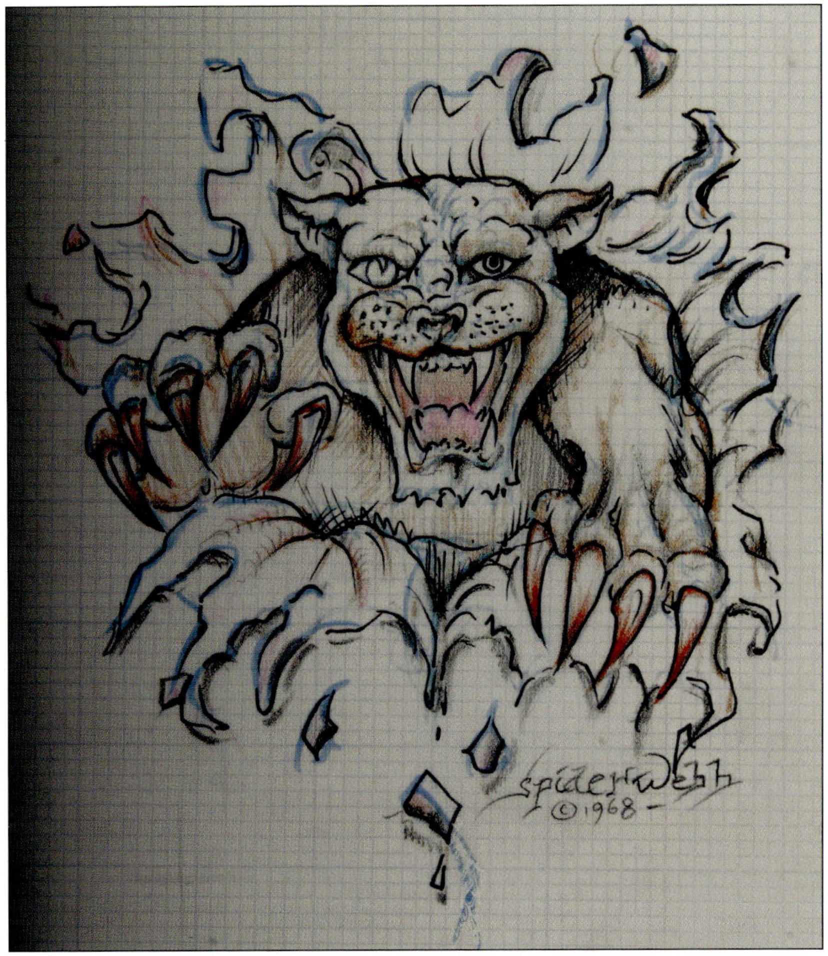


"Looking Up Her Skirt I Saw Her Tonsils." Pencil on Vellum paper, 11" x 17". 1968.

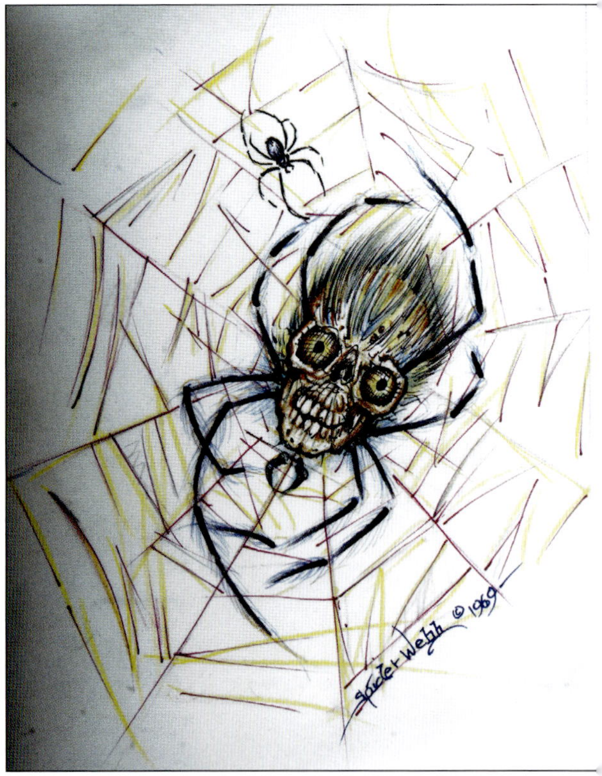


"Beat Them to Death For Exercise." Pencil on Vellum paper, 9" x 12". 1969.

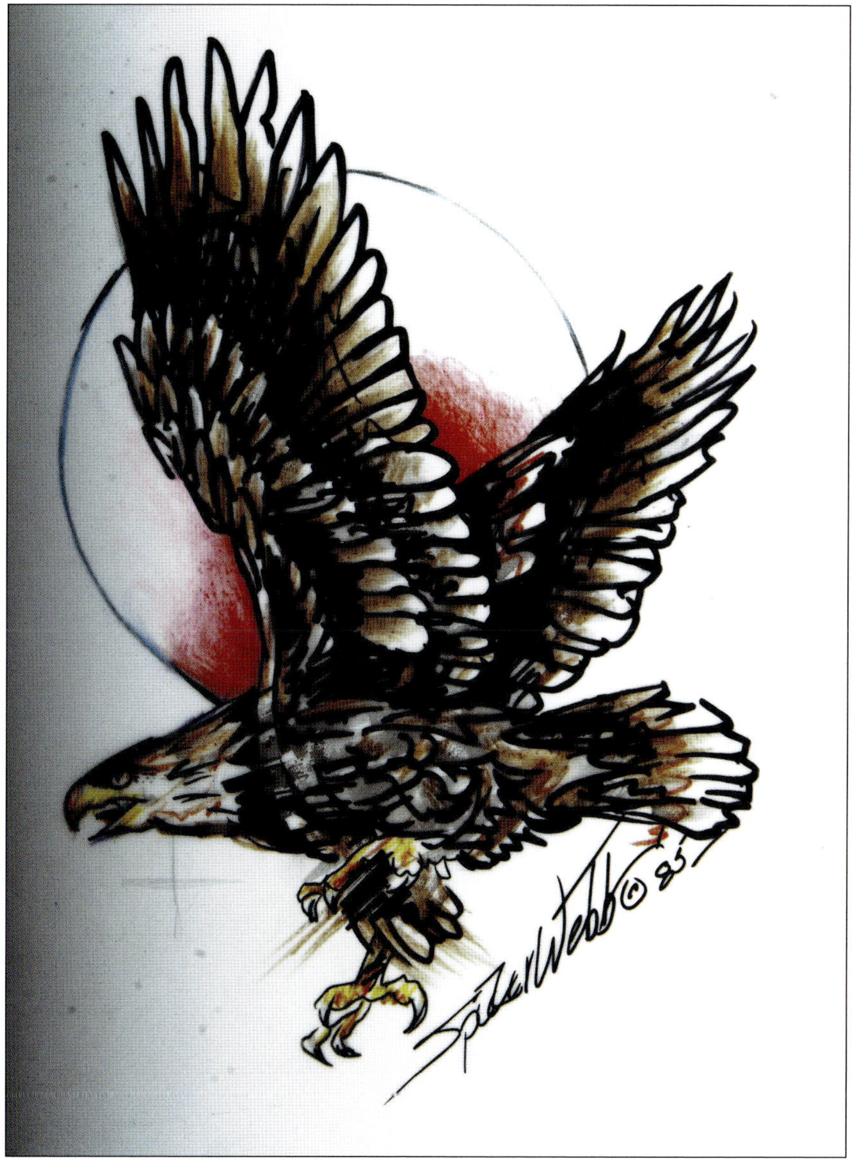

"Hate In My Veins." Pencil on Vellum paper, 8 1/2" x 11". 1985.

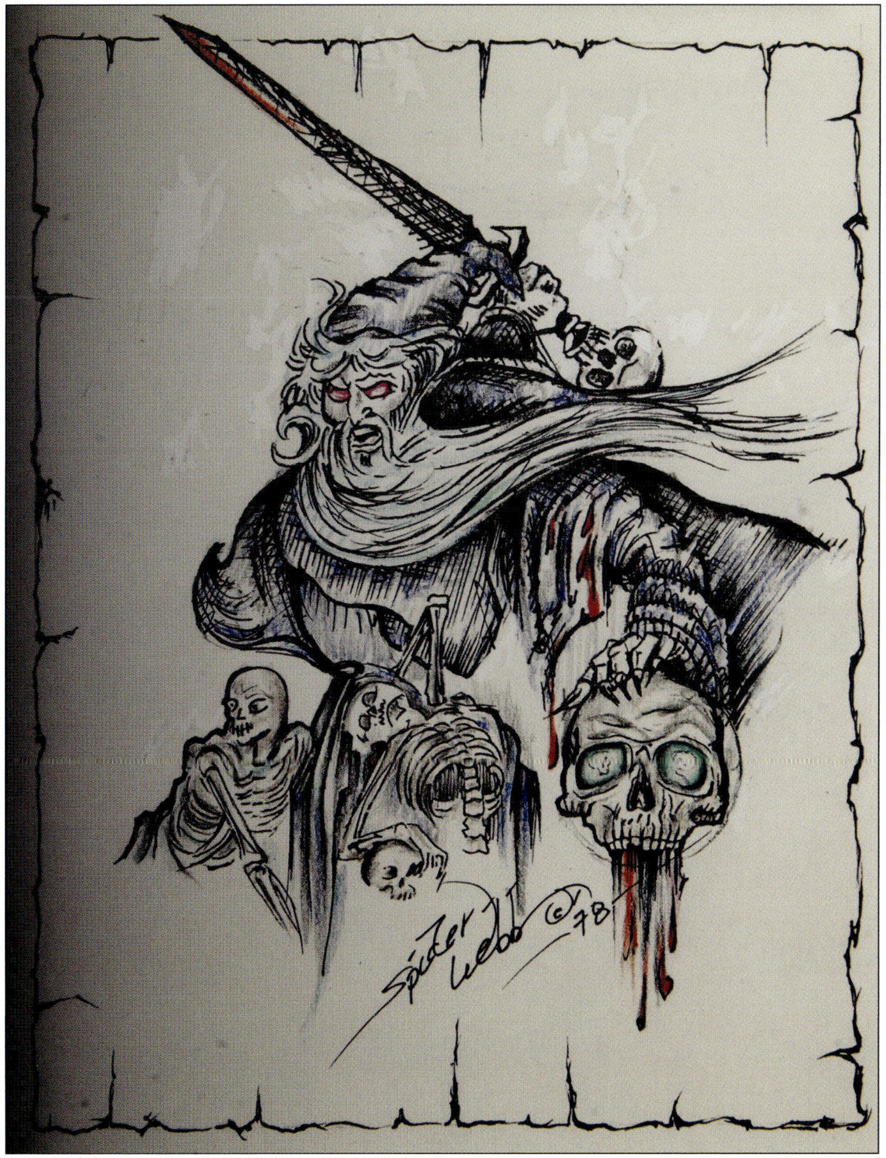

"Sick and Evil." Pencil on Vellum paper, 8 1/2" x 11". 1978.

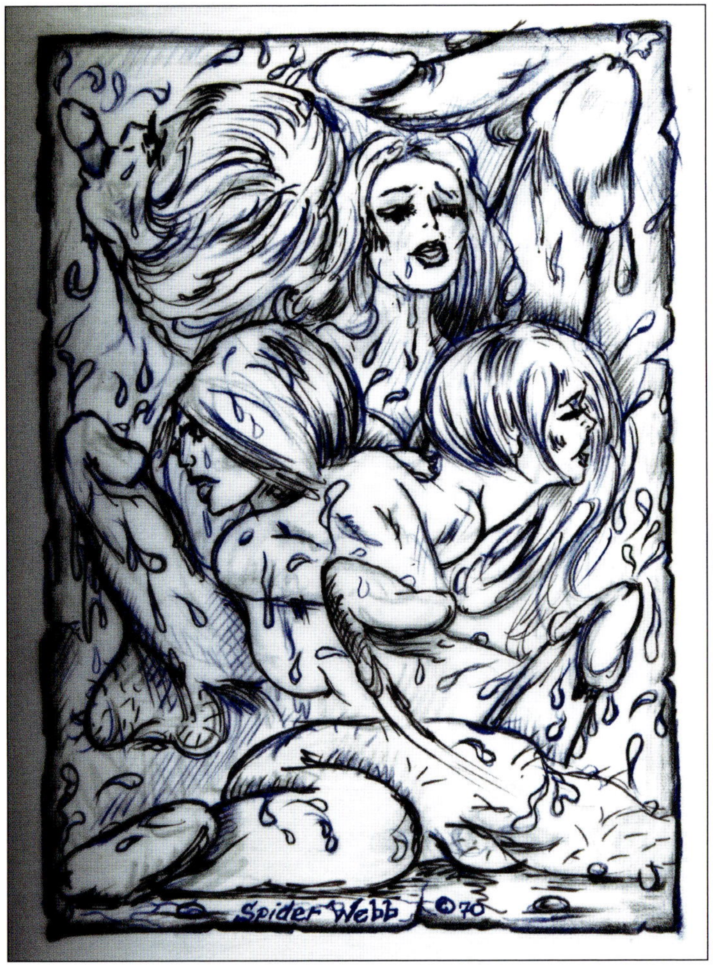


"I Can't Feel Anything Anymore." Pencil on Vellum paper, 8 1/2" x 11". 1970.

After I fainted I never believed I'd wake up having inter-racial sex with the dead...but you never know.

—*S.W.*

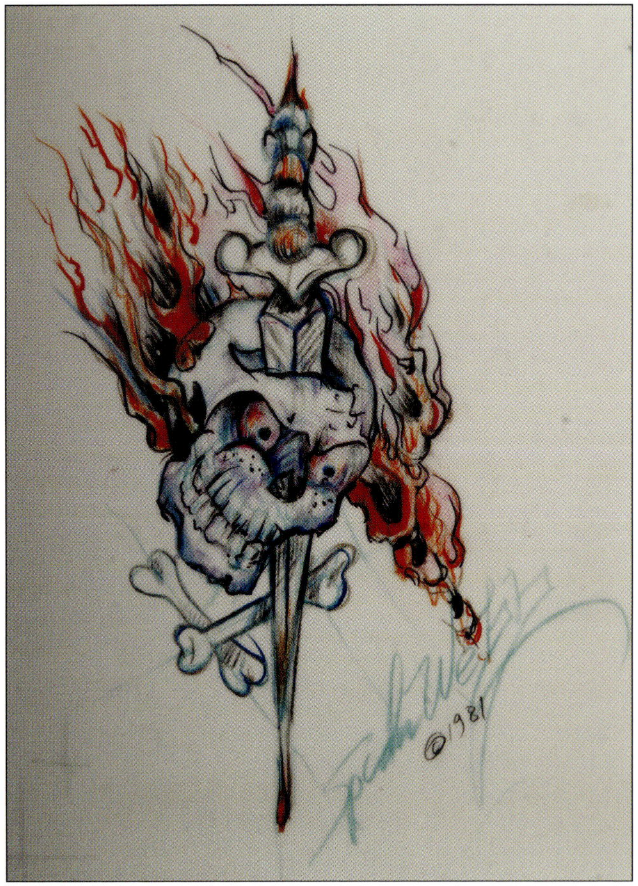


"Knowing and Believing Share a Wavelength." Pencil on Vellum paper, 8 1/2" x 11". 1981.

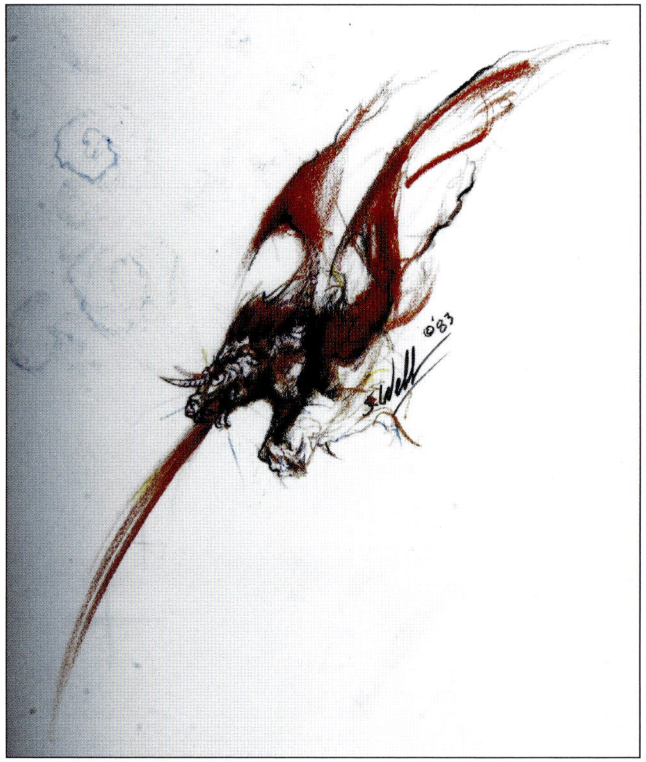

"Good Manners and Respect – Always Out Numbered." Pencil on Vellum paper, 8 1/2" x 11". 1983.

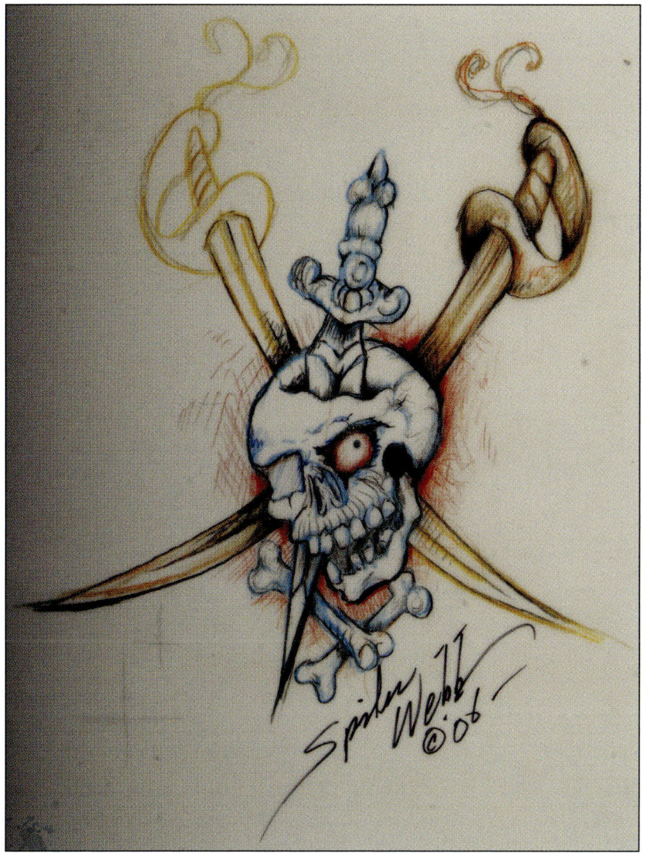

"Compromises and Missed Opportunities = Failure." Pencil on Vellum paper, 9" x 12". 2006.

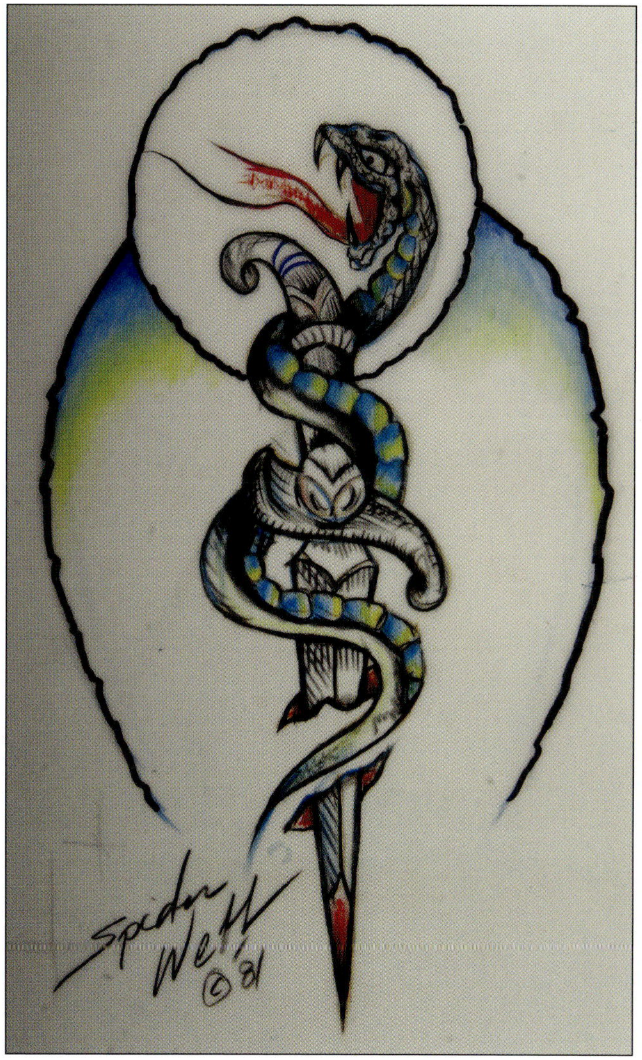

"Martial Law: The Untreated Injured." Pencil on Vellum paper, 8" x 10". 1981.

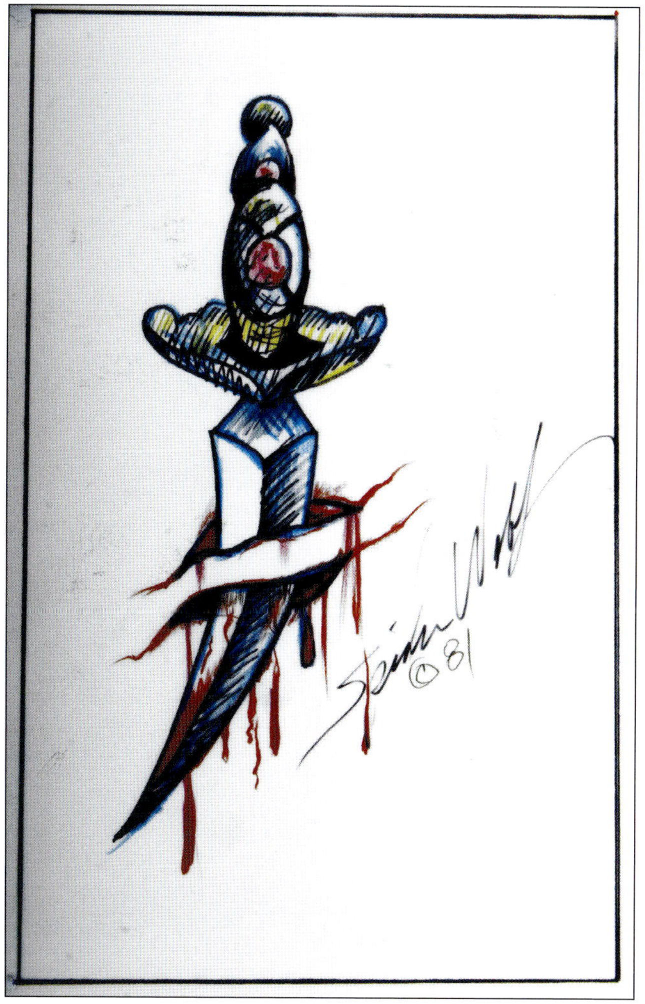

"Human Senses and Instincts, No Substitutes." Pencil on Vellum paper, 8" x 10". 1981.

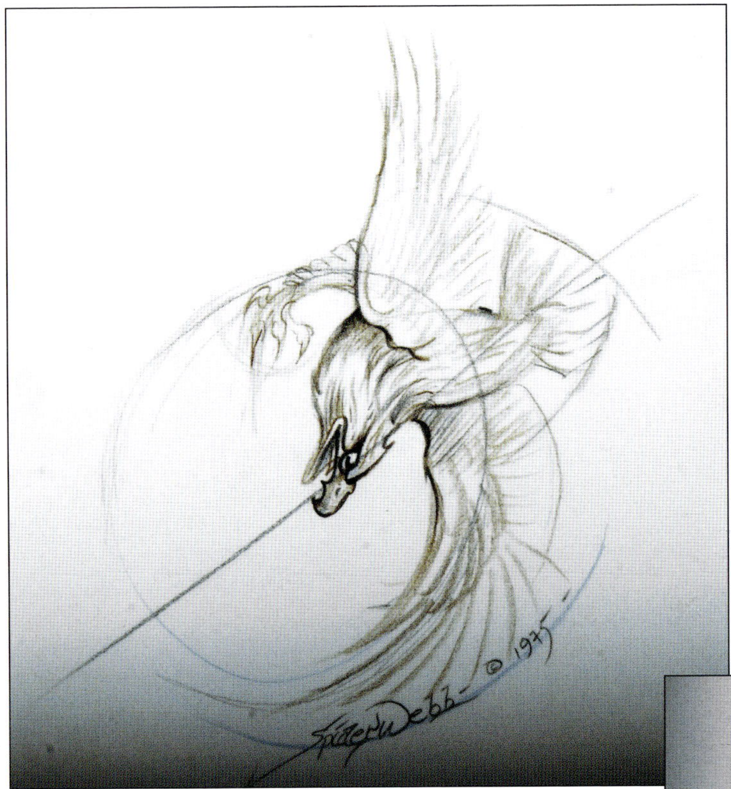

“Vanquisher of Heart.” Pencil on Vellum paper, 9" x 12". 1975.

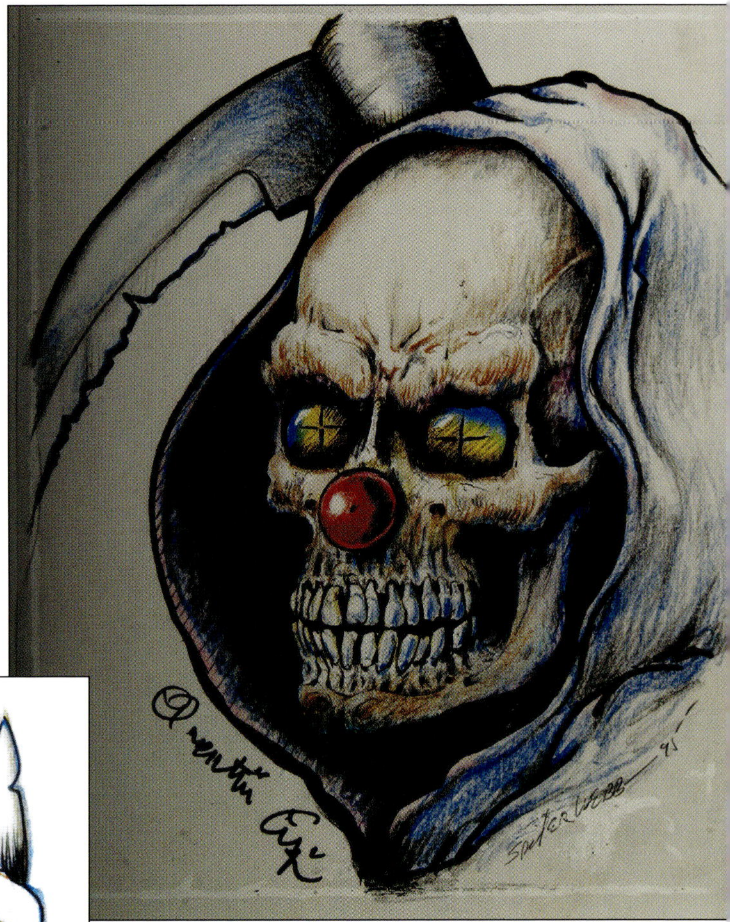

“Looking Back Seeing Only Yesterday’s Tears.” Mixed media on Archers paper, 9" x 12". 1995. *Signed Spider Webb – Quentin Crisp.*

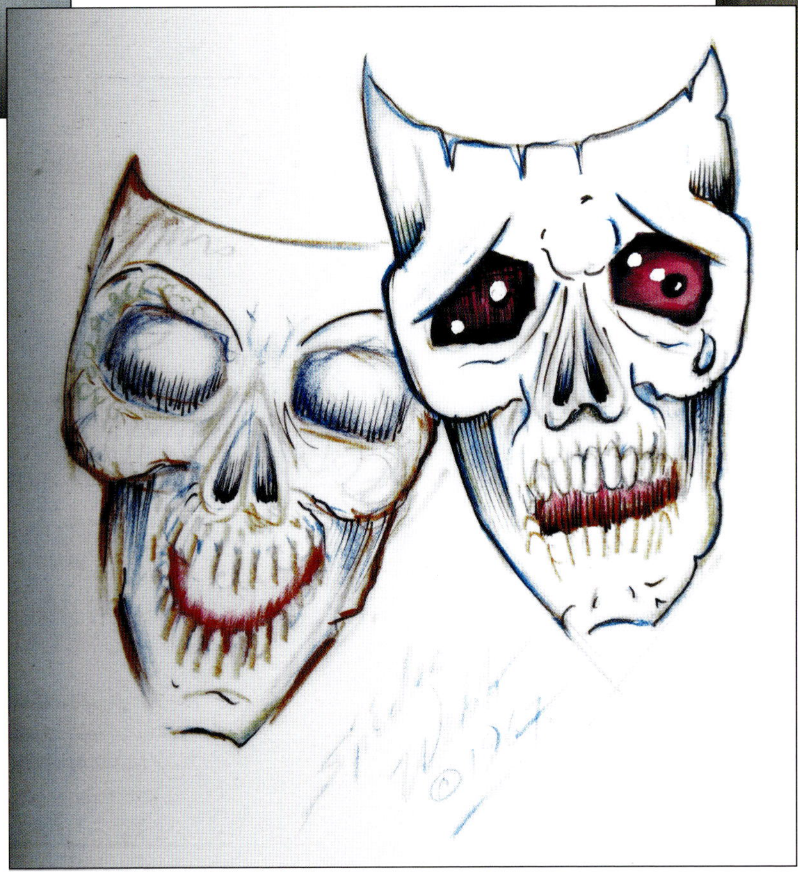

“Separated By a Veil.” Pencil on Vellum paper, 9" x 12". 1967.

Seat belts? Why, I’d rather wear a neck brace.

—*S.W.*

You can always punch yourself in the face to make it look as though you've been beaten.

—*S.W.*

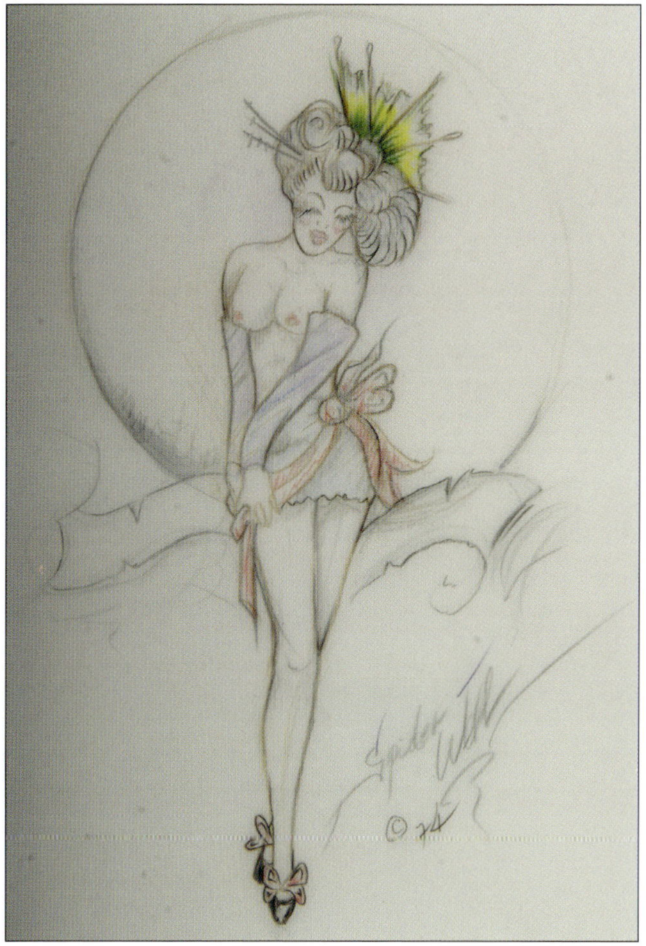

"Out of All Proportion." Pencil on Vellum paper, 8" x 11". 1974.

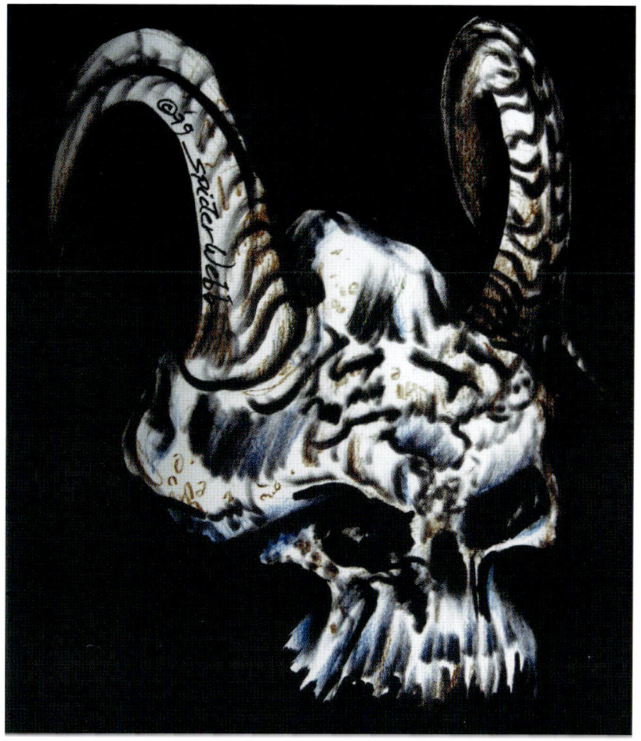

"Explosive Emotional Reaction." Ink on paper, 9" x 12". 1979.

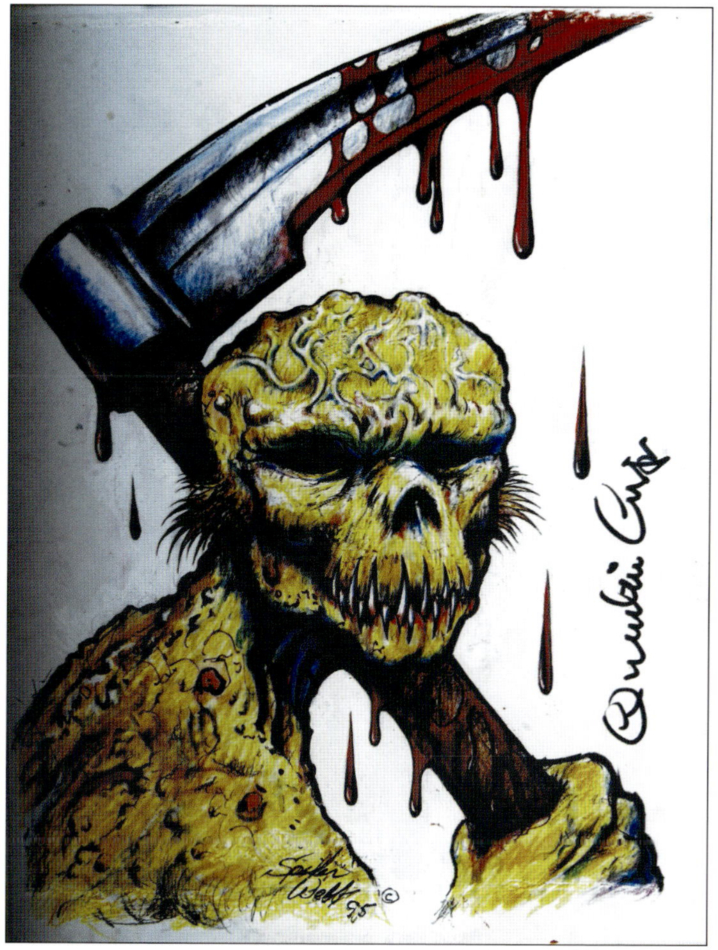

"Making Your Heart Hurry." Mixed media on Archers paper, 9" x 12". 1995.
*Signed Spider Webb – Quentin Crisp.*

Community, harmony, balance, and wholeness, just a few of the reasons I wanted to kill for the government.

—*S.W.*

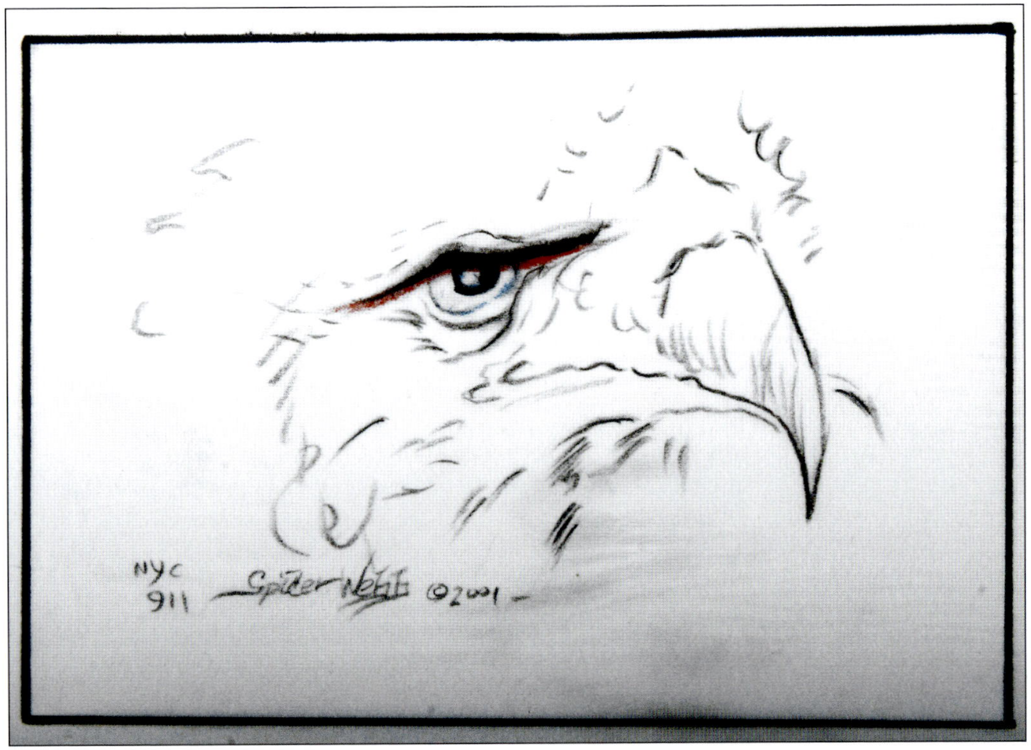


"Sundials Keeping Lost Time." Pencil on Vellum paper, 11" x 17". 2001.

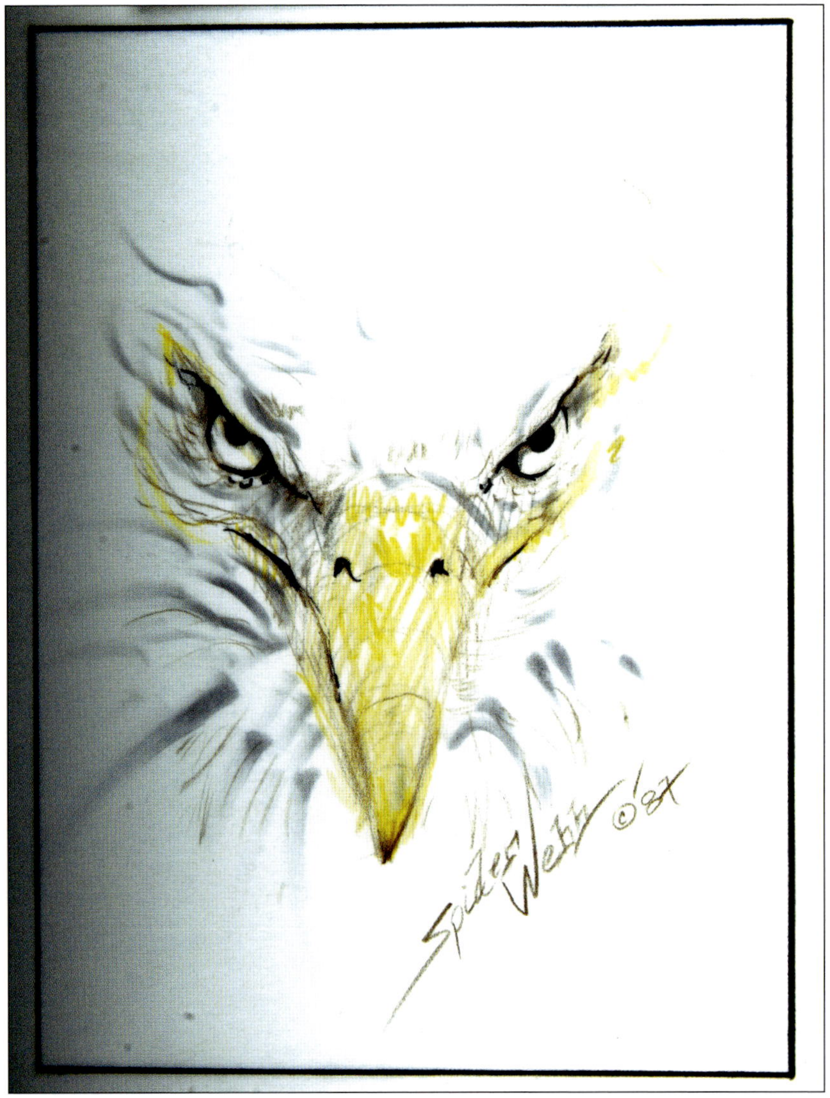


"Hour Glasses Measuring Silence." Pencil on Vellum paper, 11" x 17". 1987.

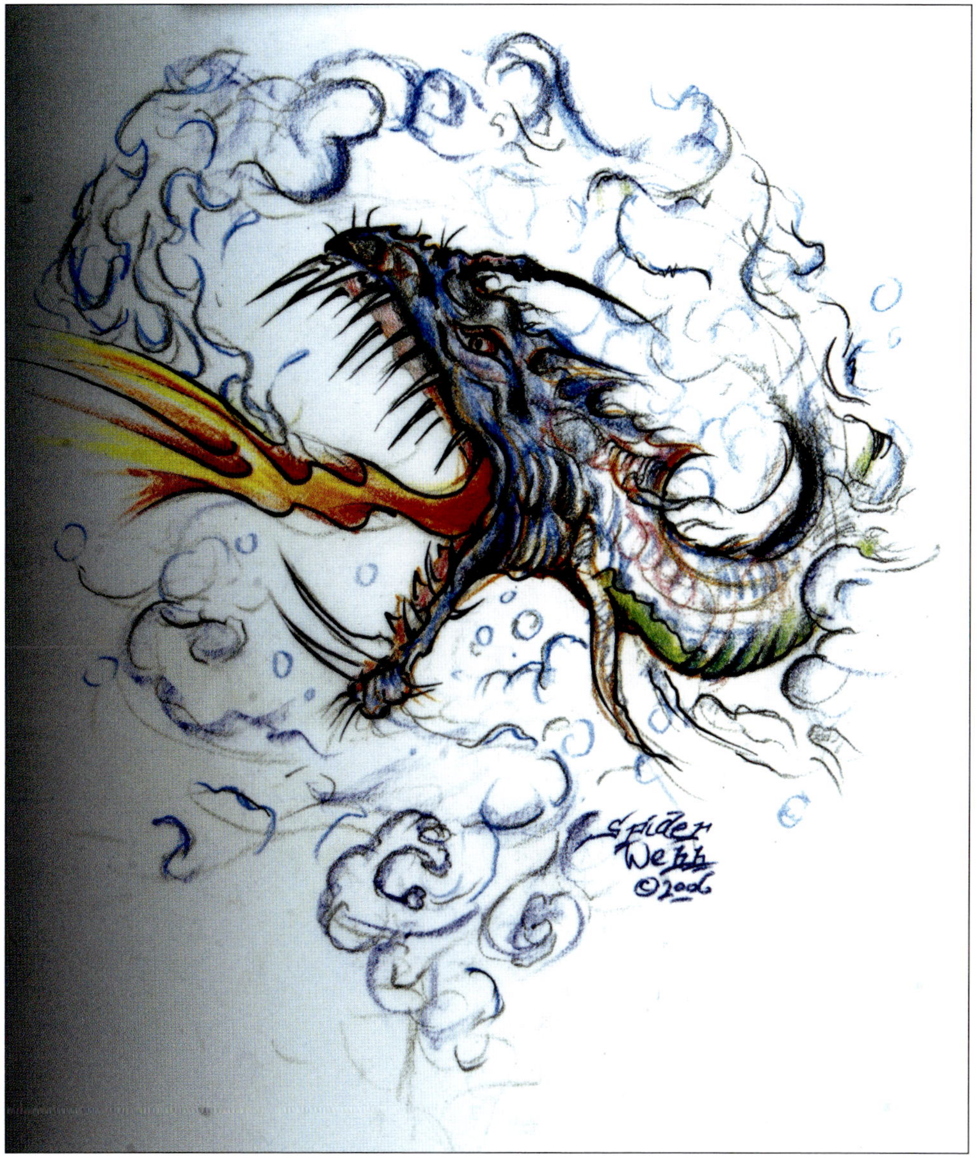


"Keep This Object Carefully." Pencil on Vellum paper, 8 1/2" x 11". 2006.

Without mysteries how do you expect to learn anything?

—*S.W.*

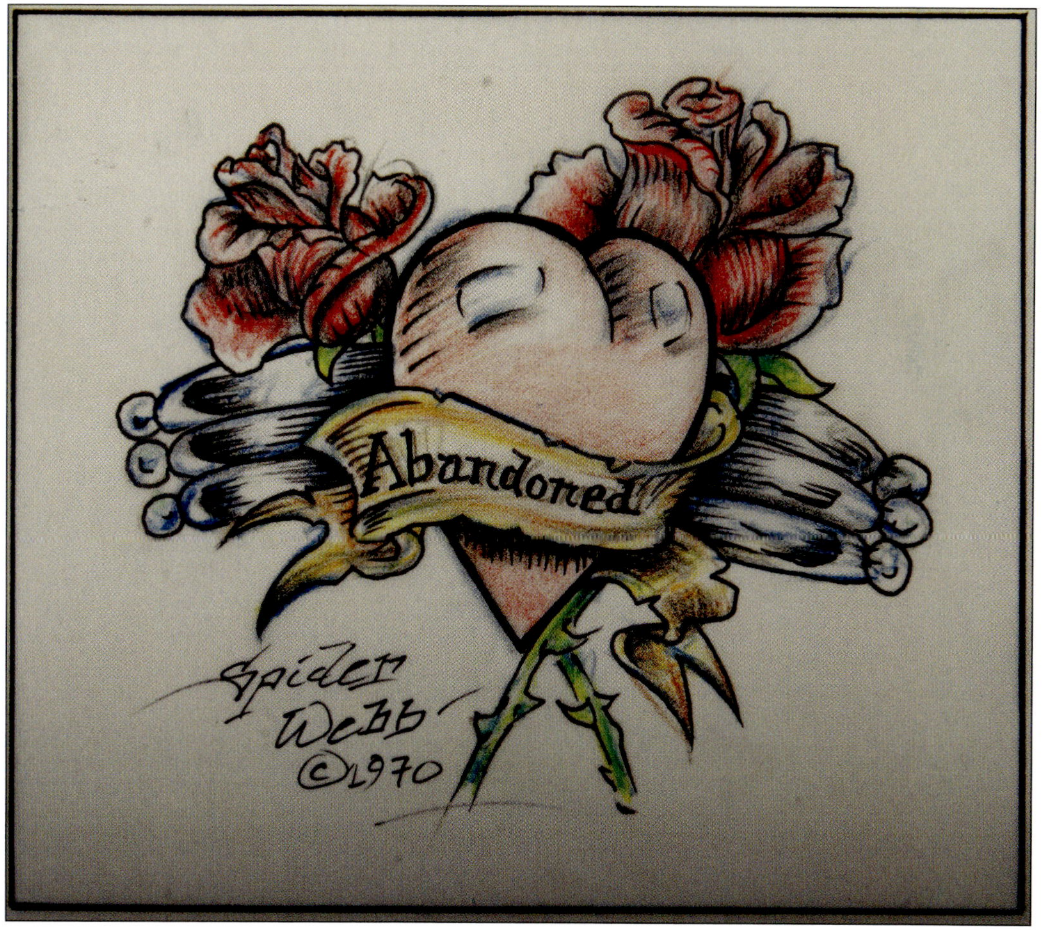


"Metaphysics Through the Skin." Pencil on Vellum paper, 9" x 12". 1970.

"Evil Done, Evil Returned." Pencil on Vellum paper, 9" x 12". 1968.

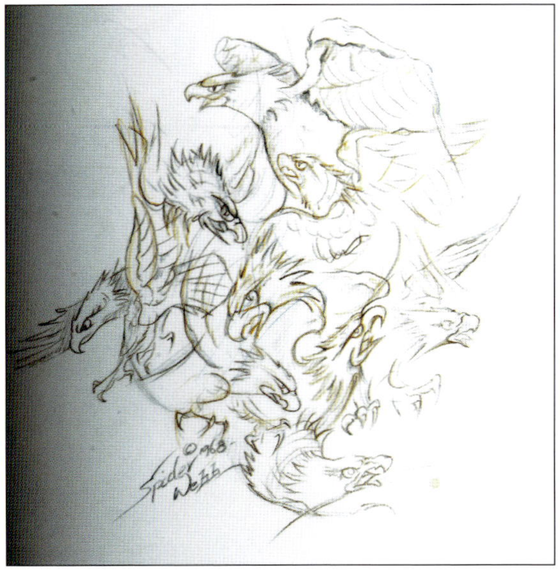

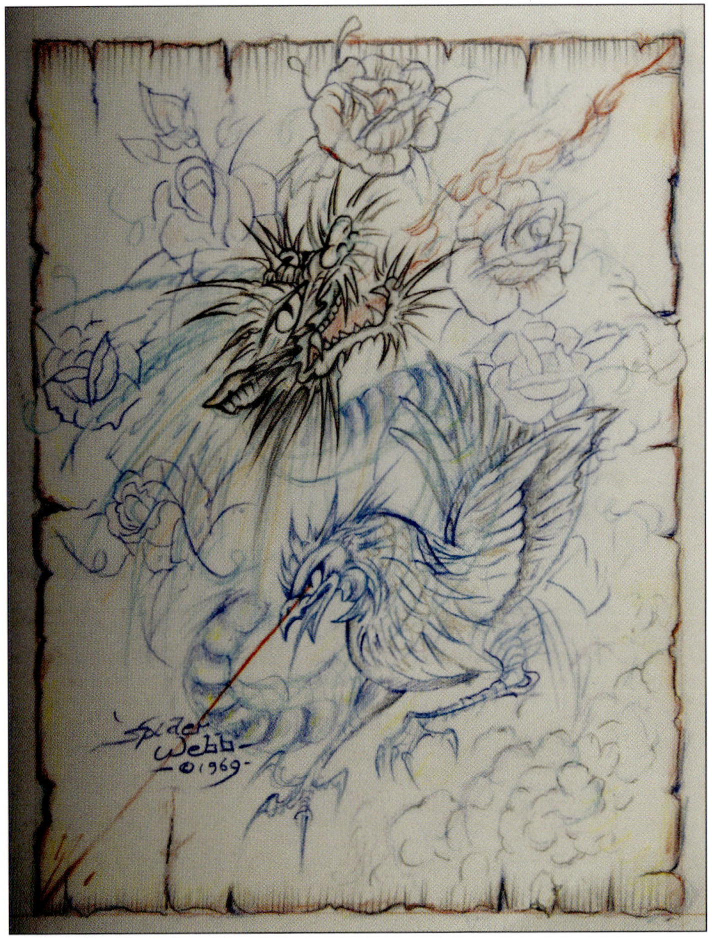


"Go Peddle Your Little Trinkets II." Pencil on Vellum paper, 9" x 12". 1969.

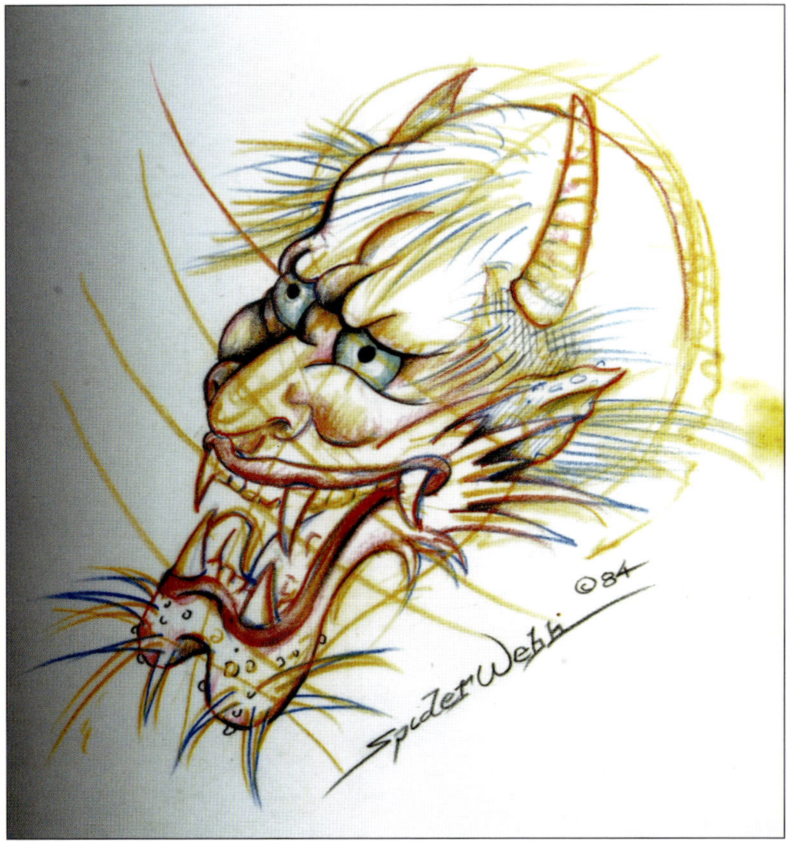


"Not Forbidden: Allowable." Pencil on Vellum paper, 9" x 12". 1984.

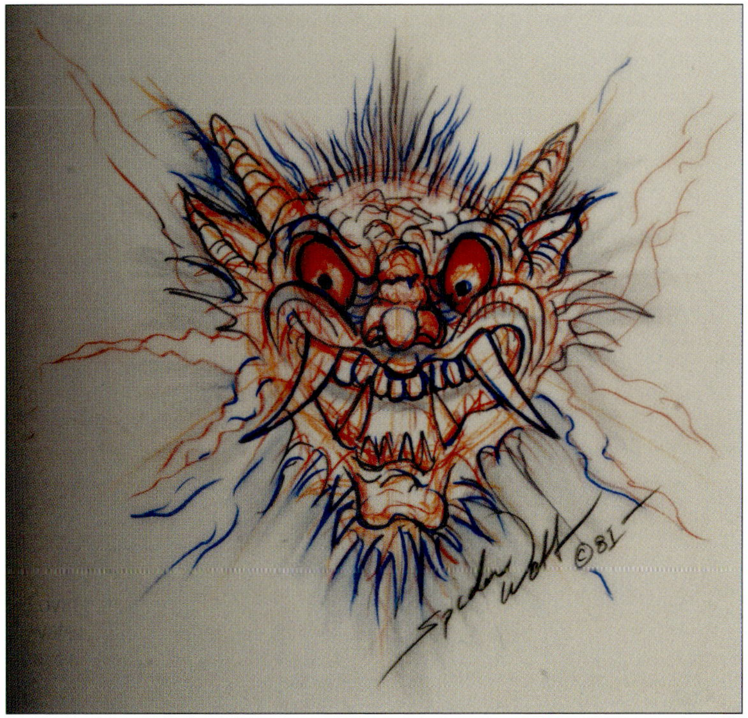

"Violating All His Laws." Pencil on Vellum paper, 11" x 17". 1981.

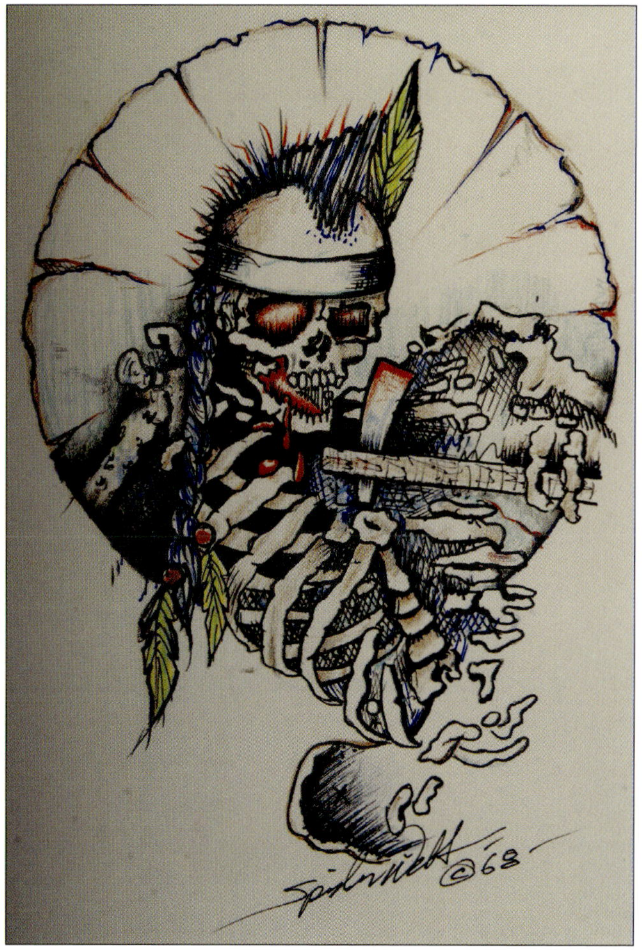

"Unleashed Power Changing Everything." Pencil on Vellum paper, 9" x 12". 1968.

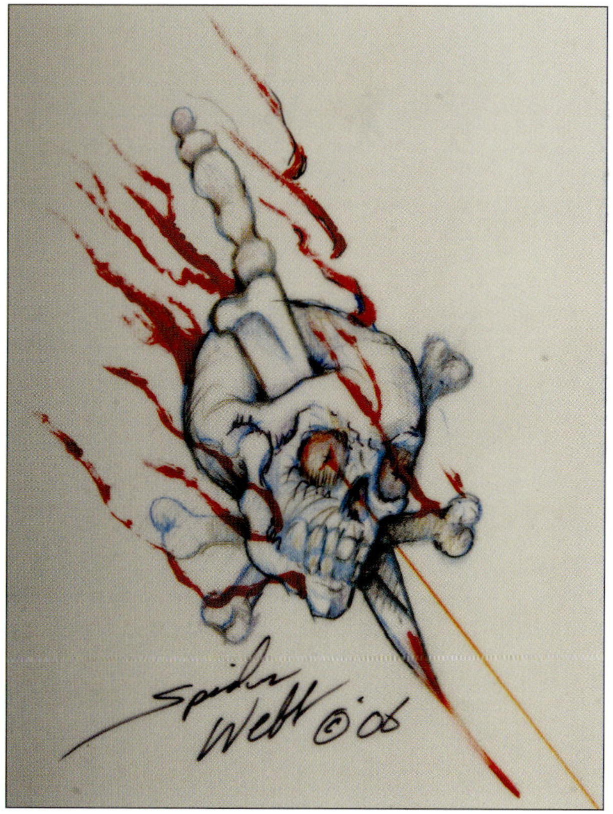

"A Belief in Magic Could Explain Everything." Pencil on Vellum paper, 9" x 12". 2006.

Somewhere between smoke and mirrors I see your soul – God help us all.

—*S.W.*

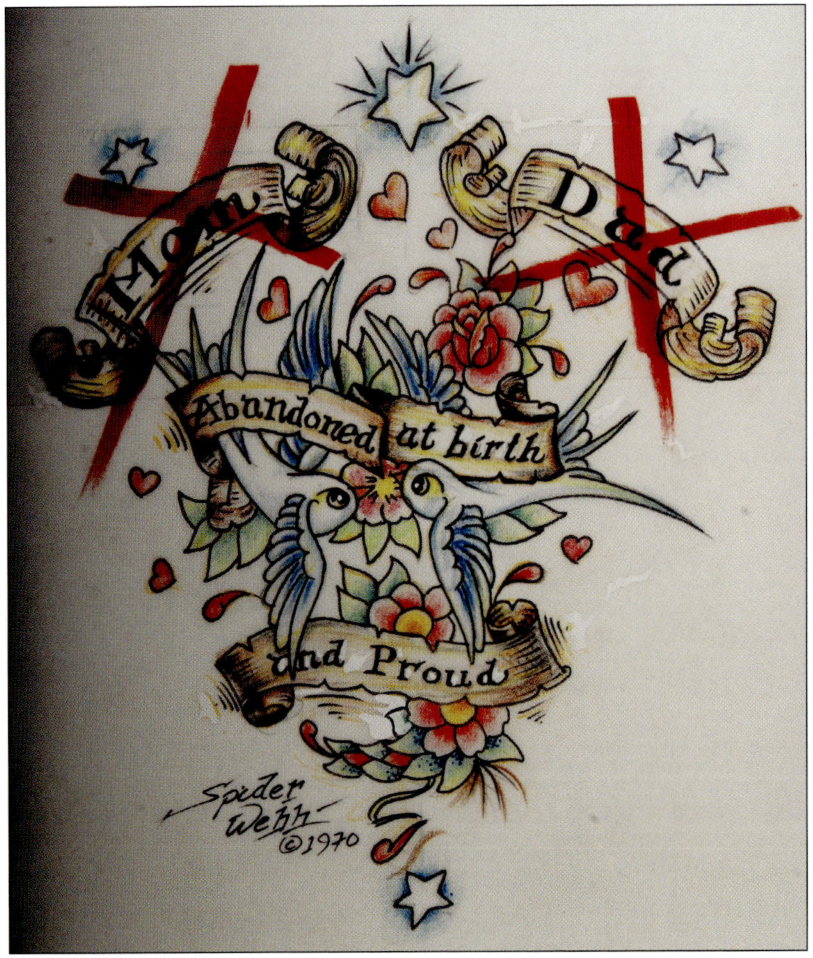


"Have a Little Fun With Yourself." Pencil on Vellum paper, 9" x 12". 1970.

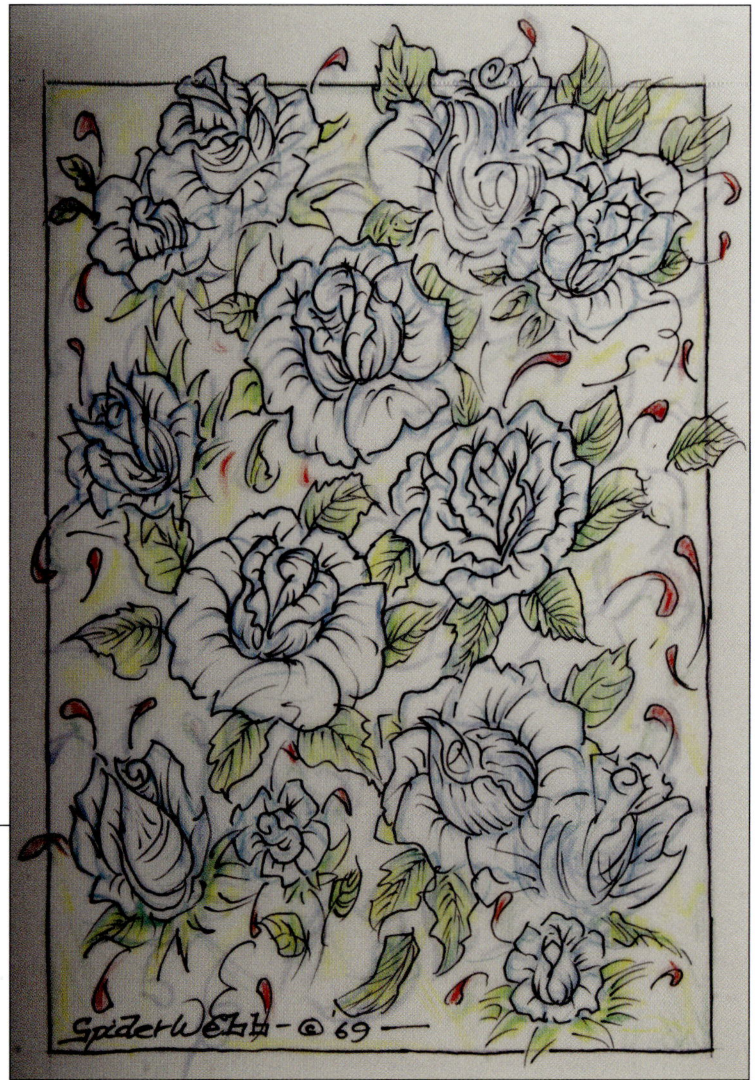


"Inspired by Angels." Pencil on Vellum paper, 9" x 12". 1969.

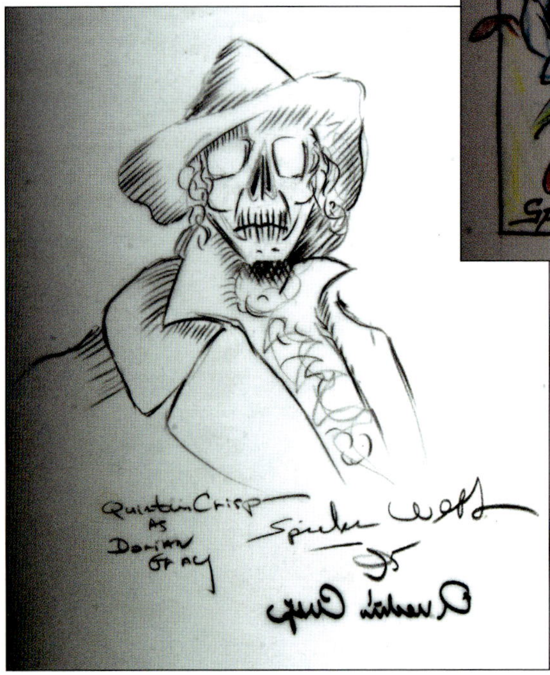


"No Reservations in Hell." Pencil on paper, 8 1/2" x 11". 1995. *Signed Spider Webb – Quentin Crisp* (signed on reverse).

Take the shit out of your ears and stick it in your mouth – I'm talking to you.

—*S.W.*

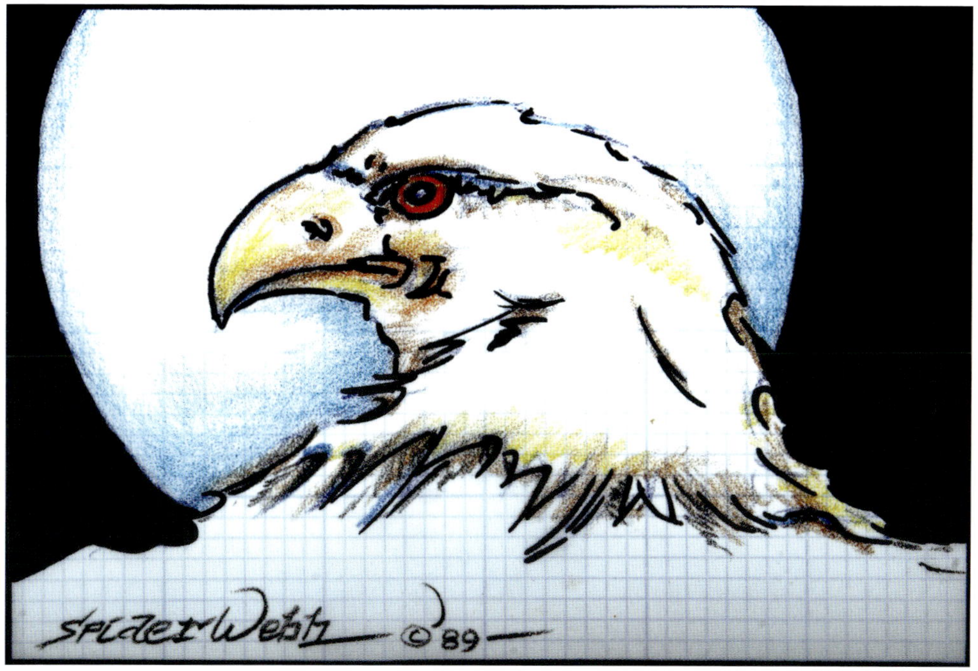


"Fairy Tales for Goats." Pencil on Vellum paper, 11" x 17". 1989.

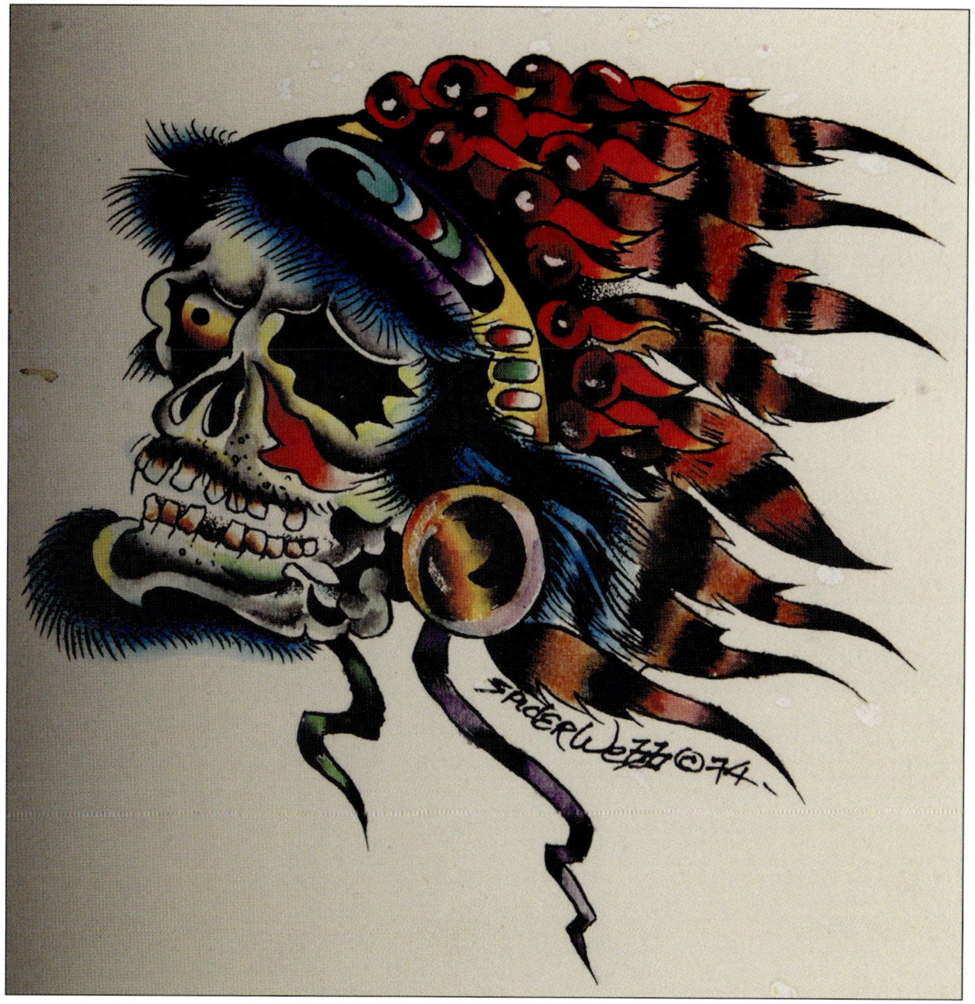


"Incredible Wasteland." Ink and watercolor on Archers paper, 9" x 12". 1974.

How can I expect to show anyone the puzzles and nuances I create?

—*S.W.*

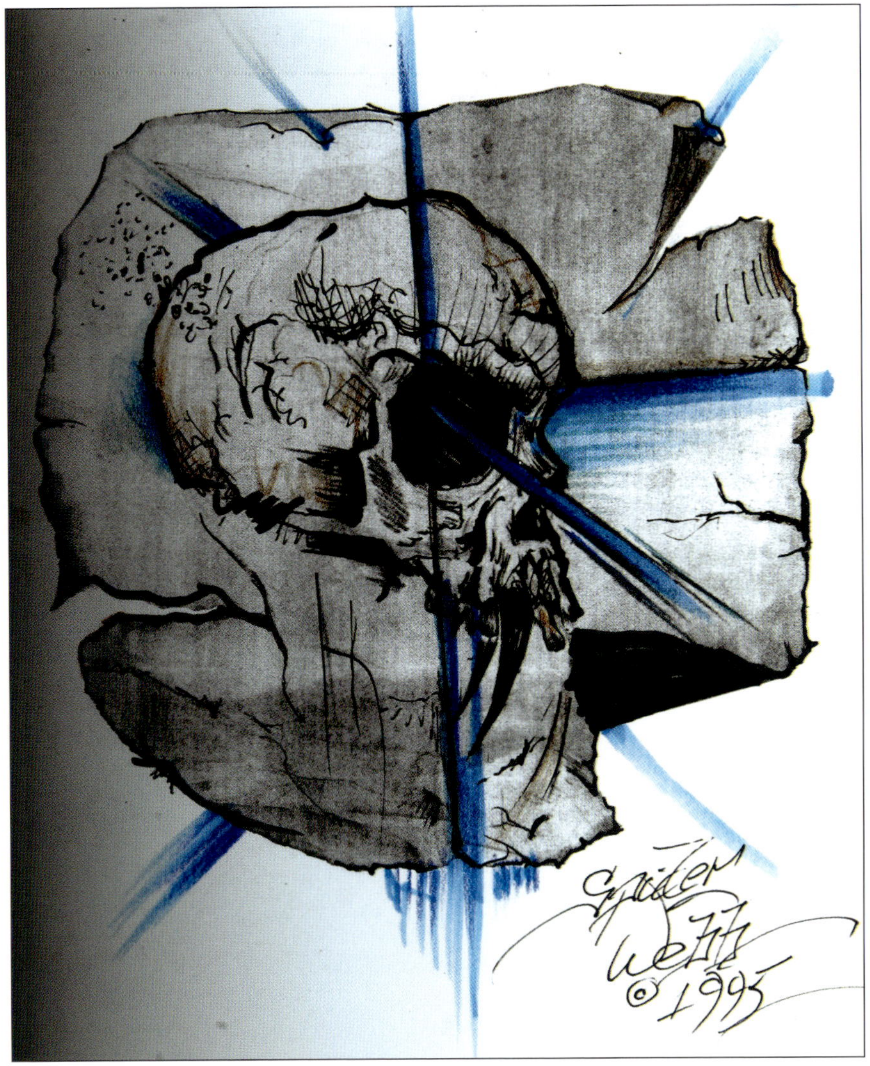

"Anonymous Content." Pencil on paper, 9" x 12". 1995.

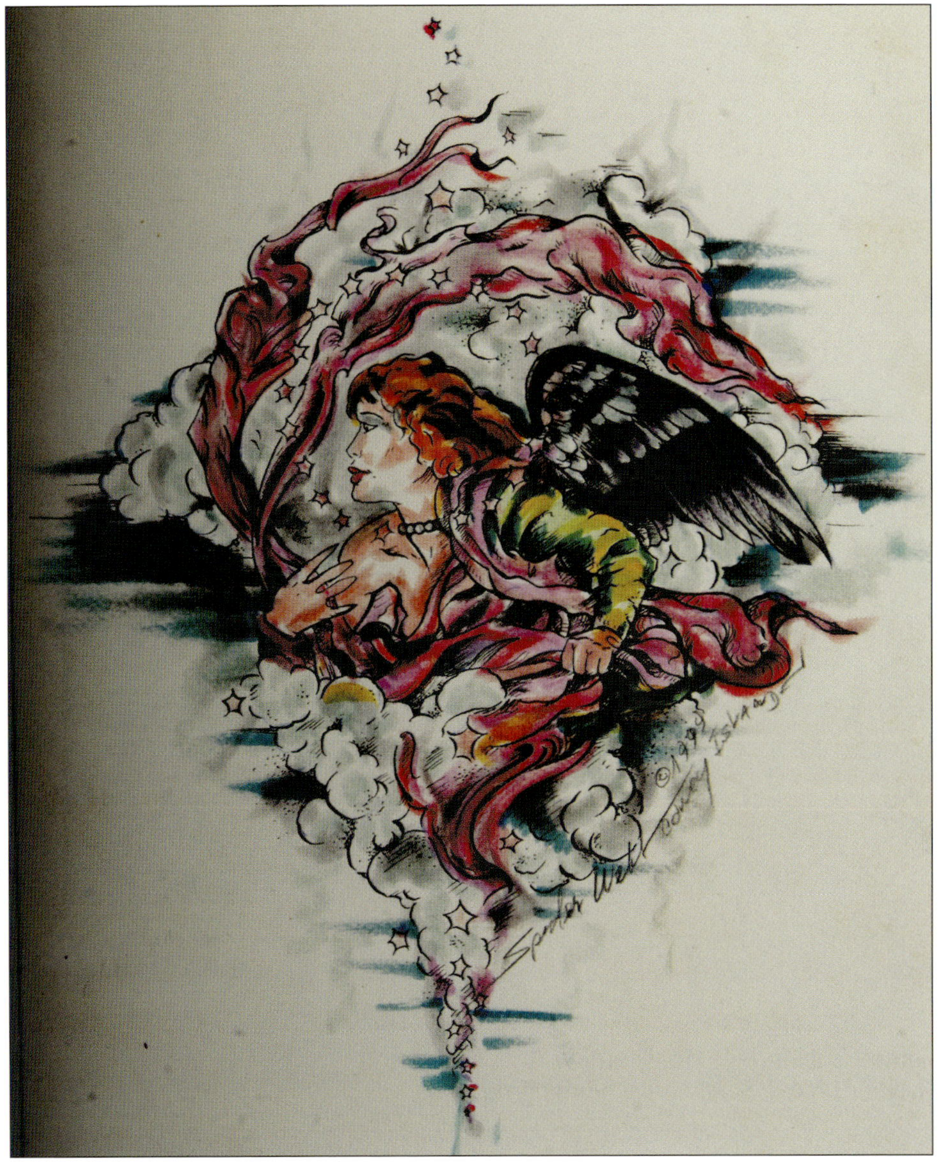

"In the Land of Hurt." Ink and watercolor on Archers paper, 9" x 12". 1999.

"Premium Soft-Core Erotic." Pencil on Vellum paper, 11" x 17". 1967.

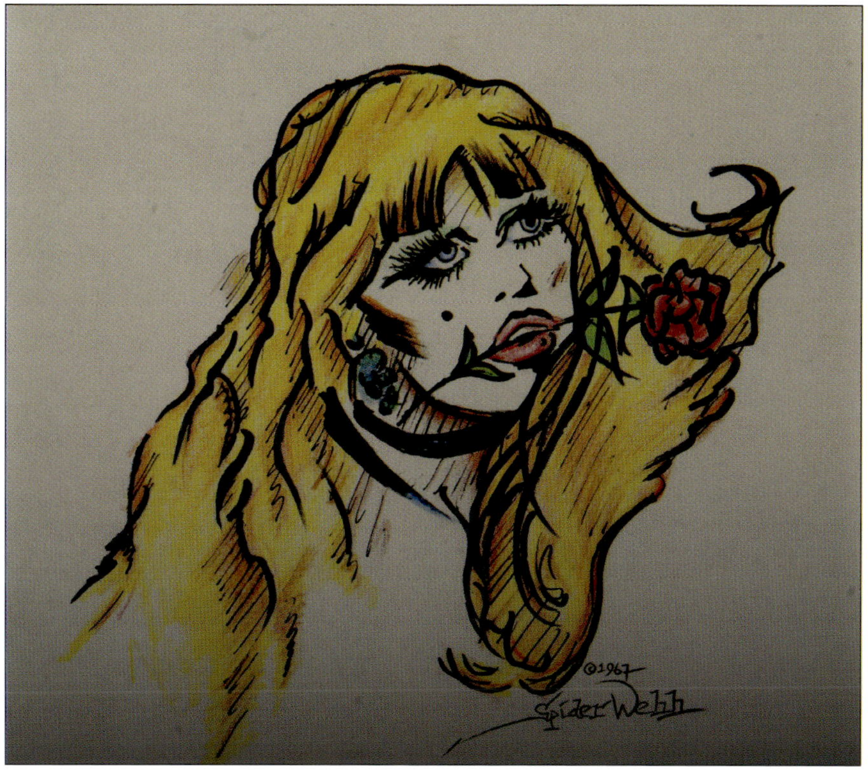


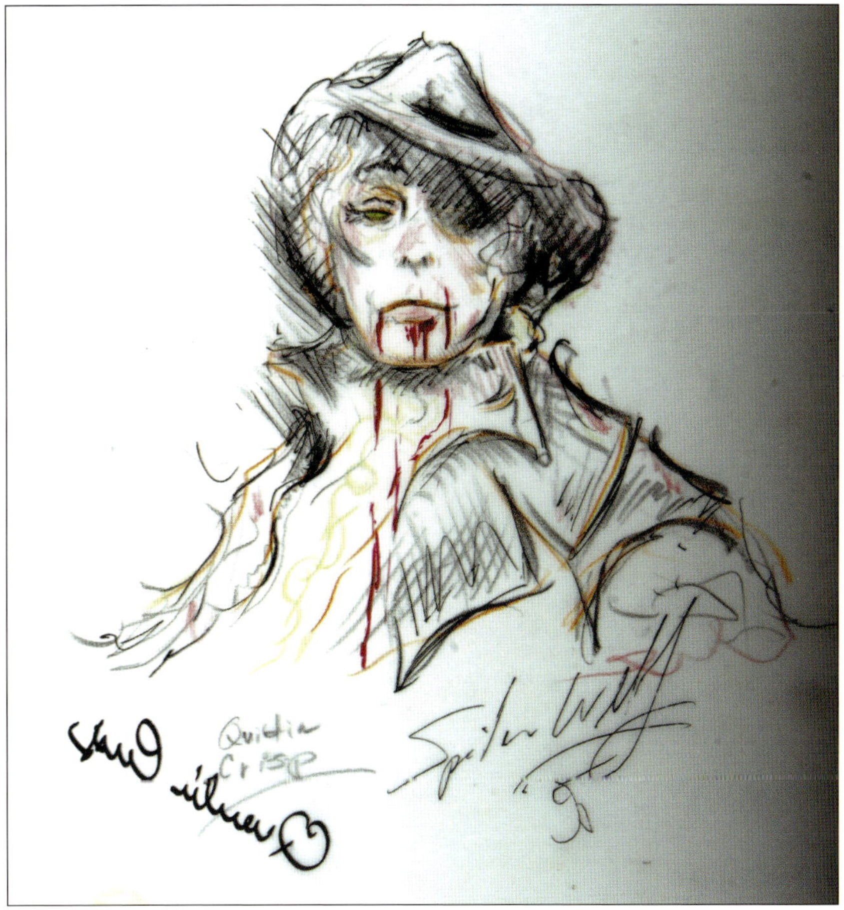

"Eventually, Who Knows?" Pencil and nail polish on paper, 9" x 12". 1996. *Signed Spider Webb – Quentin Crisp* (signed on reverse).

"Unheard Messages." Pencil on Vellum paper, 9" x 12". 1981.

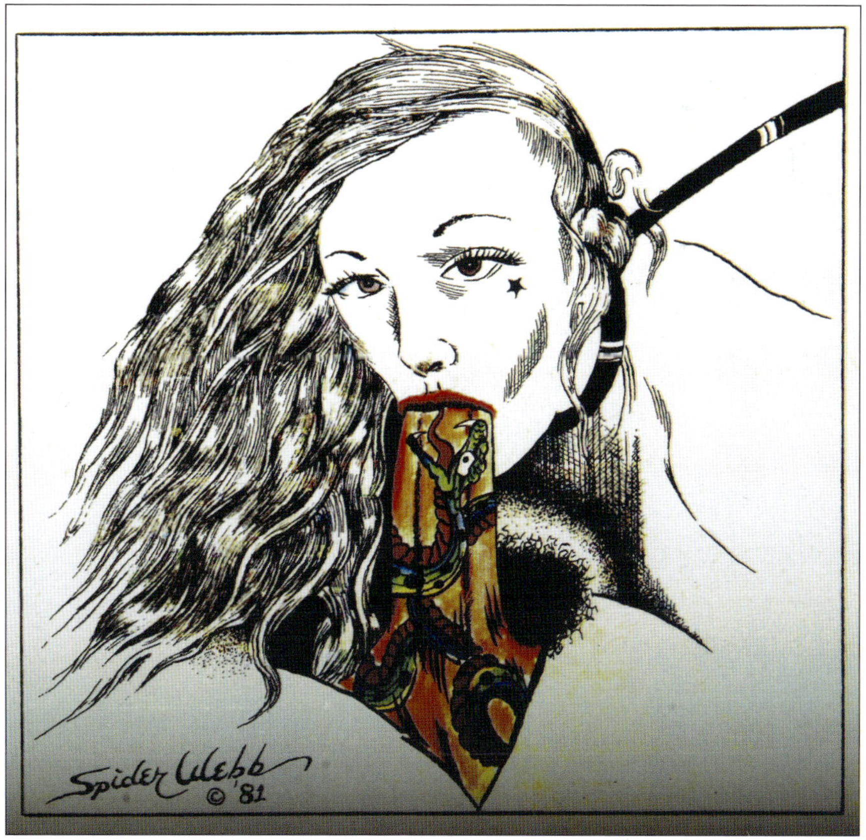

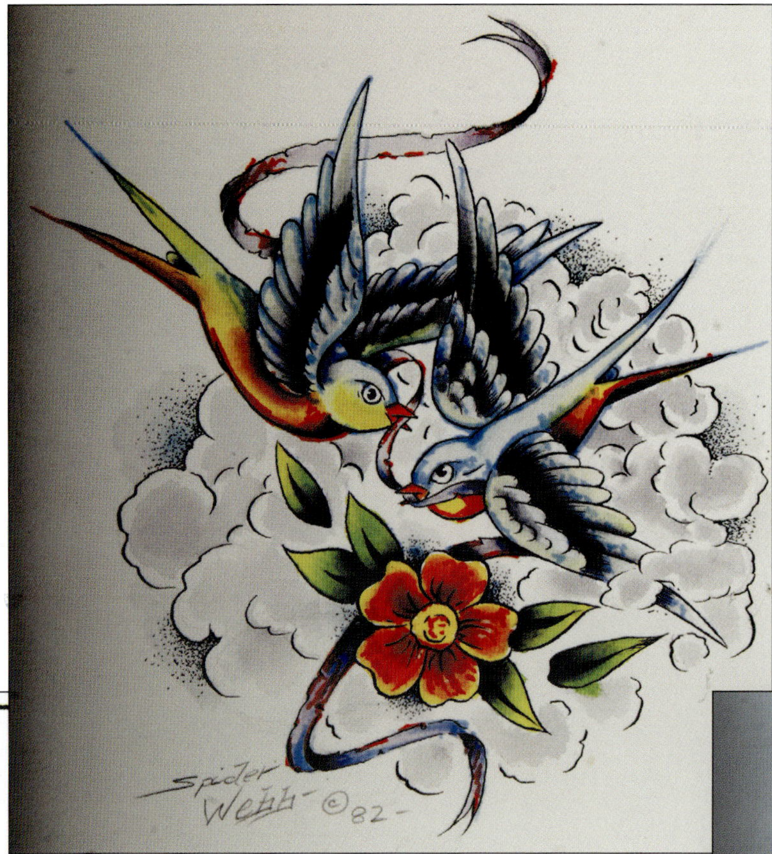


"Are You Crying." Ink and watercolor on Archers paper, 9" x 12". 1982.

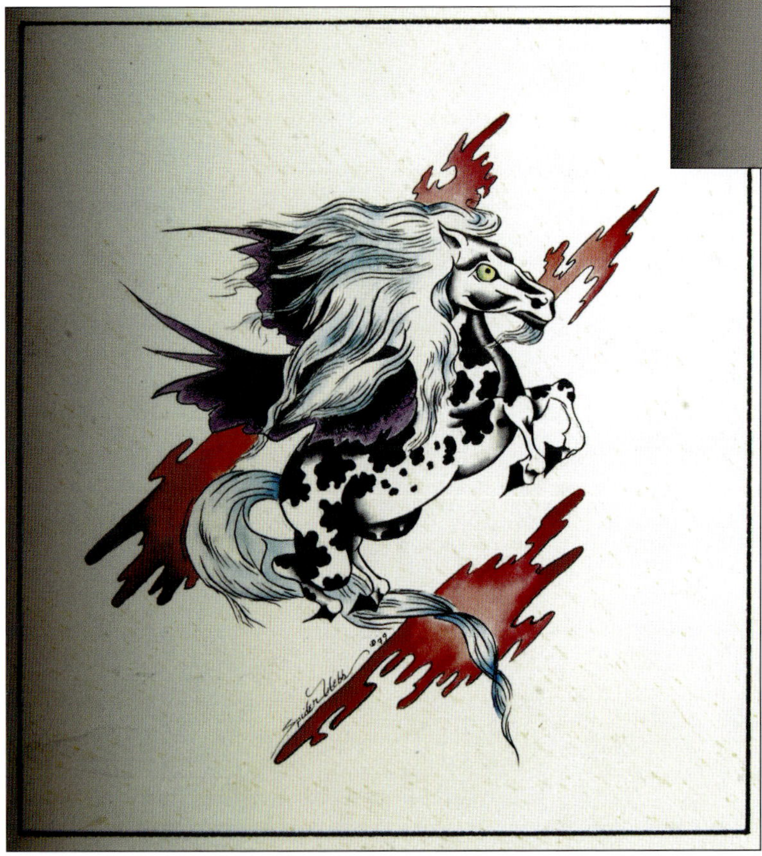

"The Freak Bar is Open." Ink and watercolor on Archers paper, 9" x 12". 1979.

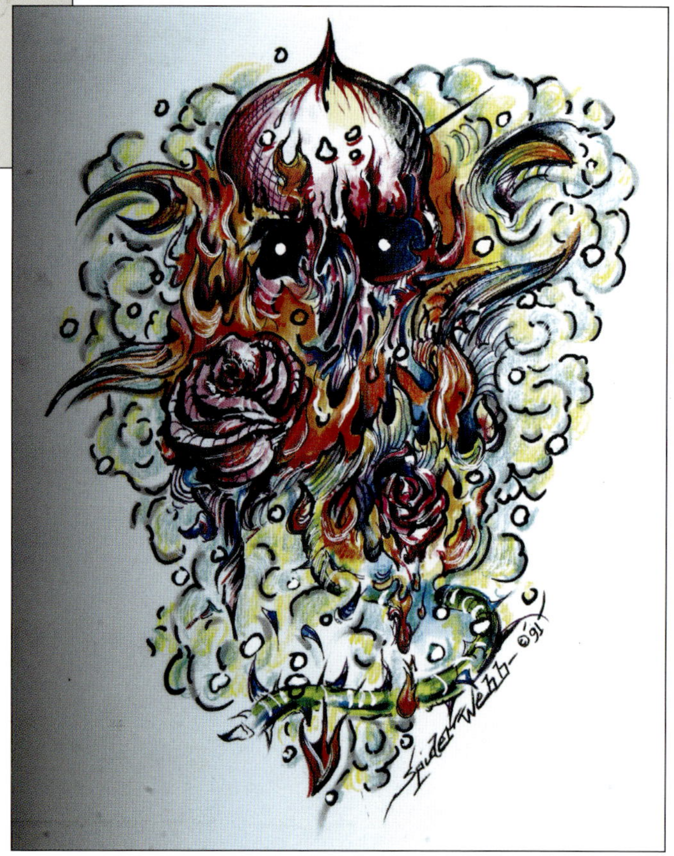

"Returning to the Mortal World." Pencil on Vellum paper, 11" x 17". 1991.

This place is full of fags, lesbos, art, and money. I think I'll move here.
—*S.W.*

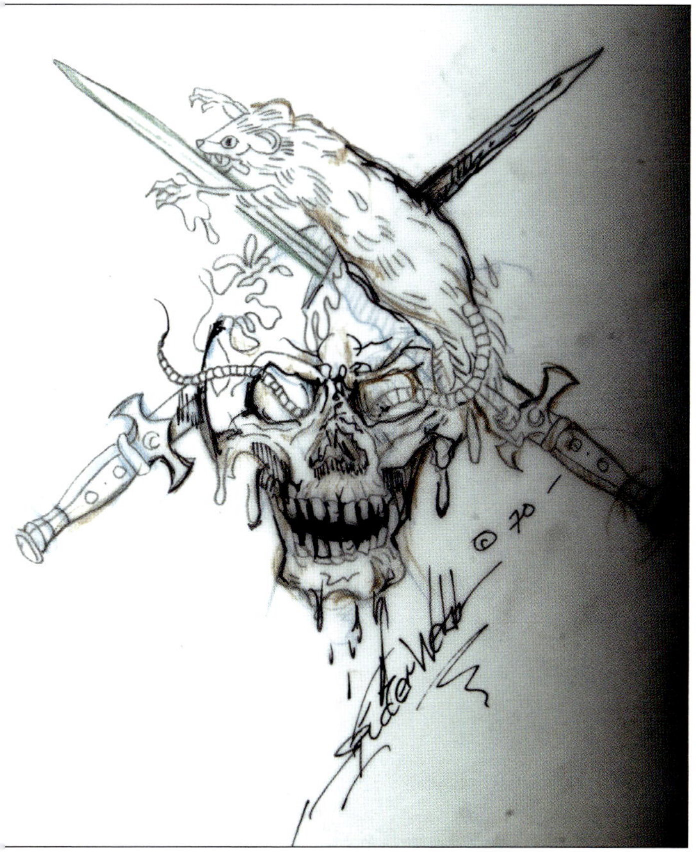

"Hopeless Longing." Pencil on Vellum paper, 9" x 12". 1970.

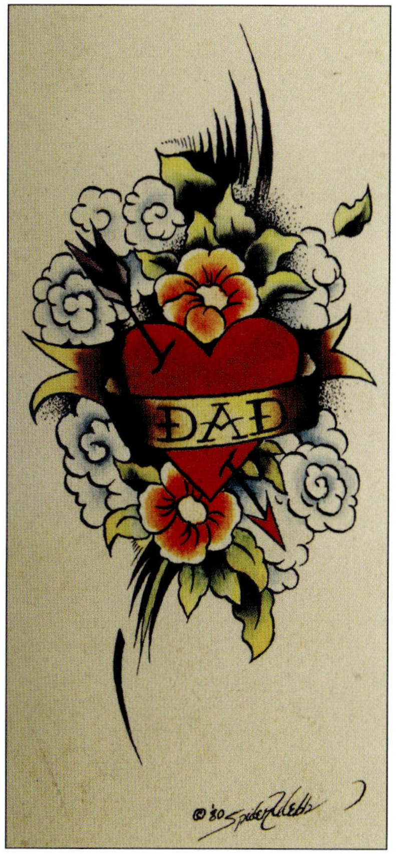


"Too Old to Have A Life of Your Own." Ink and watercolor on Archers paper, 9" x 12". 1980.

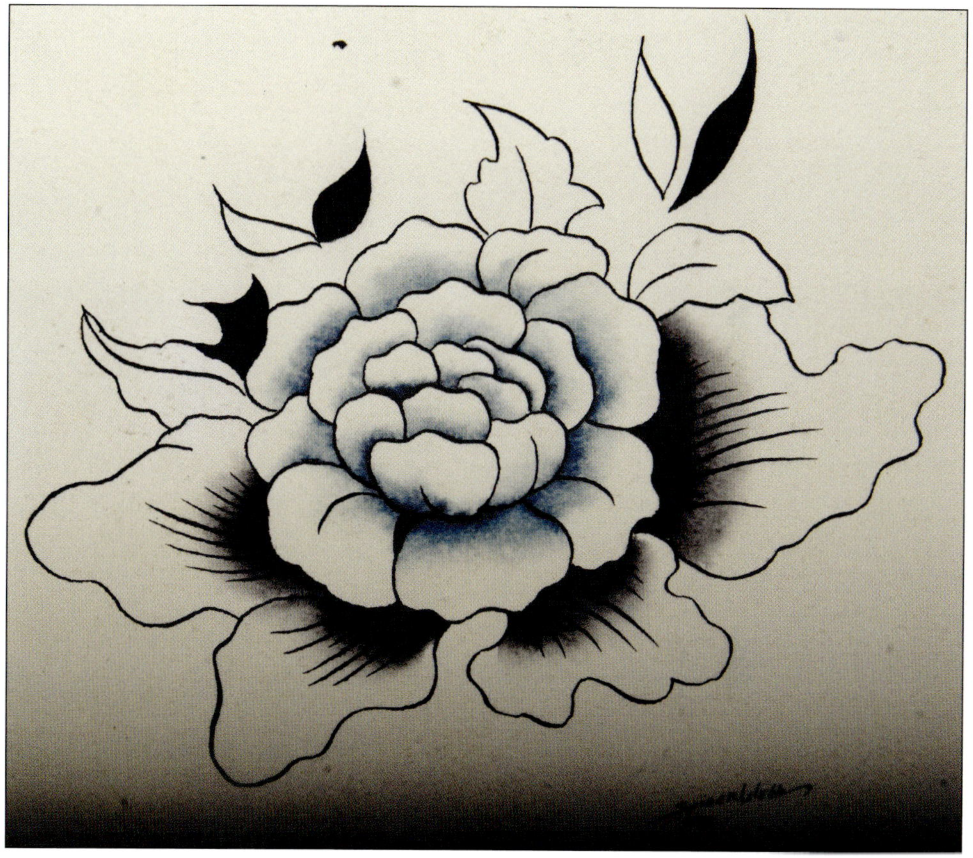

"A Nondescript Lump In My...." Ink and watercolor on Archers paper, 9" x 12". 1978.

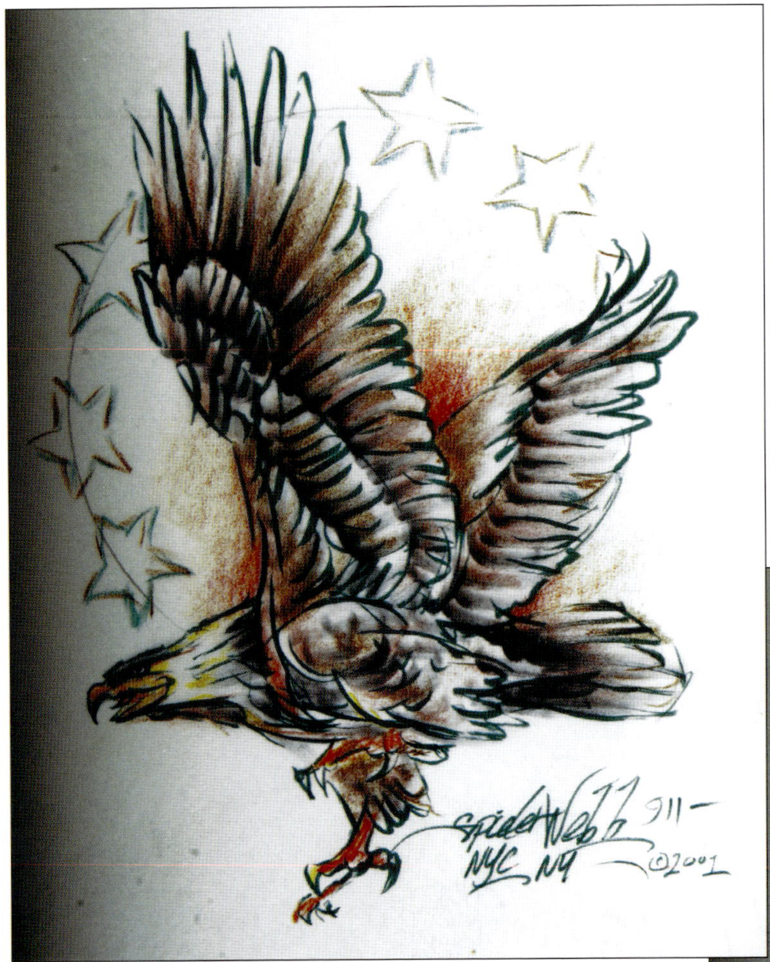

"When I'm Dead...." Pencil on Vellum paper, 9" x 12". 2001.

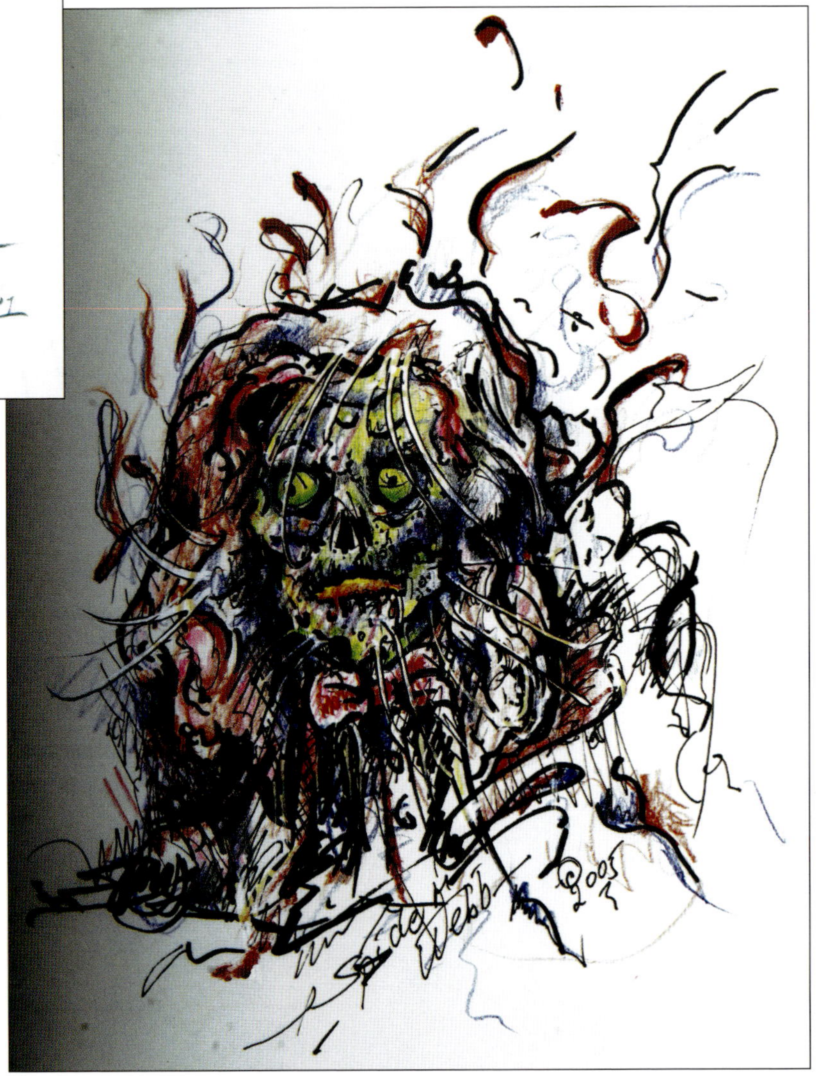

"Is A Sexual Compulsive OK?" Pencil on Vellum paper, 8 1/2" x 10". 2005.

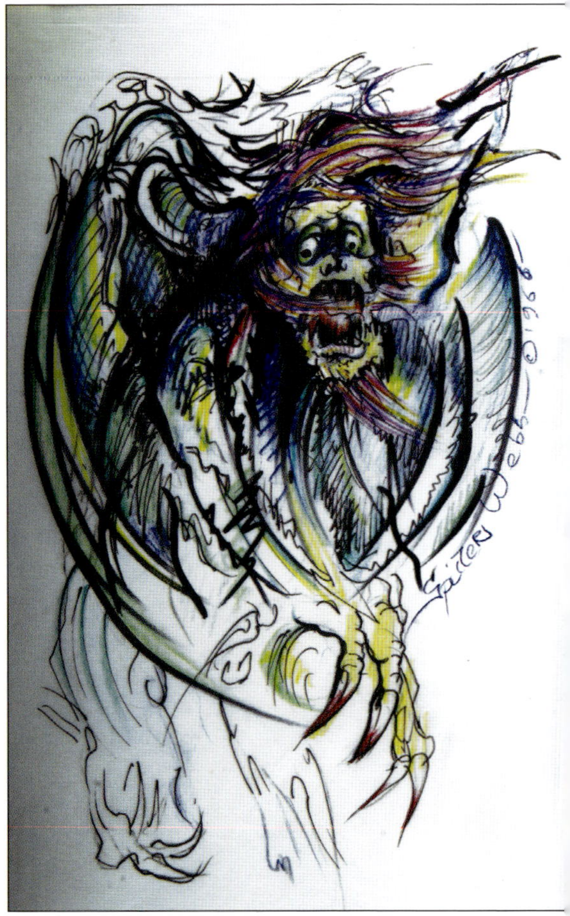

"A Traumatic Childhood." Pencil on Vellum paper, 11" x 17". 1966.

My elevator never gets to the top floor, but then again, all the goodies are in the basement.

—*S.W.*

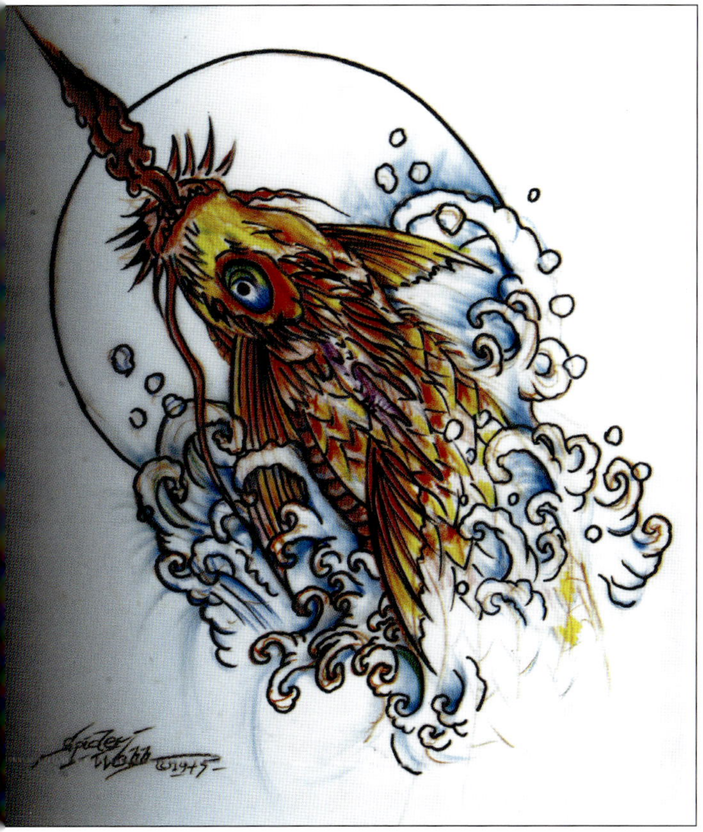

"Illicit Sex." Pencil on Vellum paper, 11" x 17". 1975.

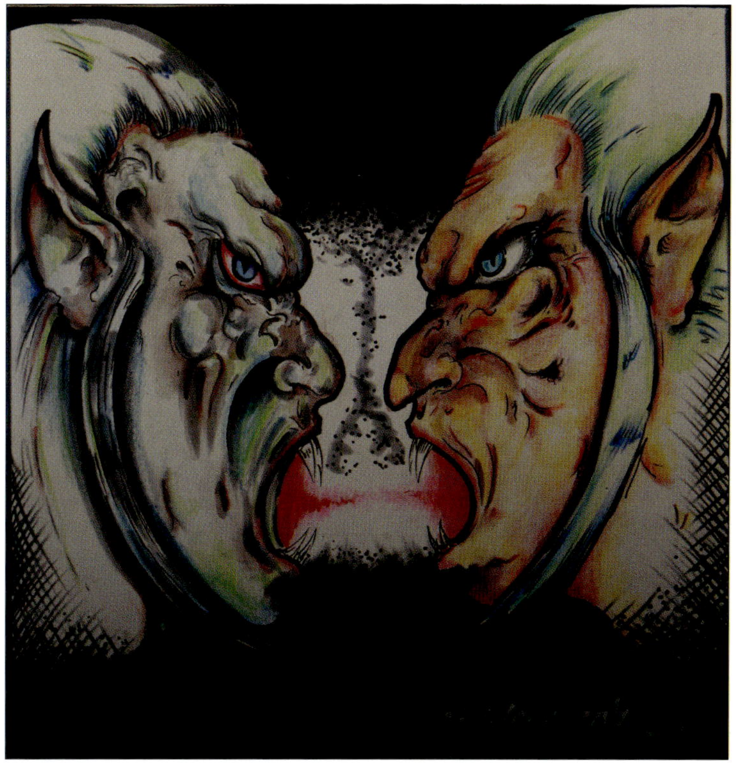

"It's Pretty Disturbing." Pencil on Vellum paper, 11" x 17". 1990.

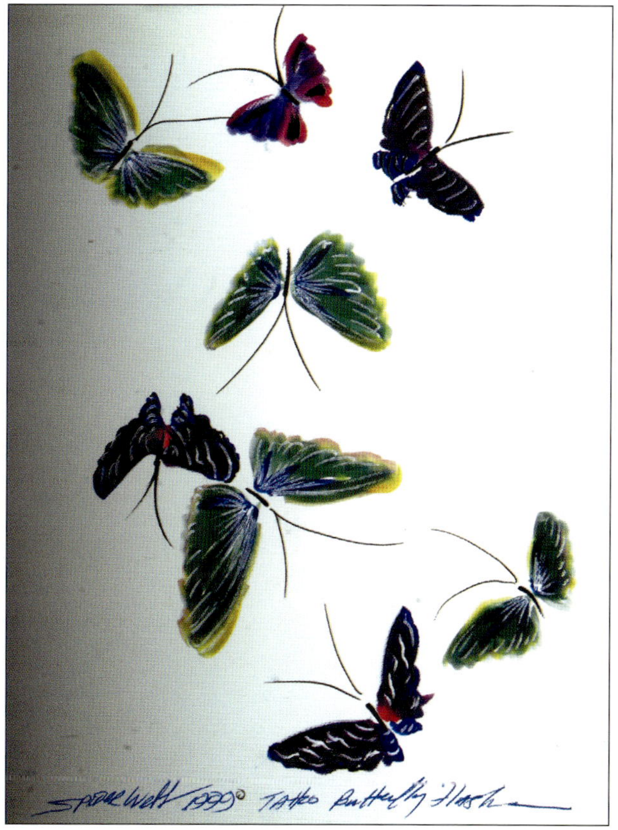

"The Biggest No-Brainer in the History of Mankind." Watercolor on paper, 9" x 12". 1999.

A shotgun blast to the face would be preferable to your bullshit.

—*S.W.*

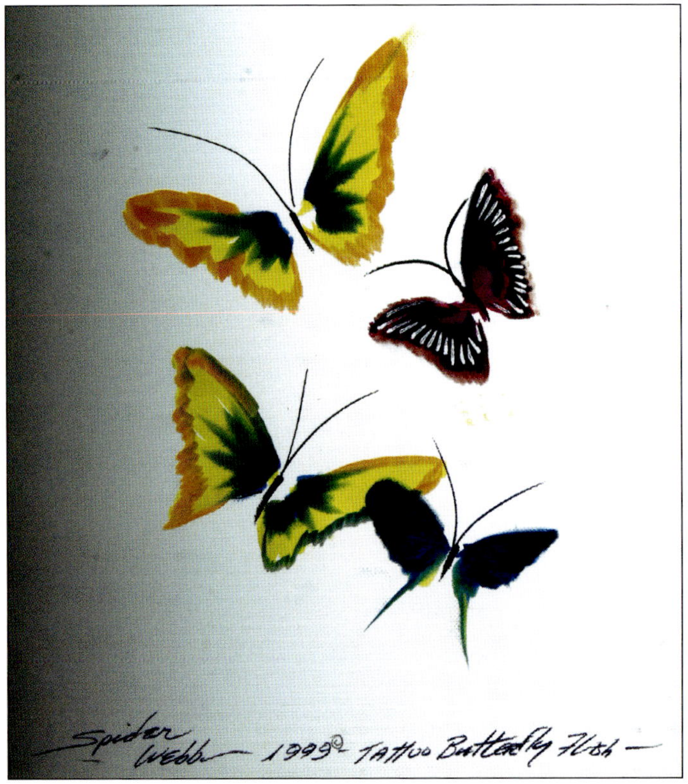


"Desperately Trying To Be Romantic." Watercolor on paper, 9" x 12". 1999.

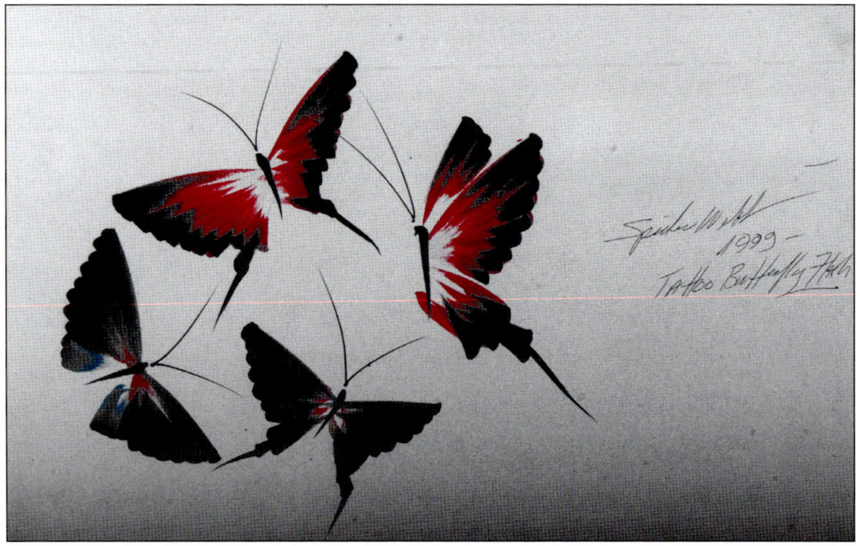

"Naive Idealism." Watercolor on paper, 9" x 12". 1999.

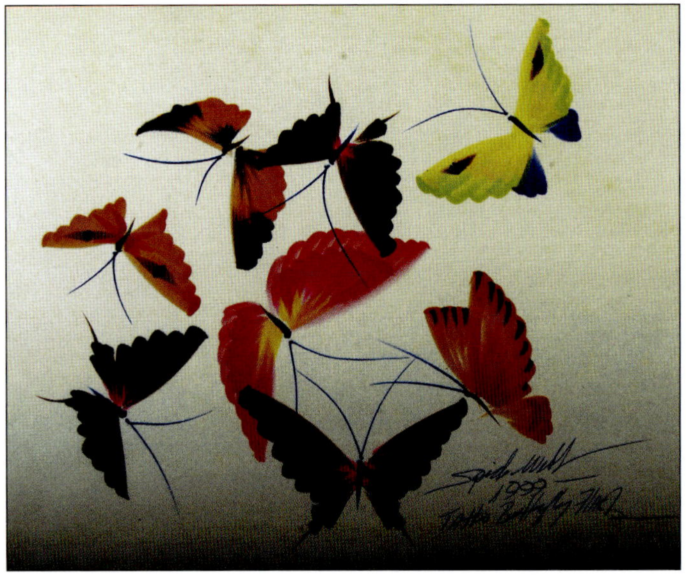

"Like Nothing I've Ever Had." Watercolor on paper, 9" x 12". 1999.

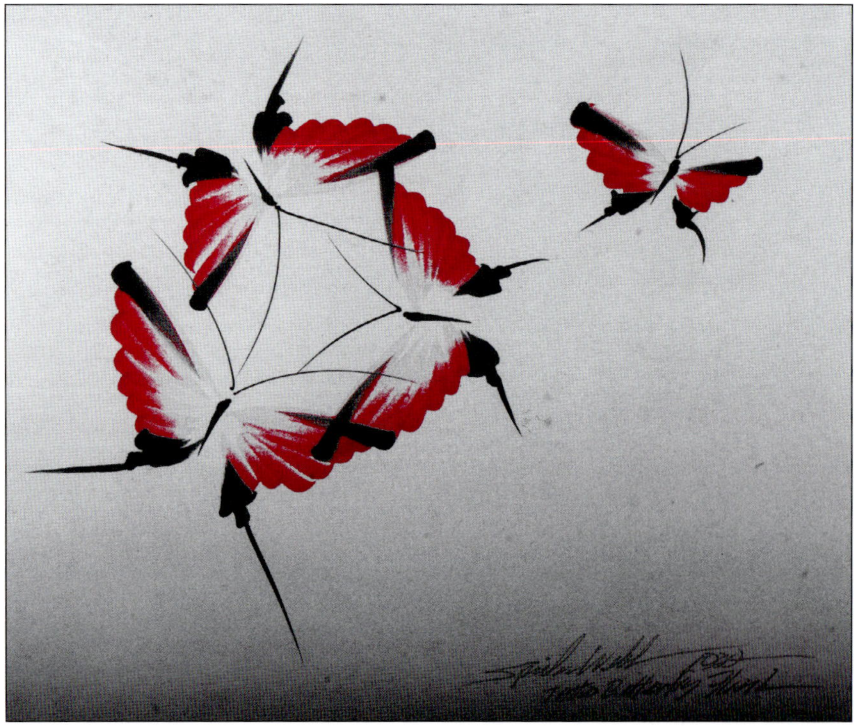

"Massive Panic Attack." Watercolor on paper, 9" x 12". 1999.

"What Part of You Belongs To Me?" Pencil on Vellum paper, 9" x 12". 1984.

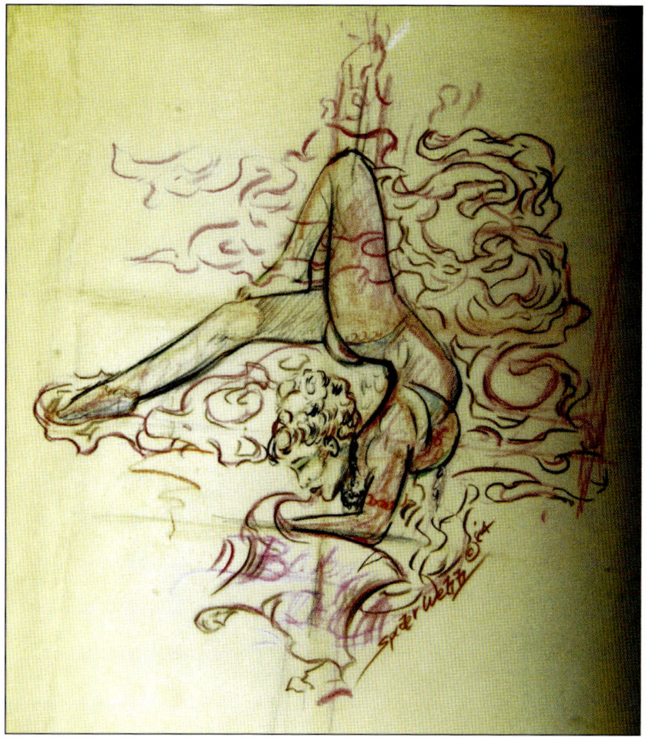

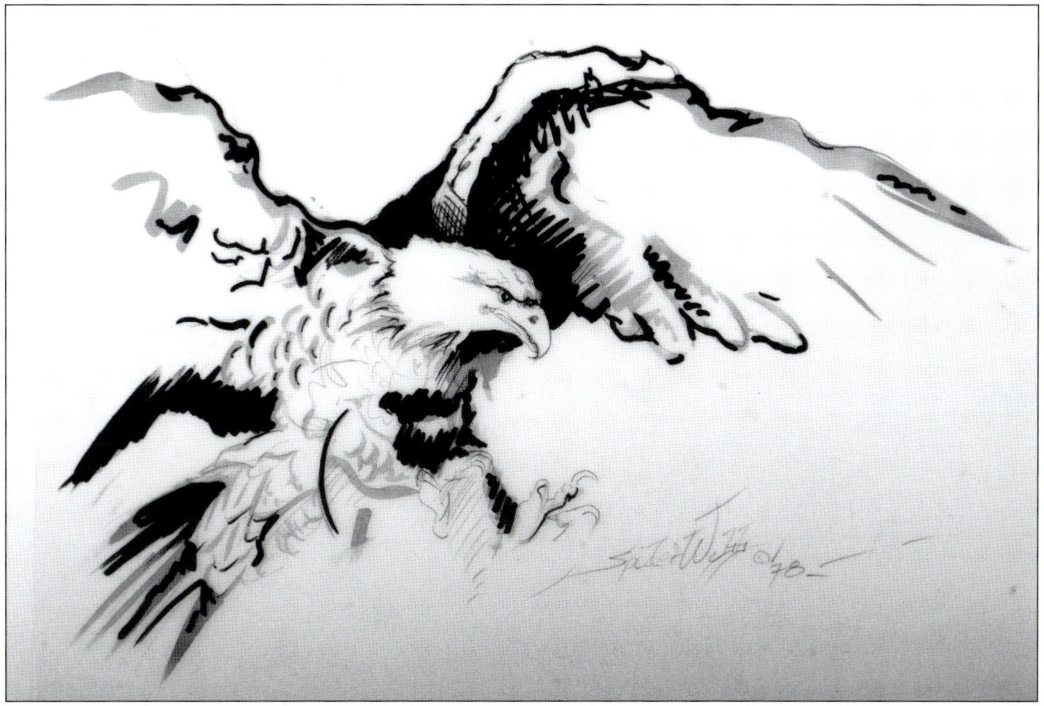

"Where Am I? What Am I?" Marker on Vellum paper, 11" x 17". 1978.

Give them everything they desire, except their freedom.
—*S.W.*

"You're Gonna Be Alright." Pencil on Vellum paper, 9" x 12". 1982.

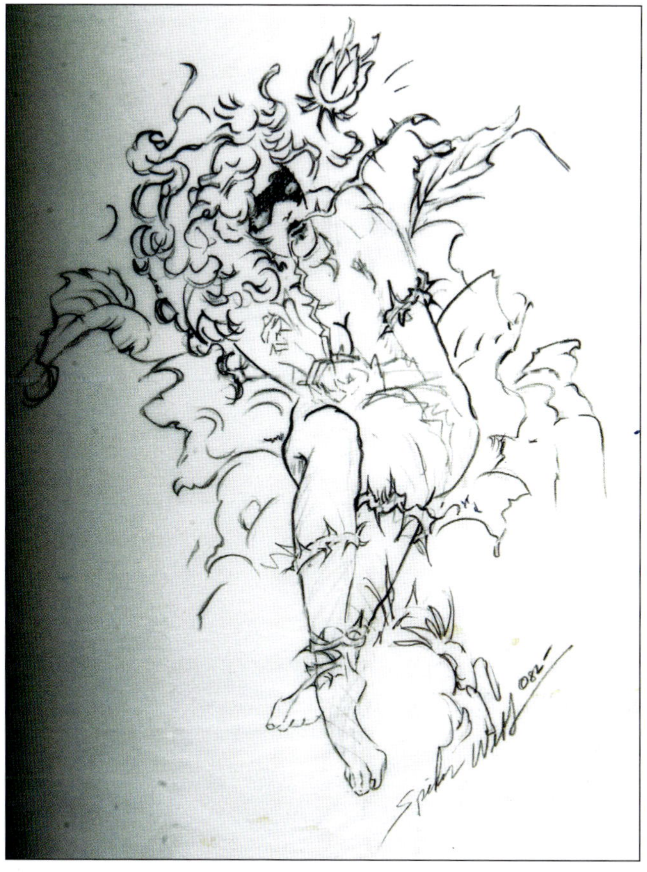

If you blow out my candle does yours shine brighter?
—*S.W.*

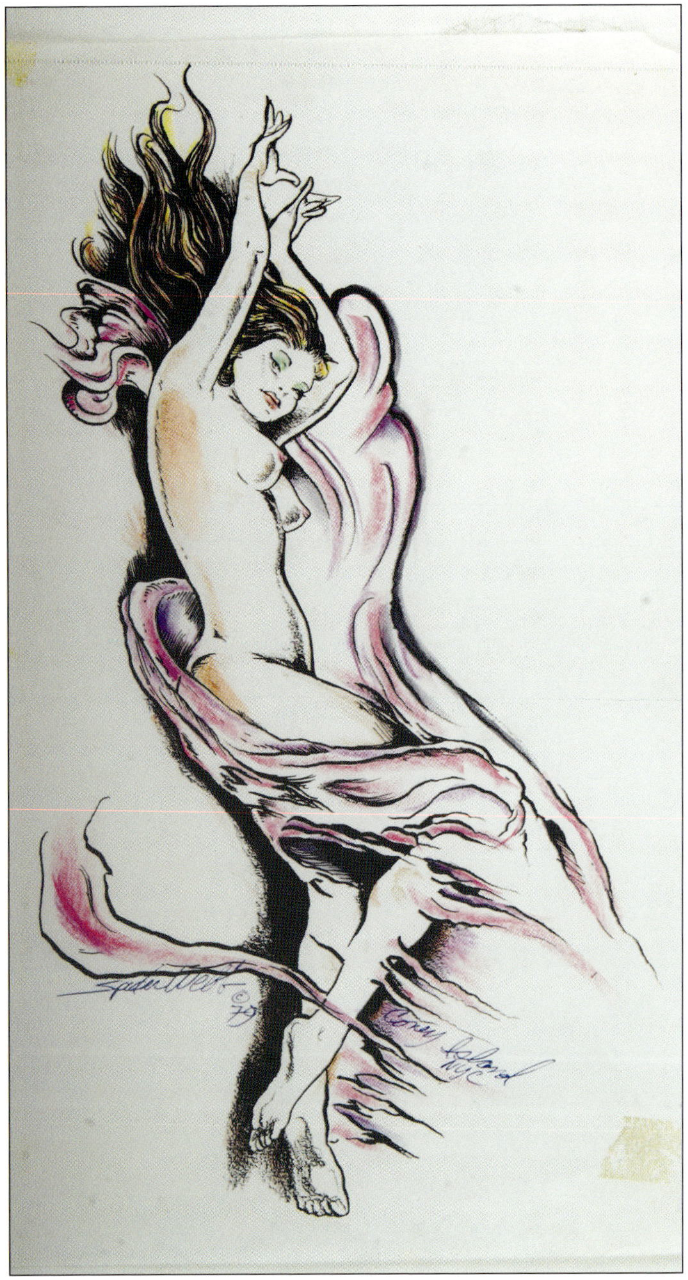

"Redefining Lame." Pencil on Vellum paper, 11" x 17". 1979.

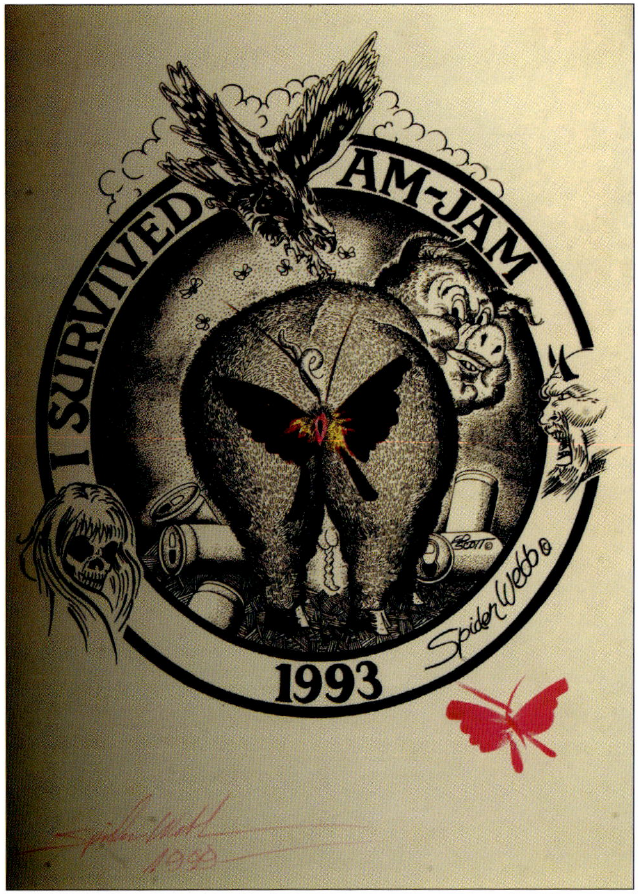


"A Curtain Fall On A Lit Stage." Ink and watercolor on paper, 11" x 17". 1993. *Signed Spider Webb – Ed Scott.*

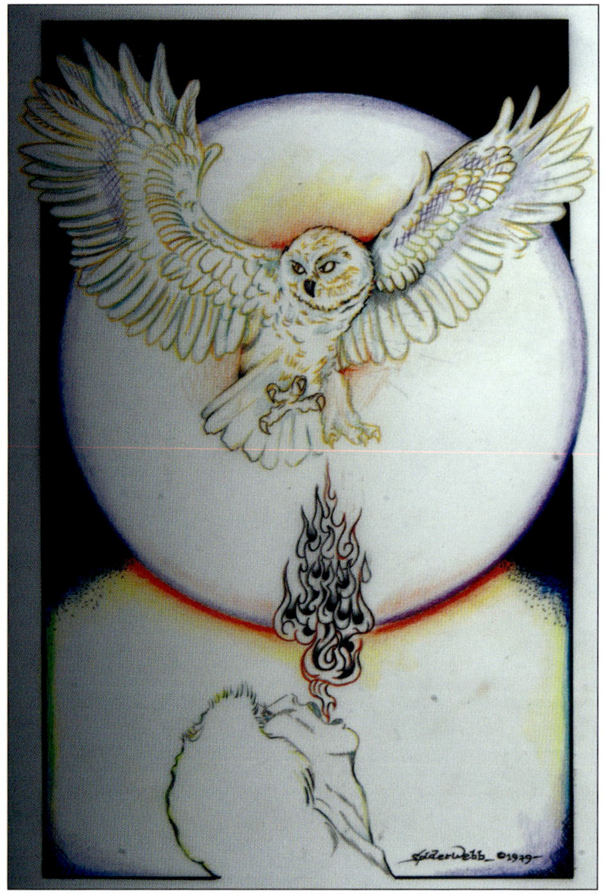

"Outside of Time." Pencil on Vellum paper, 11" x 17". 1979.

When I think of ignoble I think of a physician presiding at an execution.
—*S.W.*

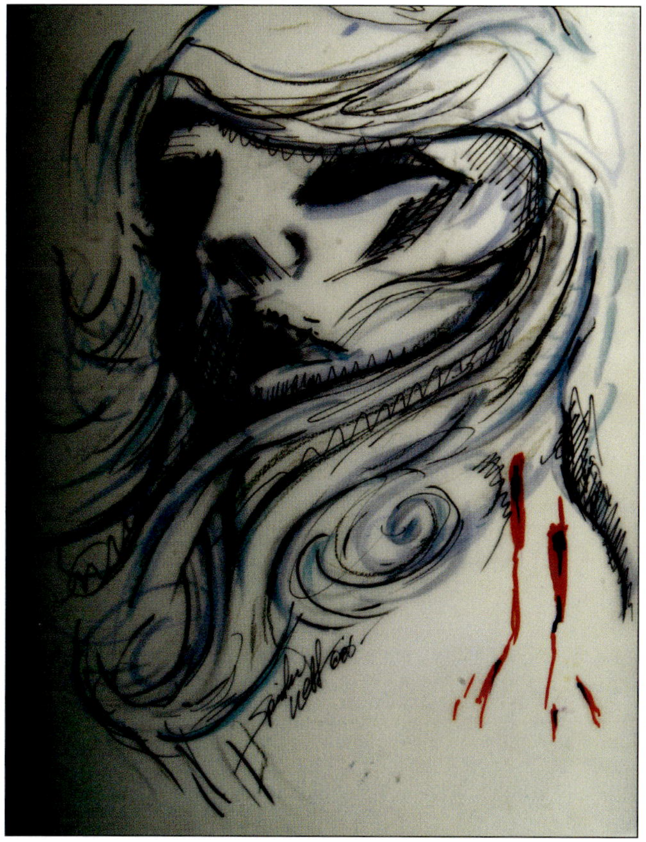

"Ecstasy in Meditation." Pencil on Vellum paper, 11" x 12". 2006.

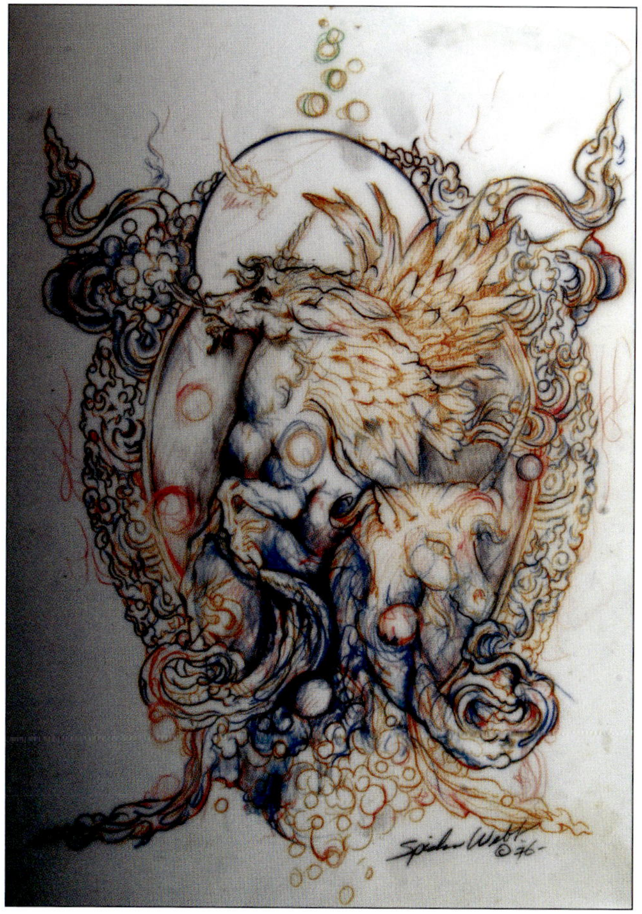

"Less Lucid." Pencil on board, 9" x 12". 1976.

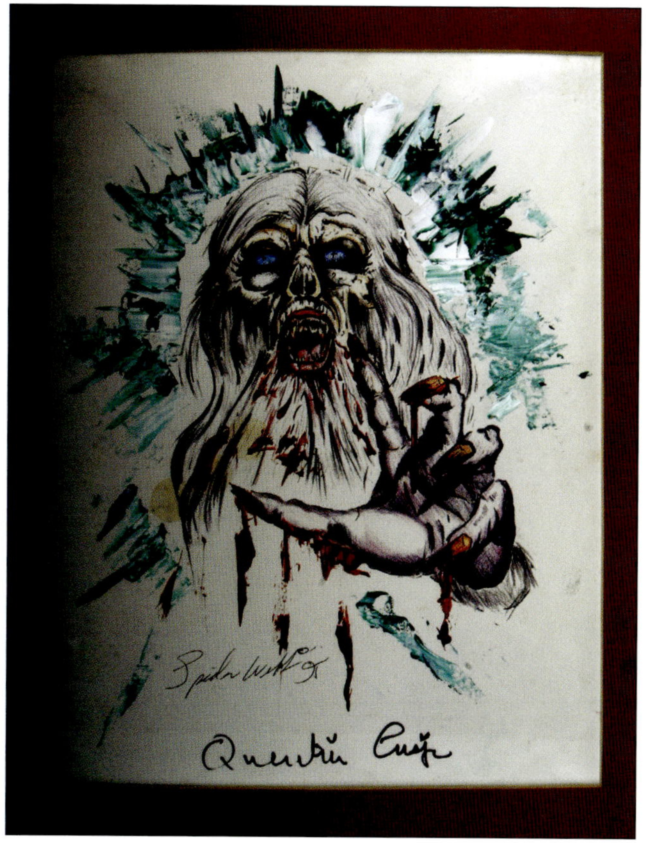

"Timeless Egoless State." Mixed media on paper, 9" x 12". 1995. *Signed Spider Webb – Quentin Crisp.*

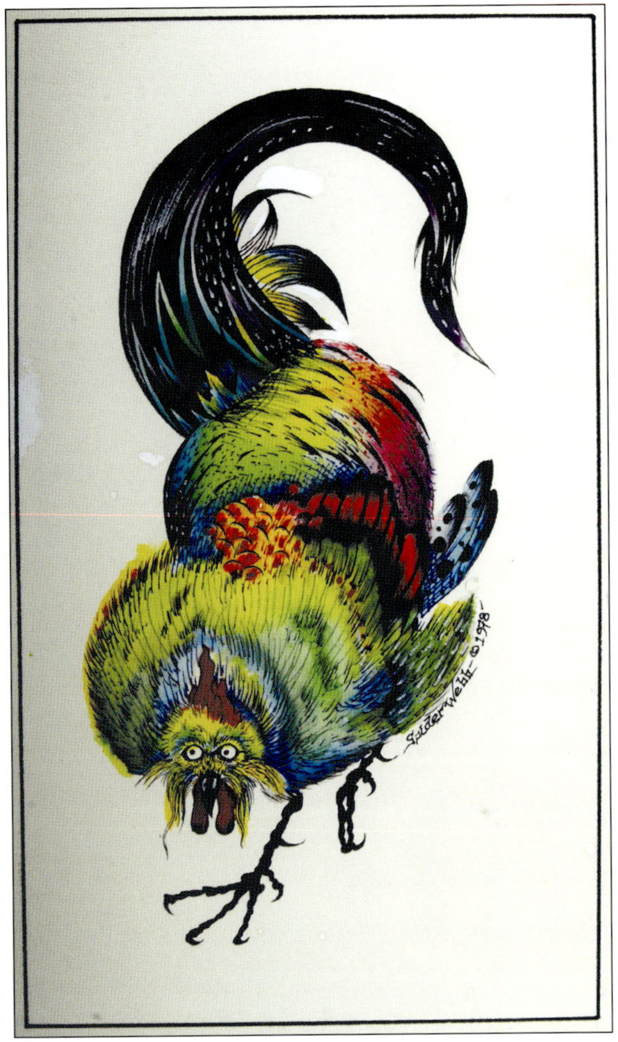

"Searching Drunks." Mixed media on Archers paper, 11" x 17". 1978.

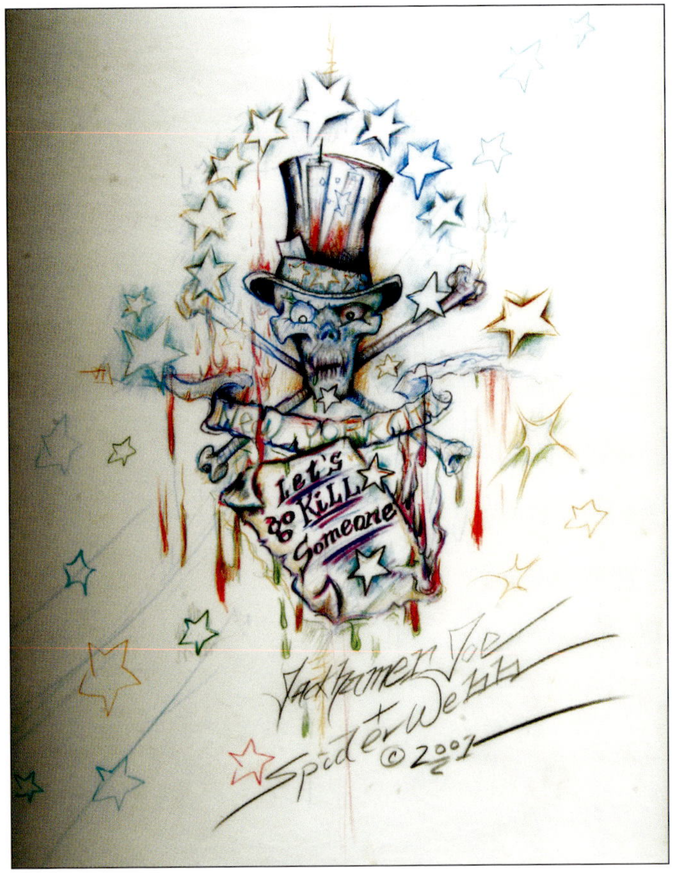


"Mastering Space." Pencil on Vellum paper, 9" x 12". 2001. *Signed Spider Webb – Jackhammer Joe.*

If blood is life...set up the glasses and lets drink the wine.
—*S.W.*

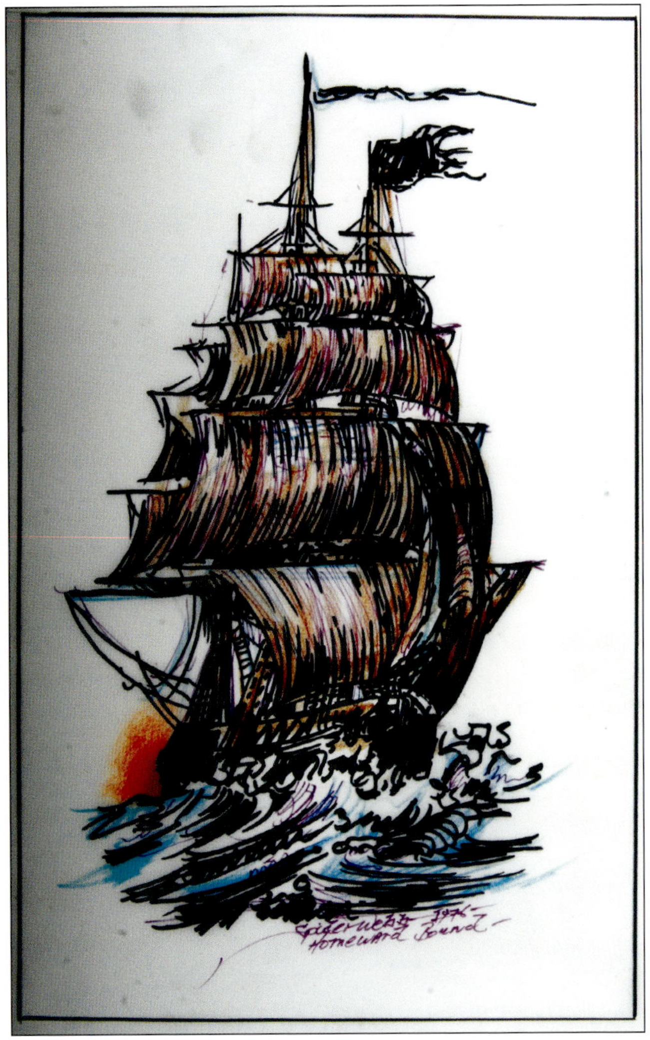

"Timeless Time." Pencil on Vellum paper, 11" x 17". 1976.

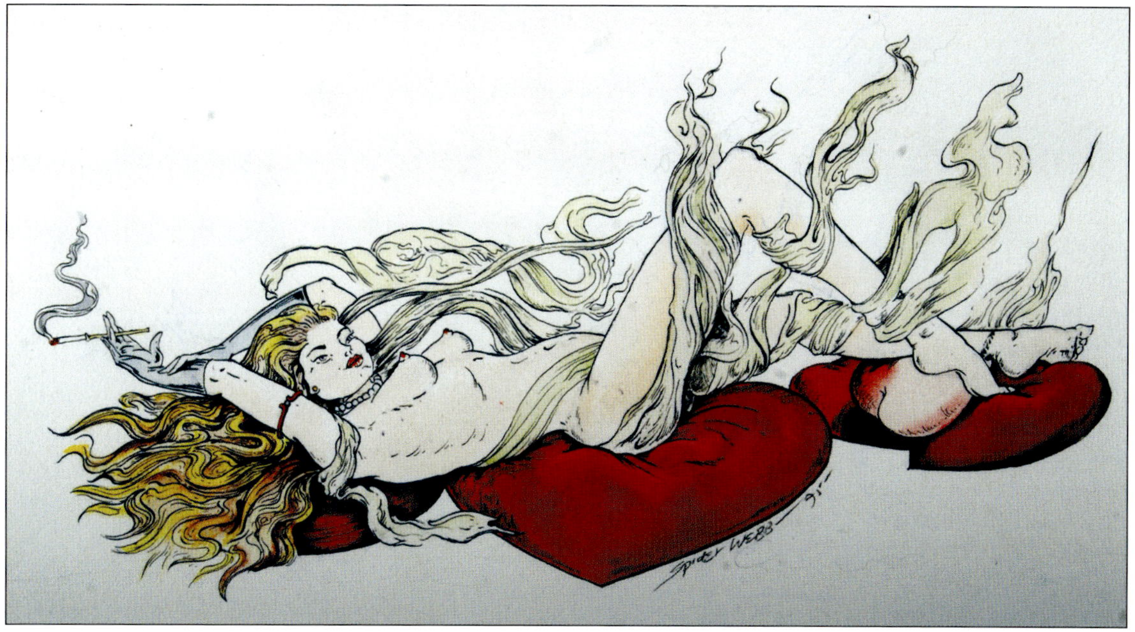

"Pitiful Little Time." Ink and watercolor on Archers paper, 18" x 20". 1995.

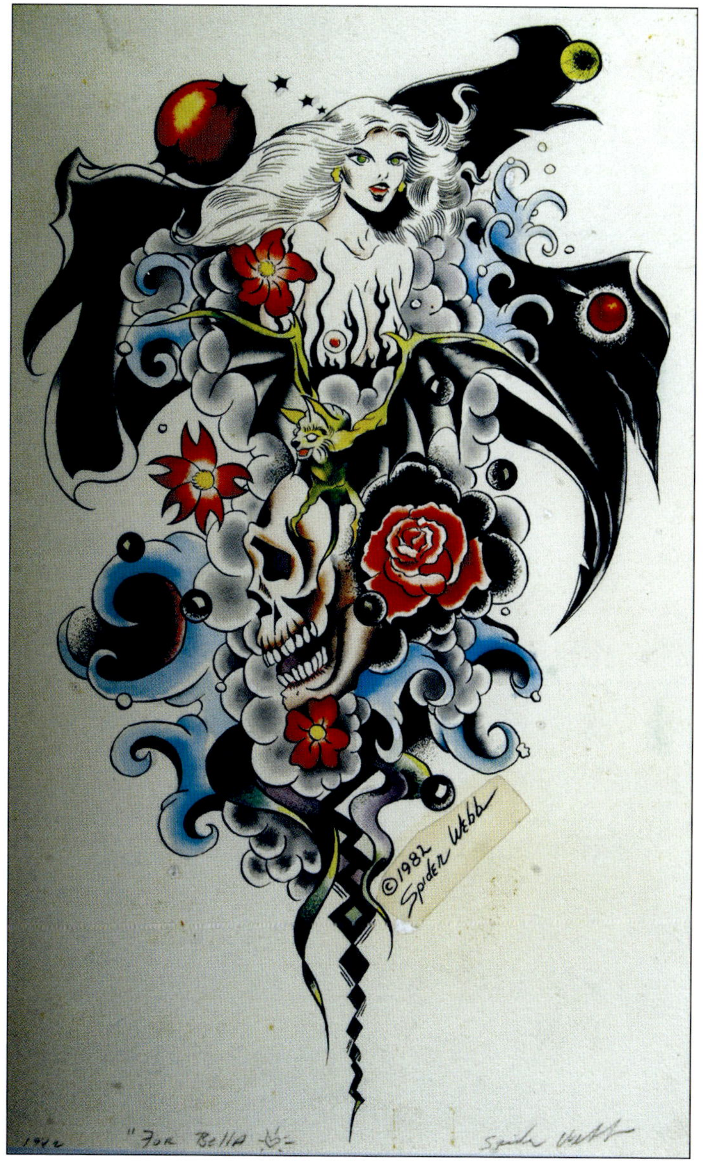


"Keys to the Mystic." Ink and watercolor on Archers paper, 18" x 20". 1982.

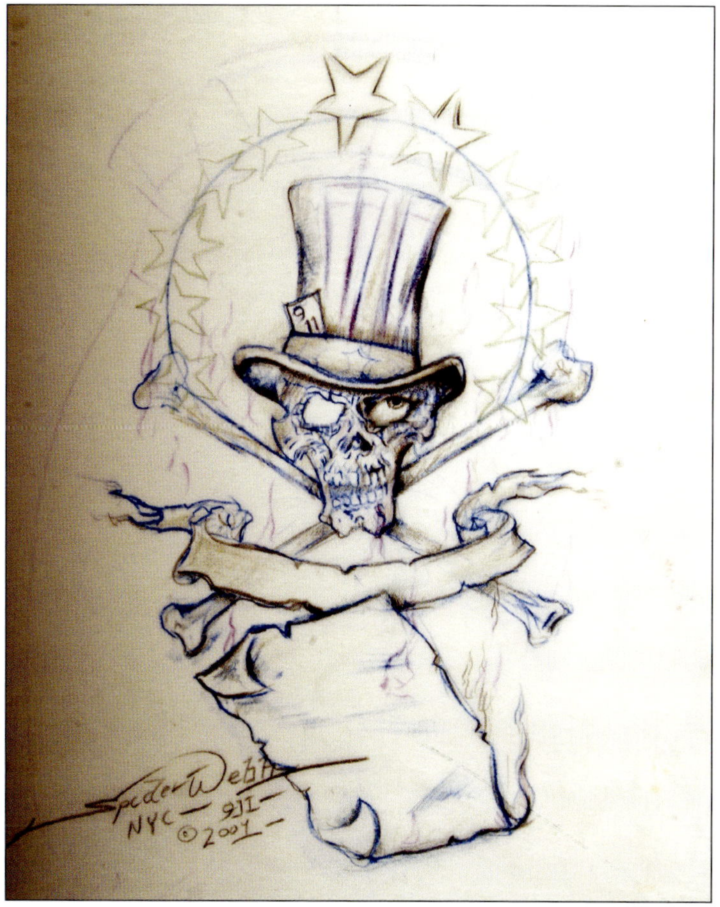


"Immediacy and Intensity." Pencil on Vellum paper, 9" x 12". 2001.

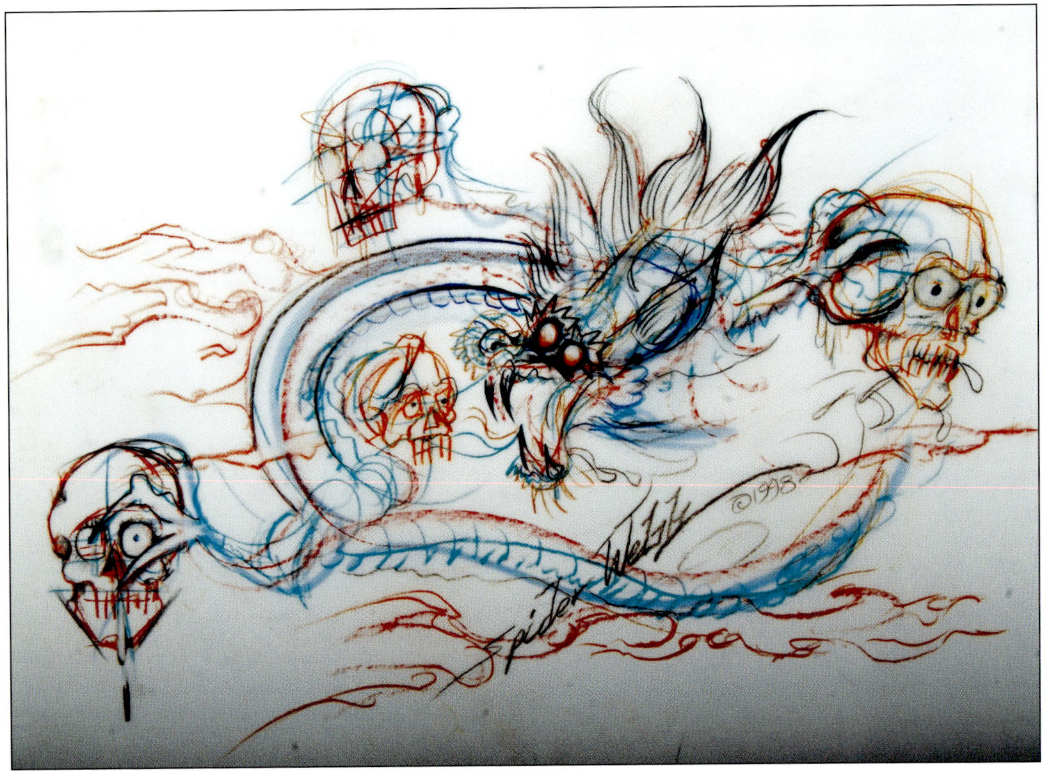


"Physical Masterpieces." Pencil on Vellum paper, 11" x 17". 1998.

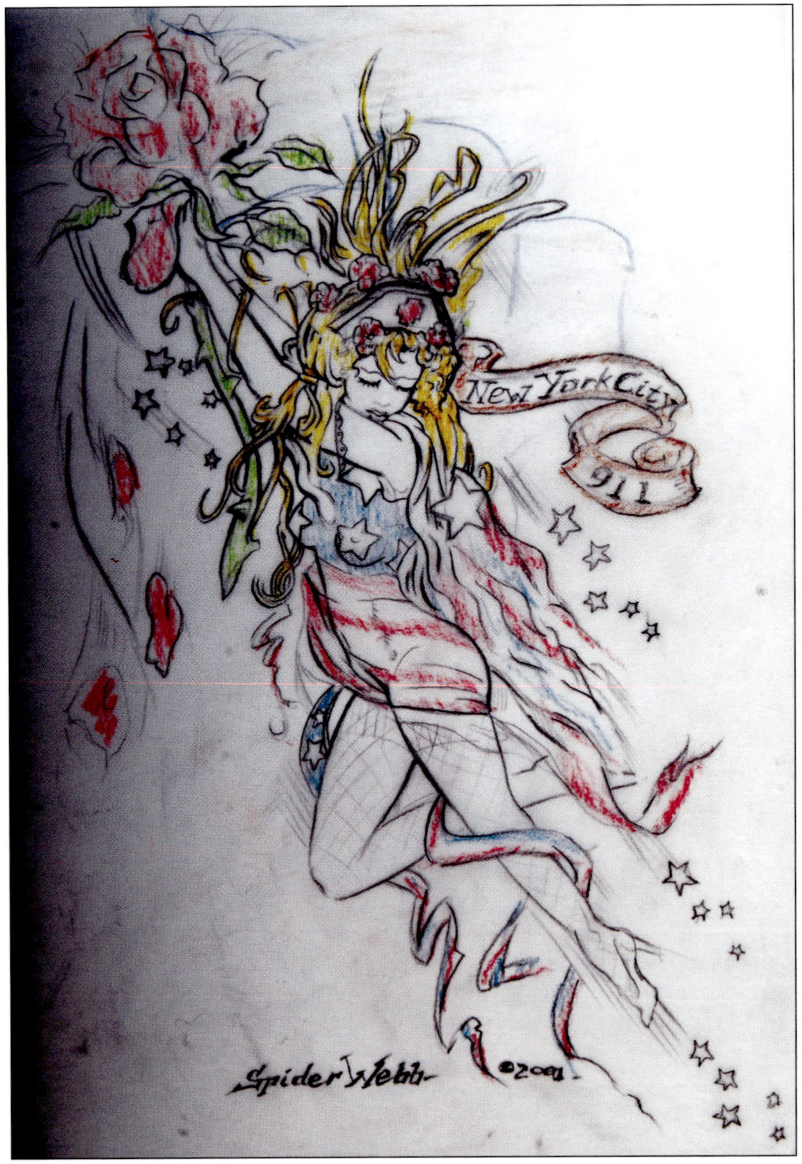


"Saint Vincent's Hospital, New York City." Pencil on paper, 11" x 17". 2001.

Your name sounds like something a prostitute might charge extra for.
—*S.W.*

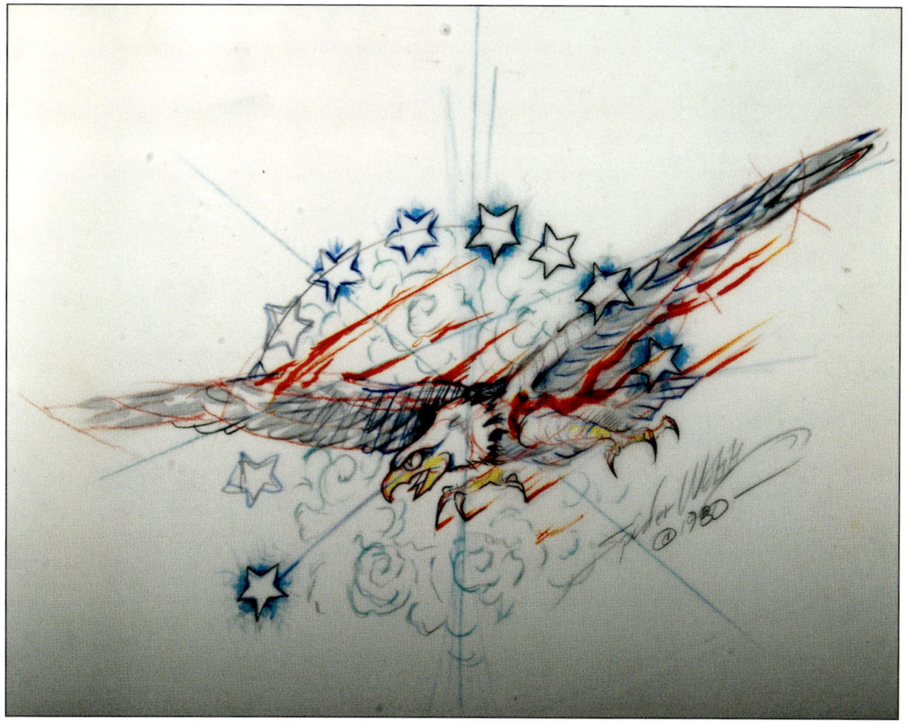

"Spiritual Ecstasy." Pencil on Vellum paper, 11" x 17". 1980.

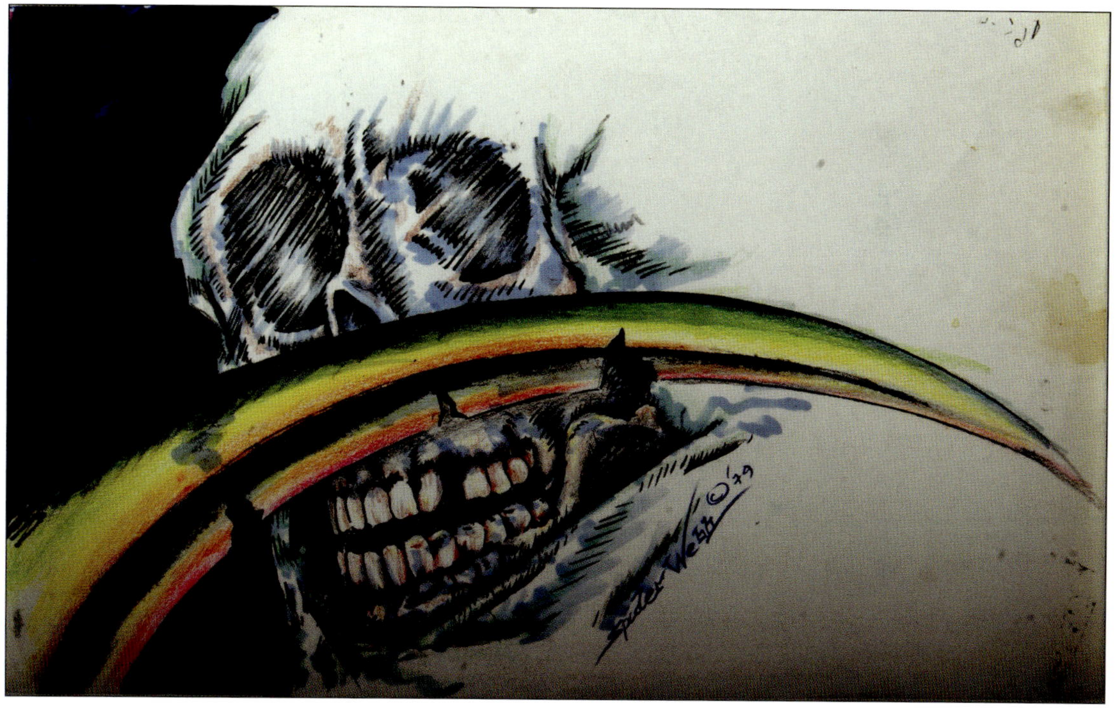

"Eradication of Fun." Ink and pencil on Vellum paper, 11" x 17". 1979.

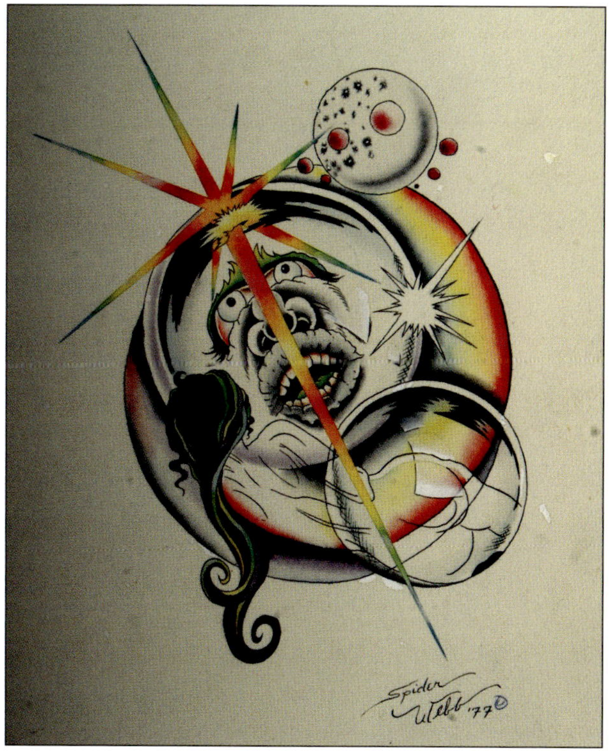

"Loving Discovery." Ink and watercolor on Archers paper, 9" x 12". 1977.

The people who changed my life didn't conform to any reality but their own.

—*S.W.*

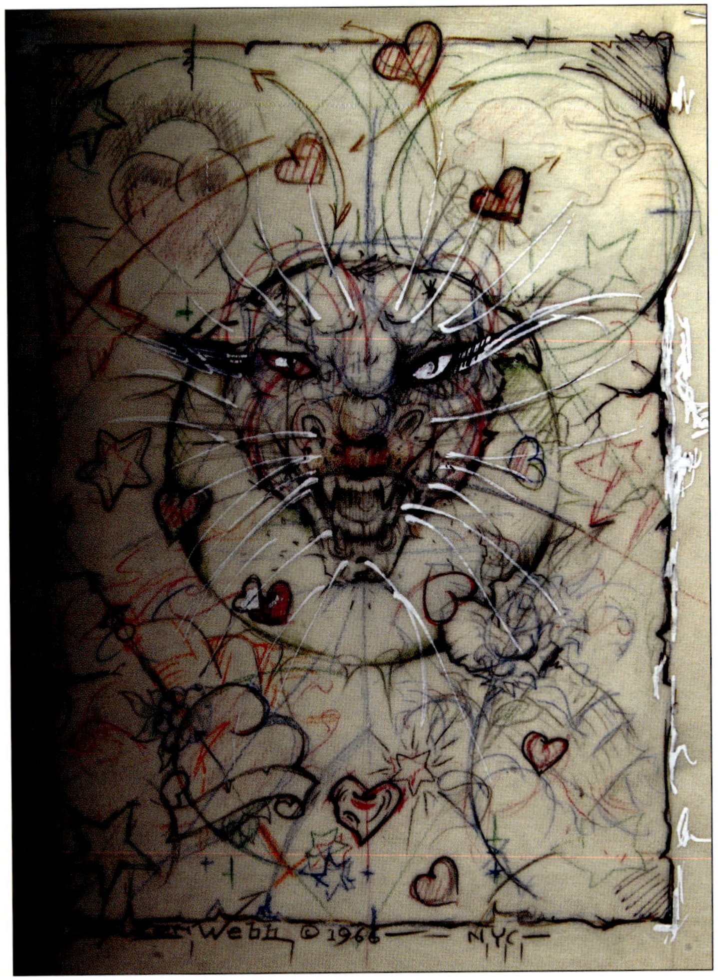

"Law of the Universe." Pencil on Vellum paper, 11" x 17". 1966.

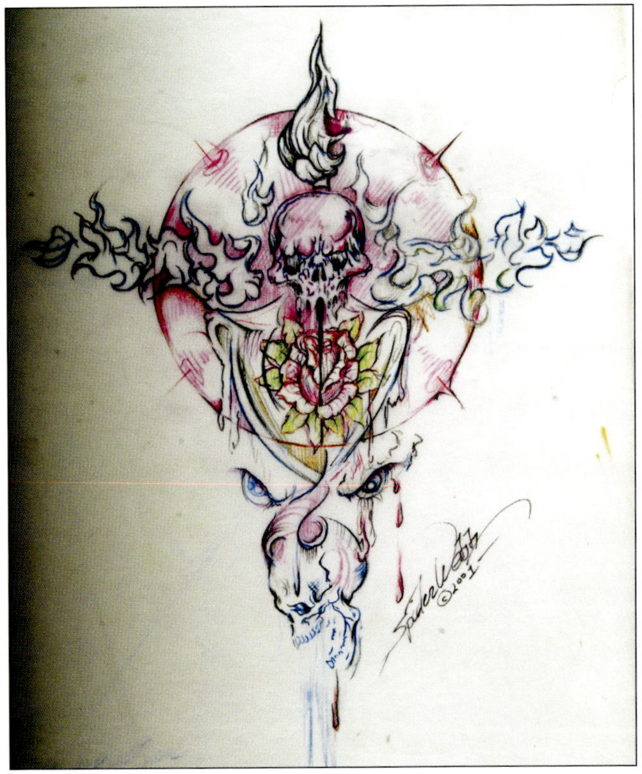

"Ceremonies." Pencil on Vellum paper, 11" x 17". 2001.

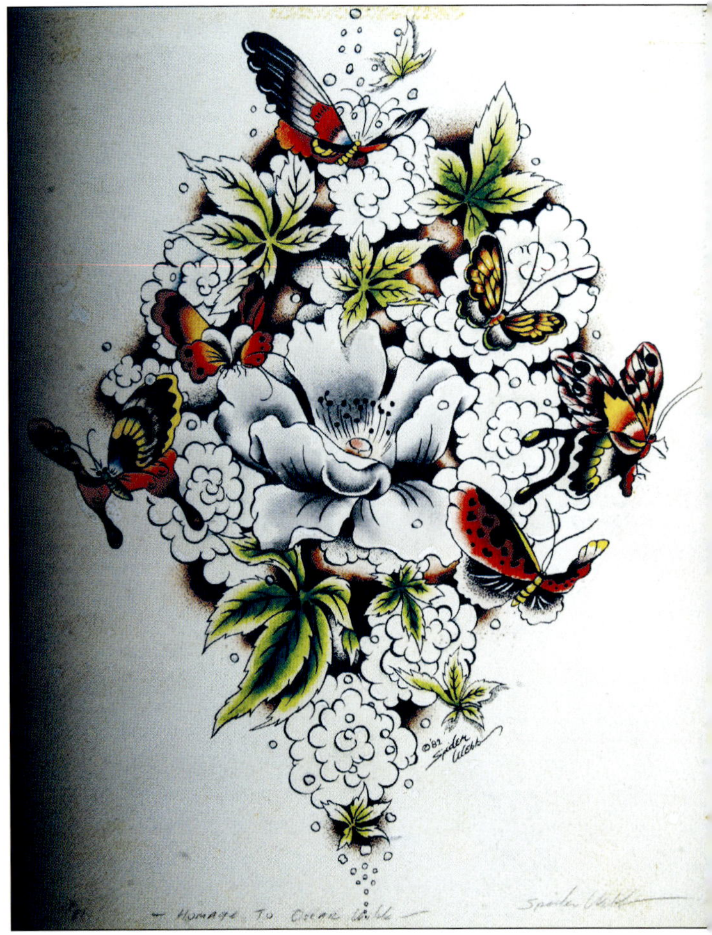

"The Universe Does Not Have Laws." Ink and watercolor on Archers paper, 18" x 20". 1981.

You must always color outside the lines with your imagination.
—*S.W.*

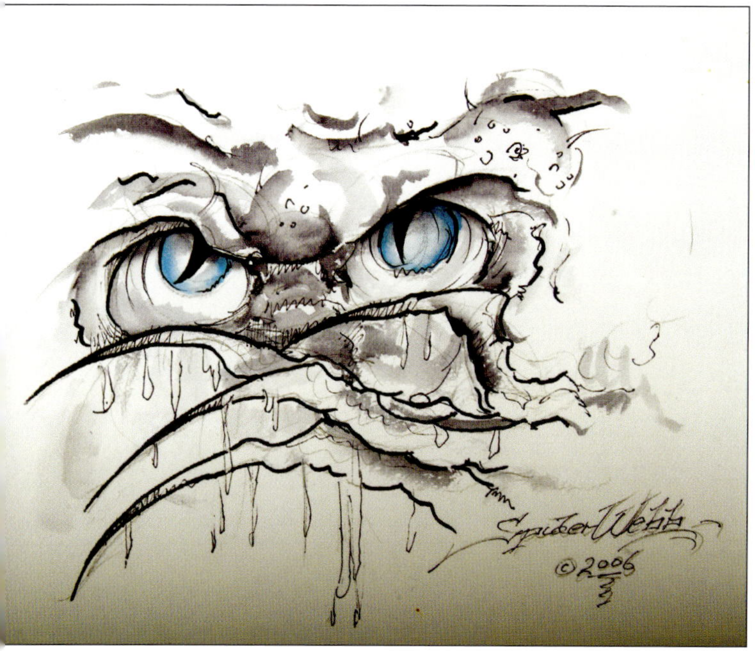


"No Vacancy Neon." Ink and pencil on Vellum paper, 11" x 17". 2006.

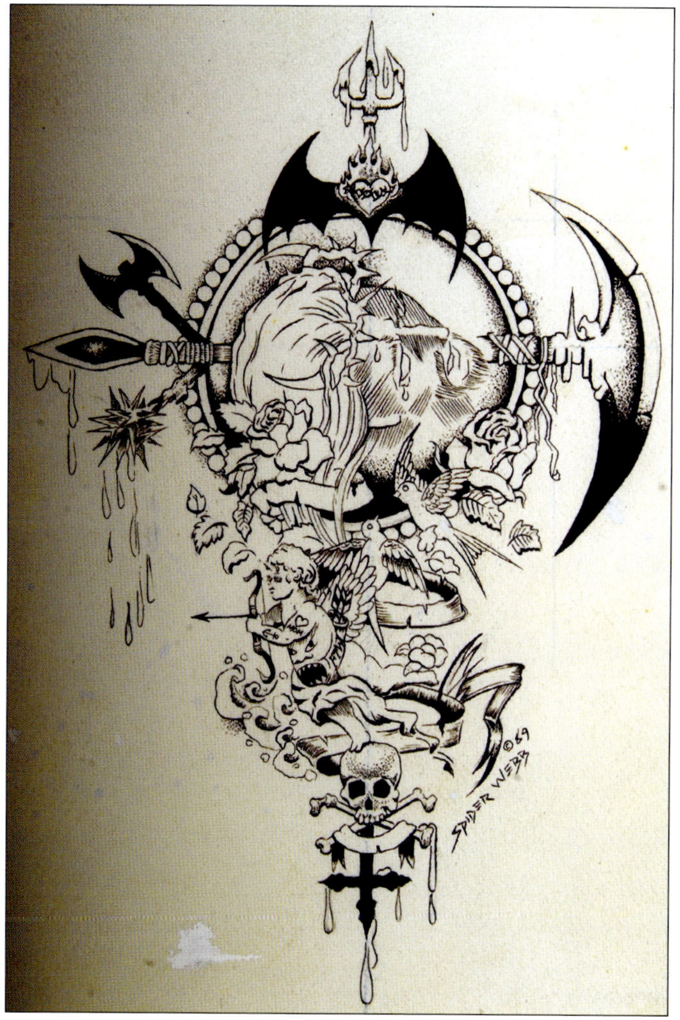


"High-Pitched Delusion." Pencil on board, 9" x 12". 1989.

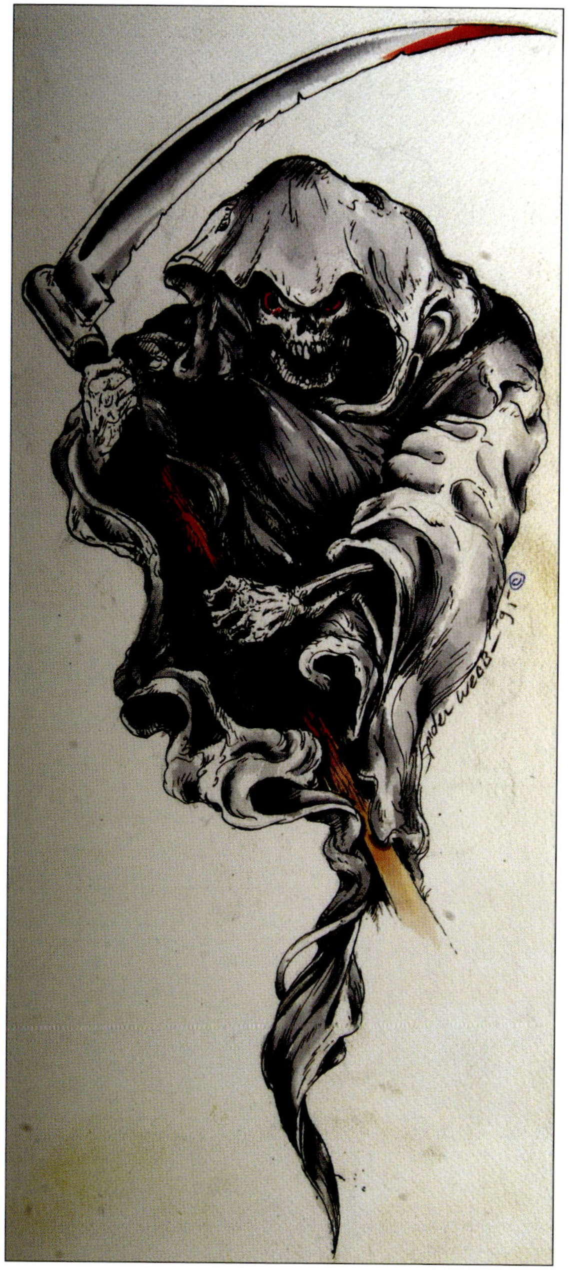

"Razor Punching Bag." Ink and watercolor on Archers paper, 12" x 16". 1995.

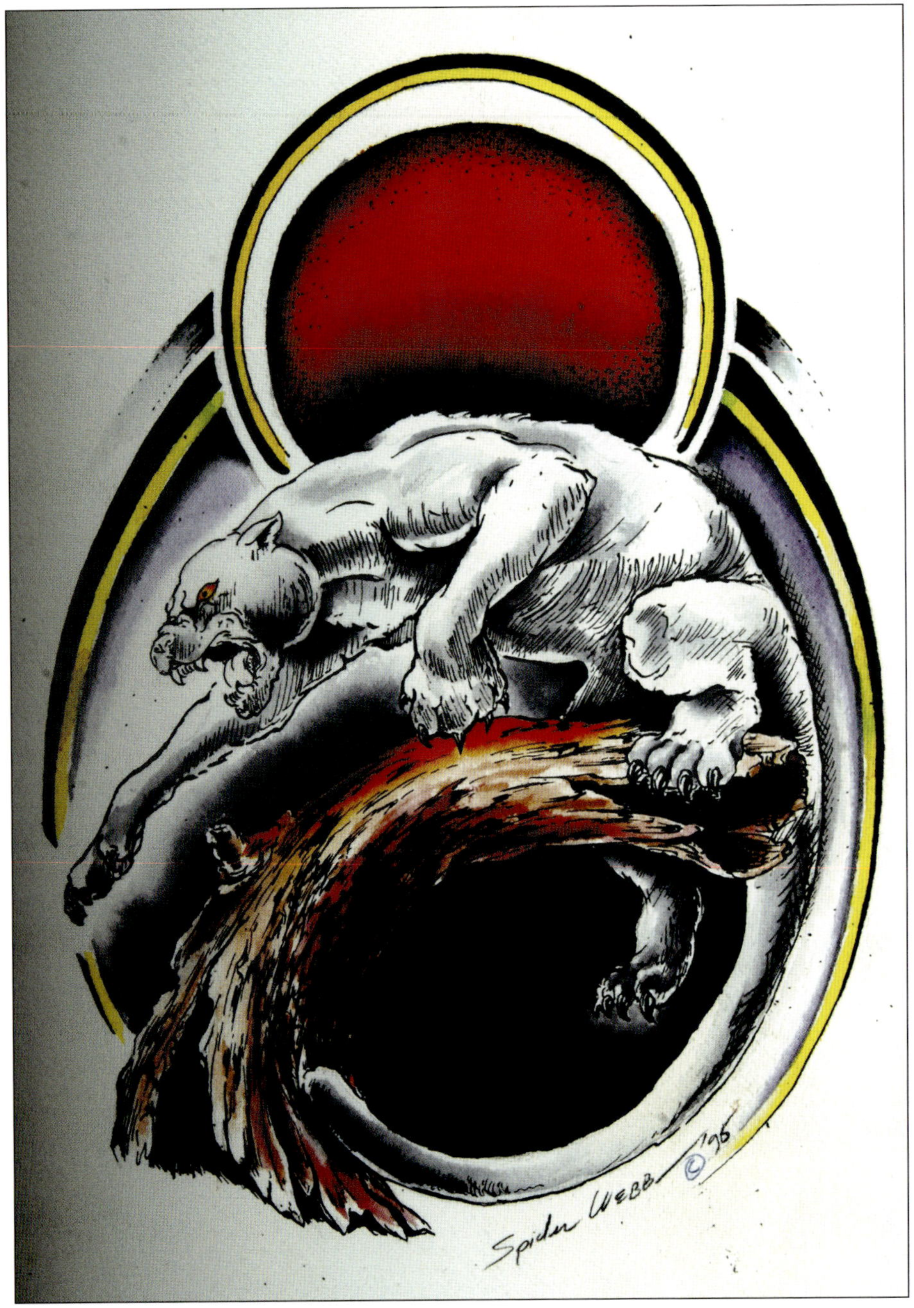

"Barbecued Brain." Ink and watercolor on Archers paper, 12" x 16". 1995.

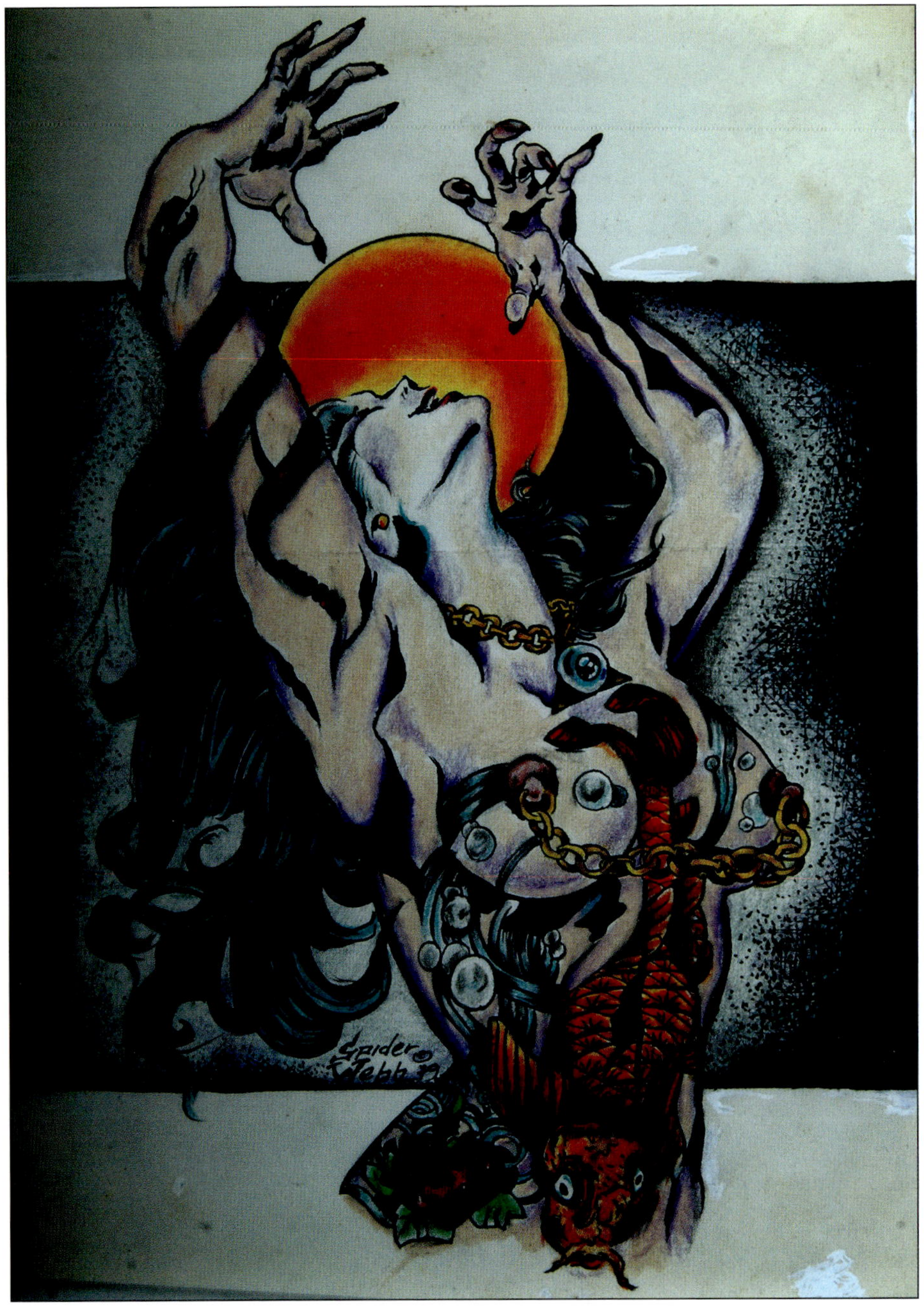

"A Dance Against Dying." Mixed media on Vellum paper, 11" x 17". 1979.

A woman's brain shrinks 8 percent during pregnancy. Who would have thought?
—*S.W.*

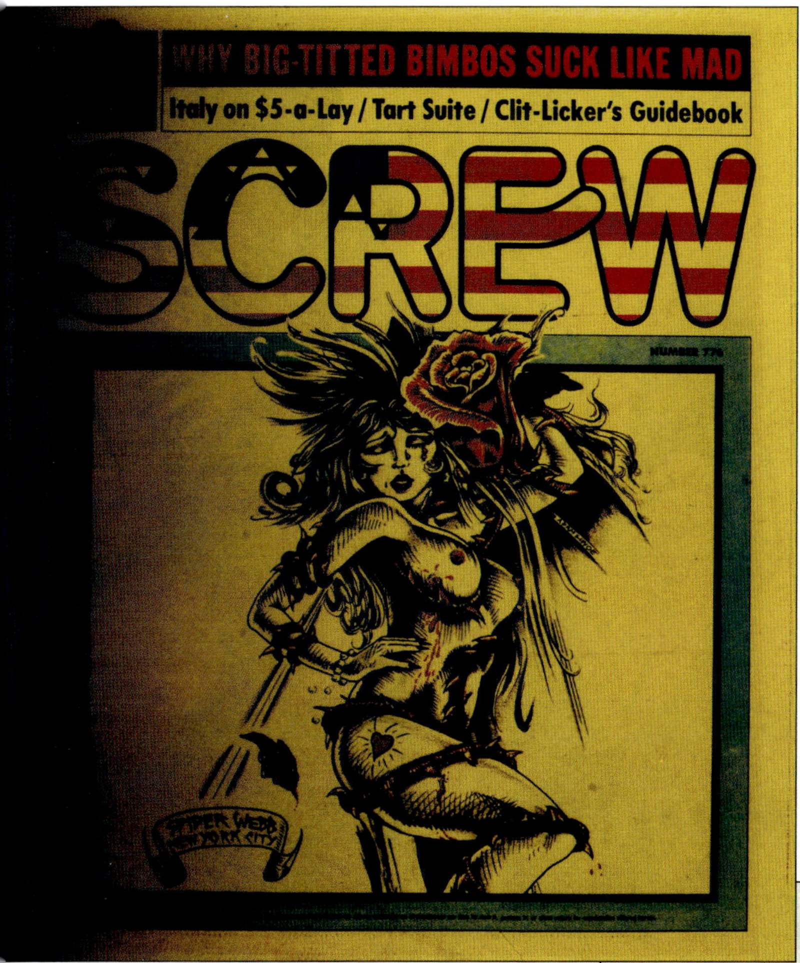


Screw cover. Original Art, Ink and water color on board. 1976.

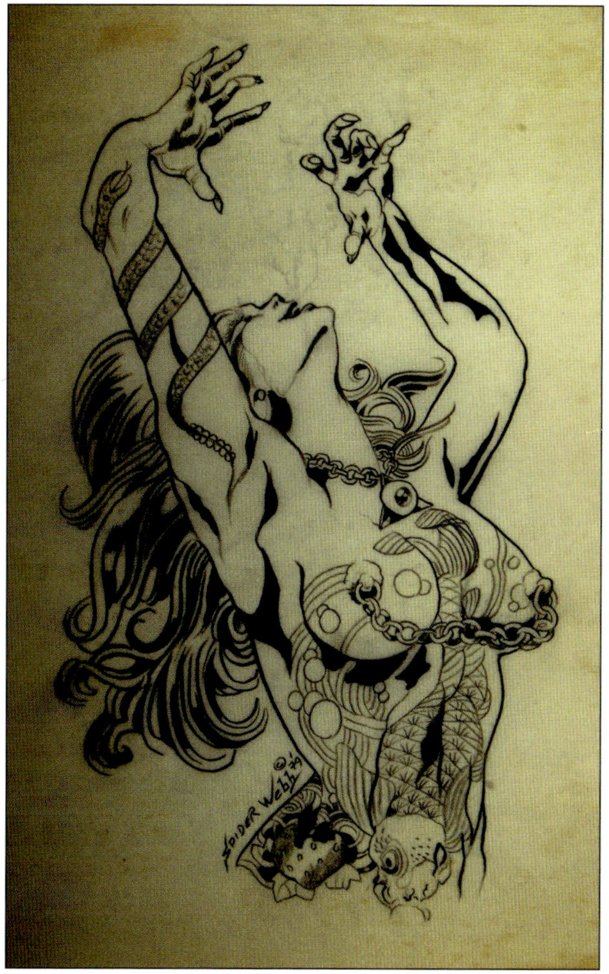

"Existence Can Be Rearranged." Pencil on Vellum paper, 11" x 17". 1979.

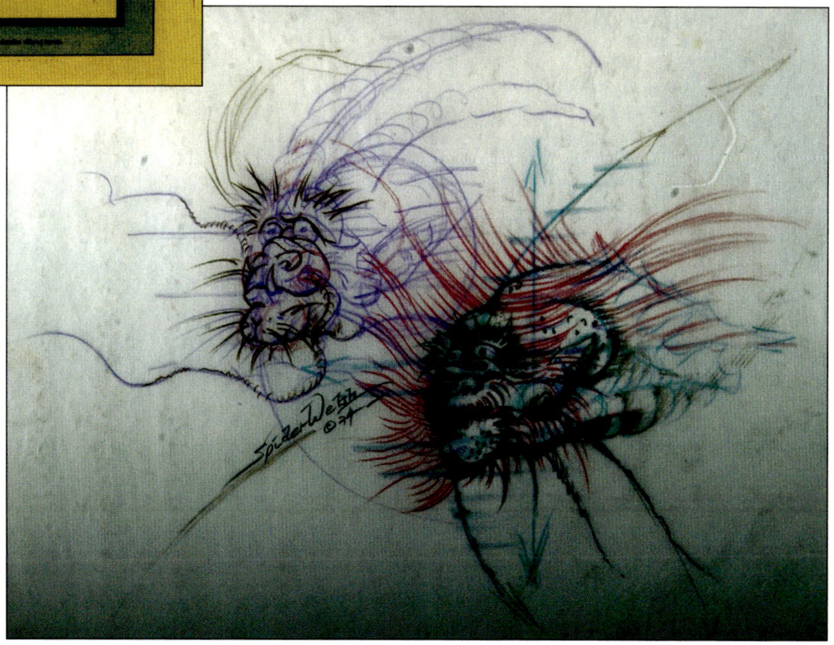

"Sobs of the Shaman." Pencil on Vellum paper, 11" x 17". 1974.

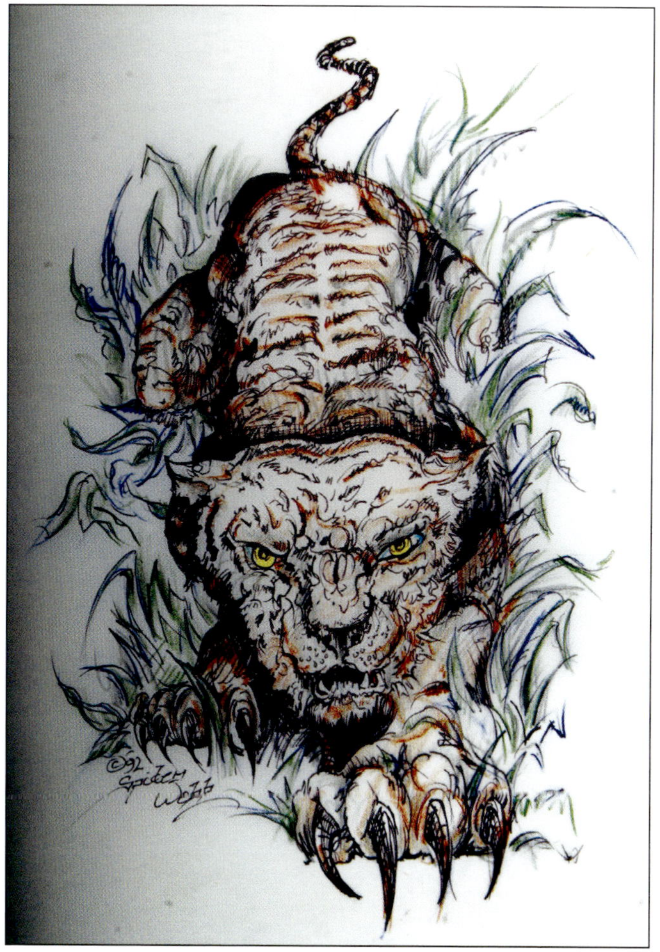

"Braid of Dried Love." Pencil on Vellum paper, 11" x 17". 1992.

I don't care about image. I don't have an image problem. I don't even have a mirror.
—*S.W.*

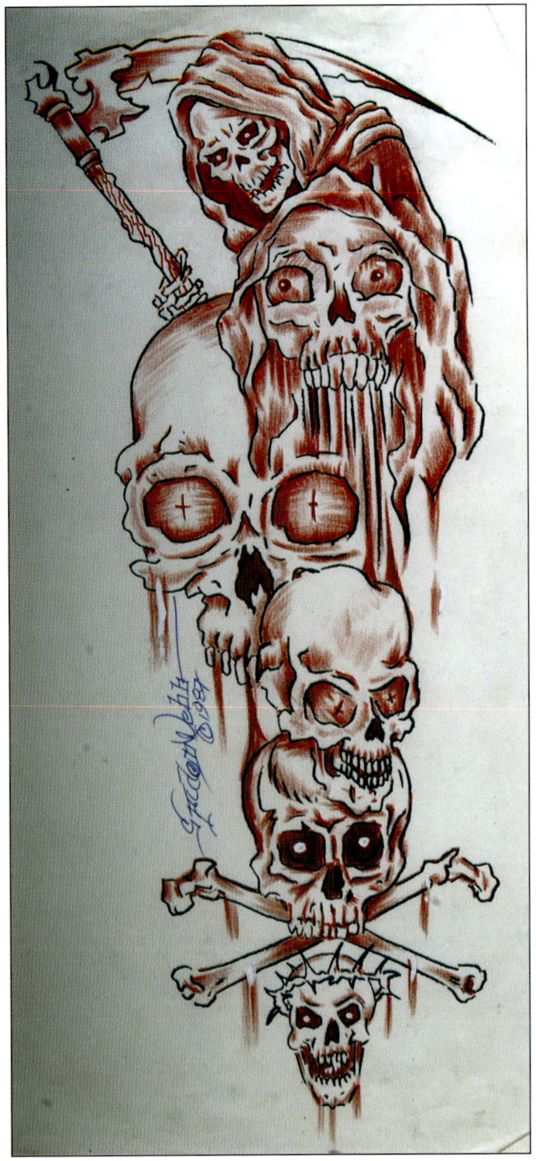

"Powerful Old Magic." Pencil on Vellum paper, 9" x 12". 1987.

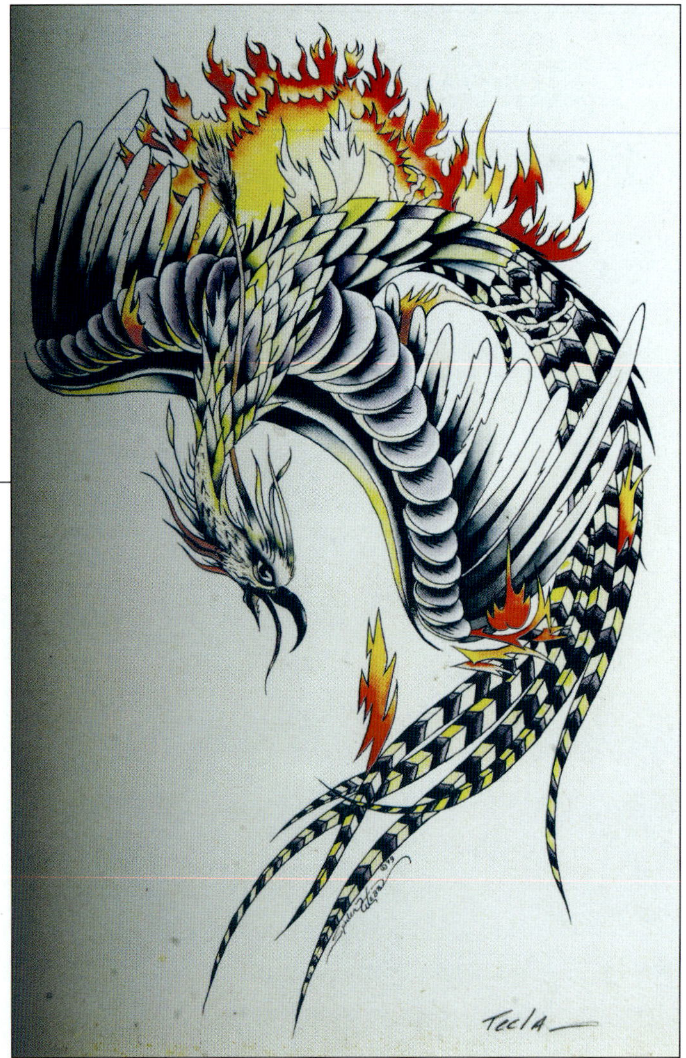

"Tecla V." Ink and watercolor on Archers paper, 20" x 24". 1979.

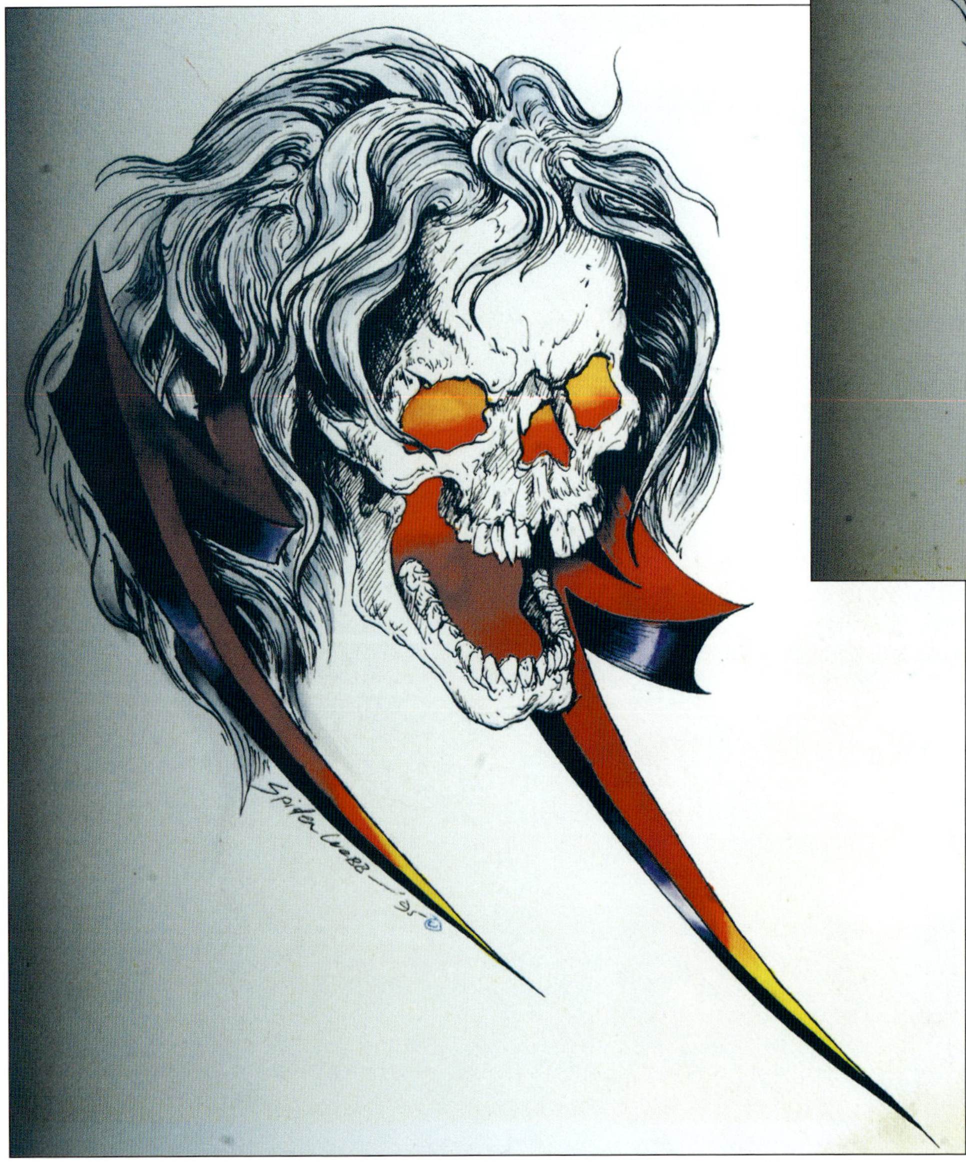

"Crazy Old Farts." Ink and watercolor on Archers paper, 20" x 24". 1995.

I ask you – would Custer like another crack at the Indians? I sure would.

—*S.W.*

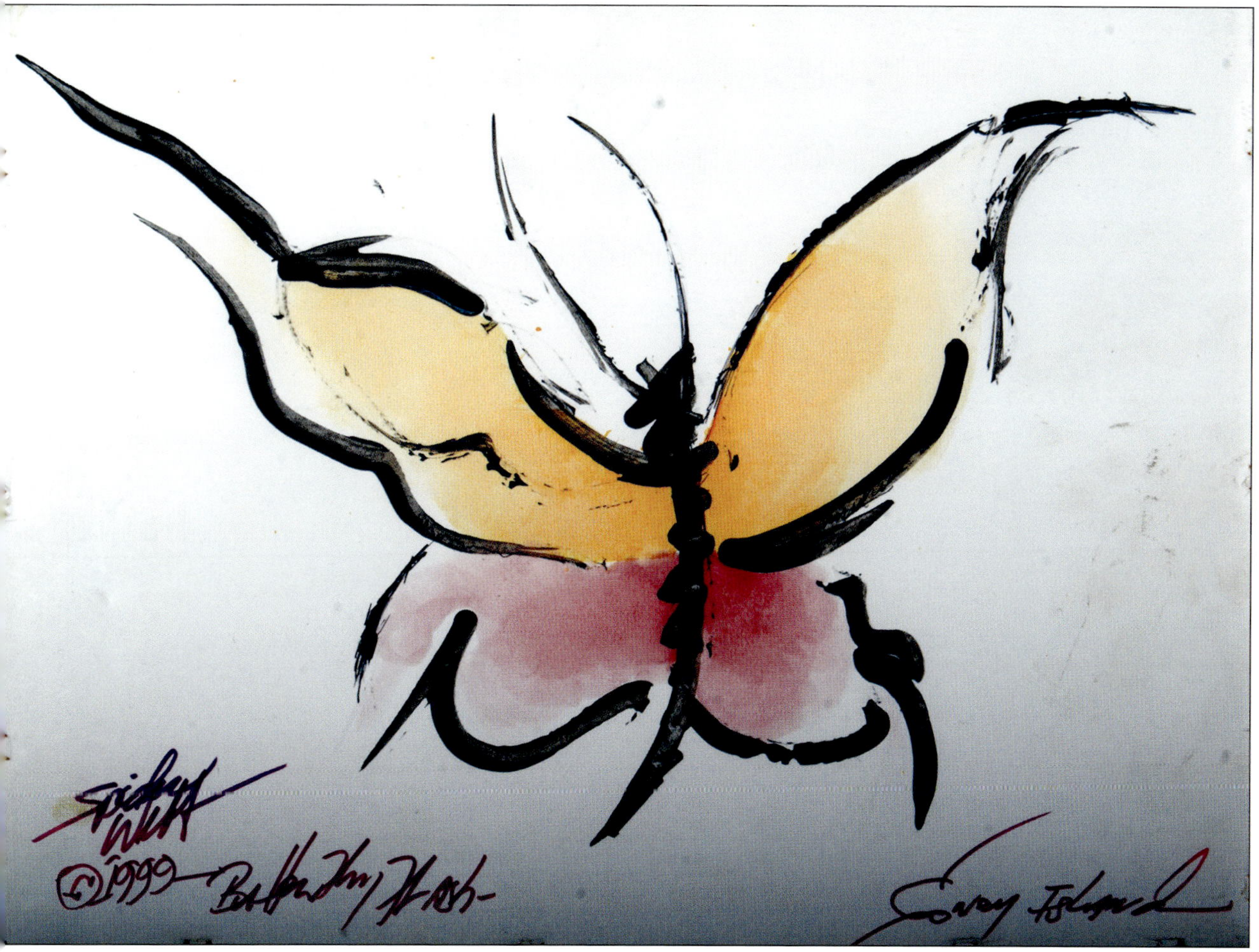

"Bedbug Jitterbug." Ink and watercolor on Vellum paper, 11" x 17". 1999.

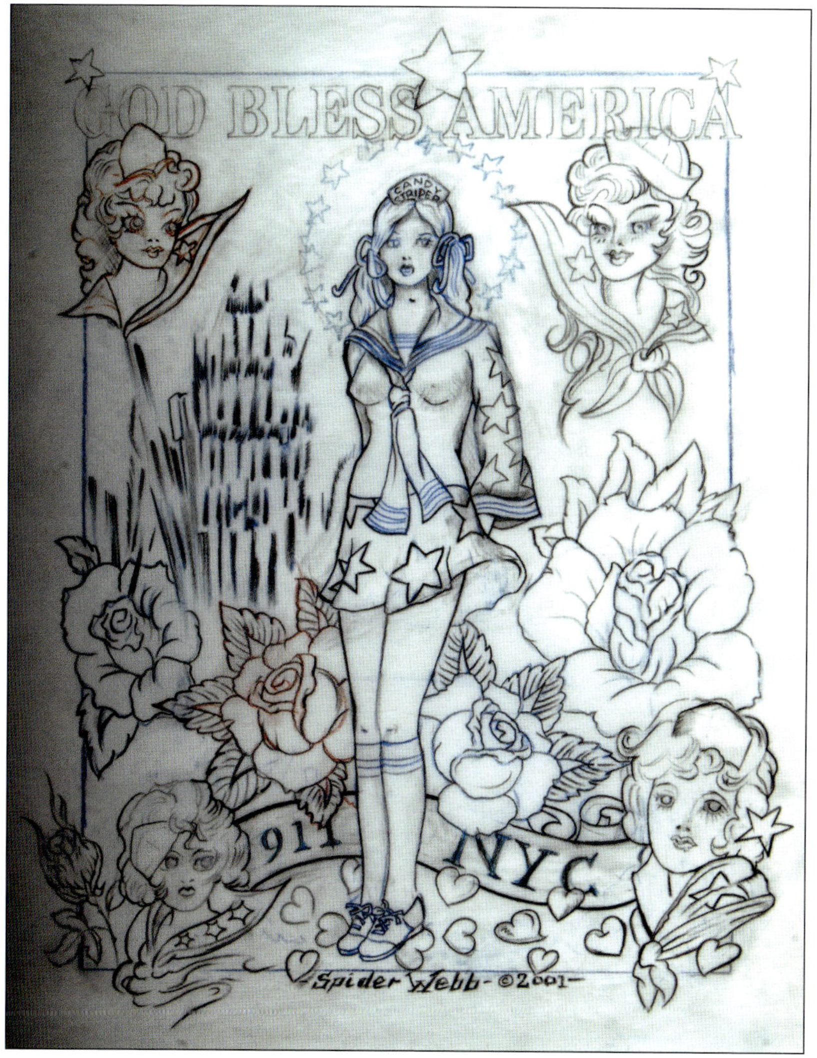


"Candy Striper." Pencil on paper, 18" x 20". 2001.

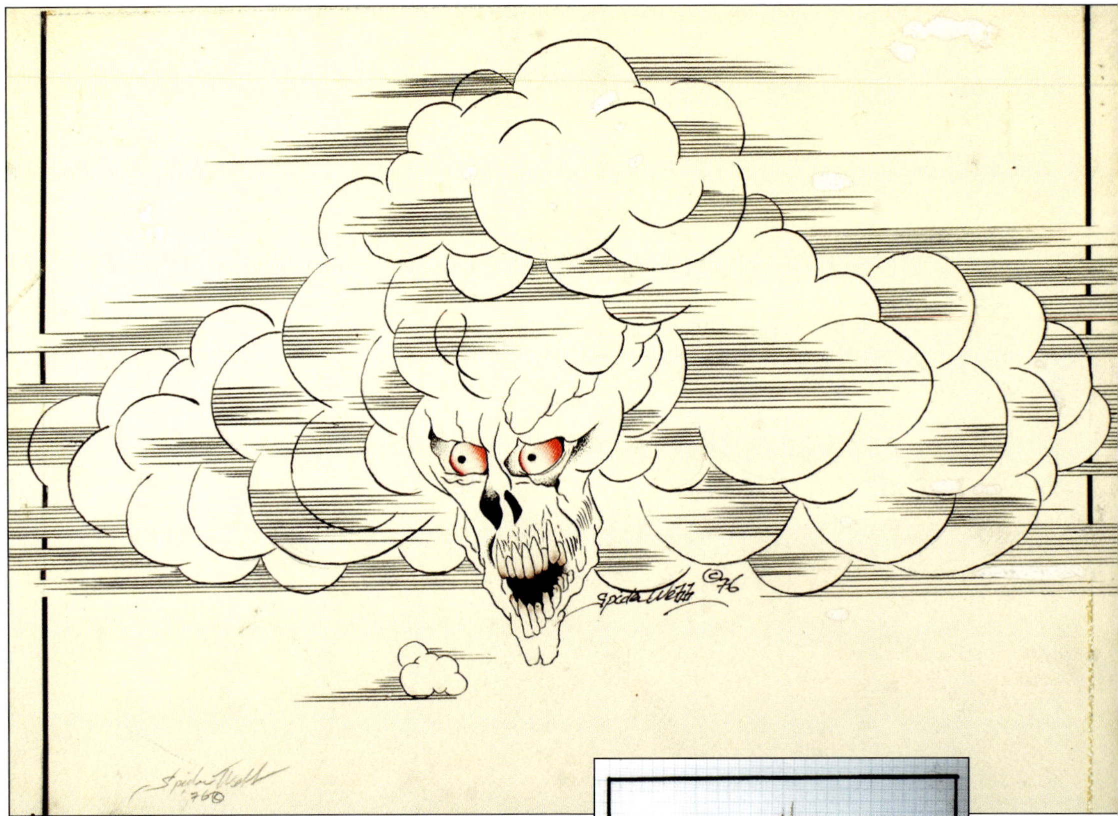

"Children in Peril." Pencil on board, 11" x 14". 1976.

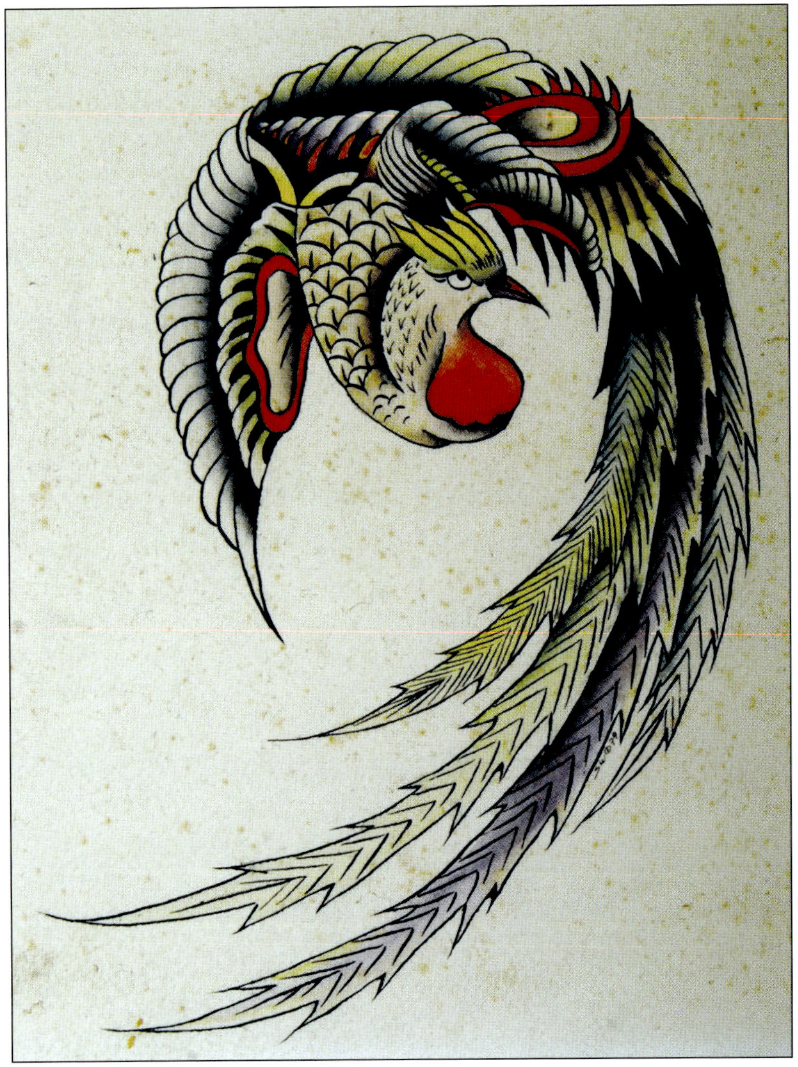

"Kisses in Black." Pencil on Vellum paper, 11" x 17". 1978.

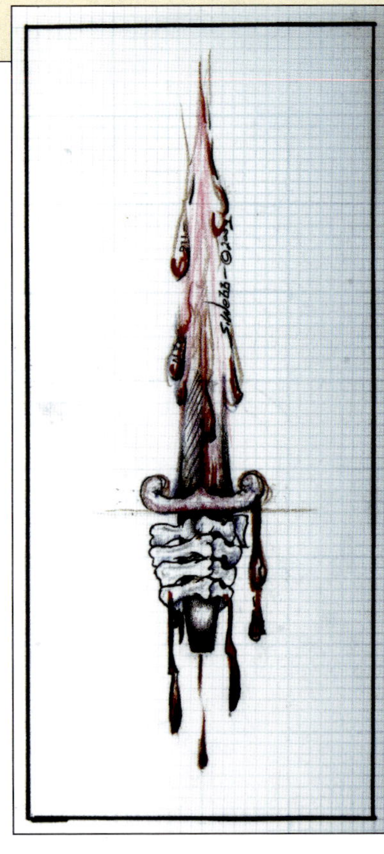

"She Smiled Triumphantly."
Pencil on Vellum paper, 8" x 10".
2001.

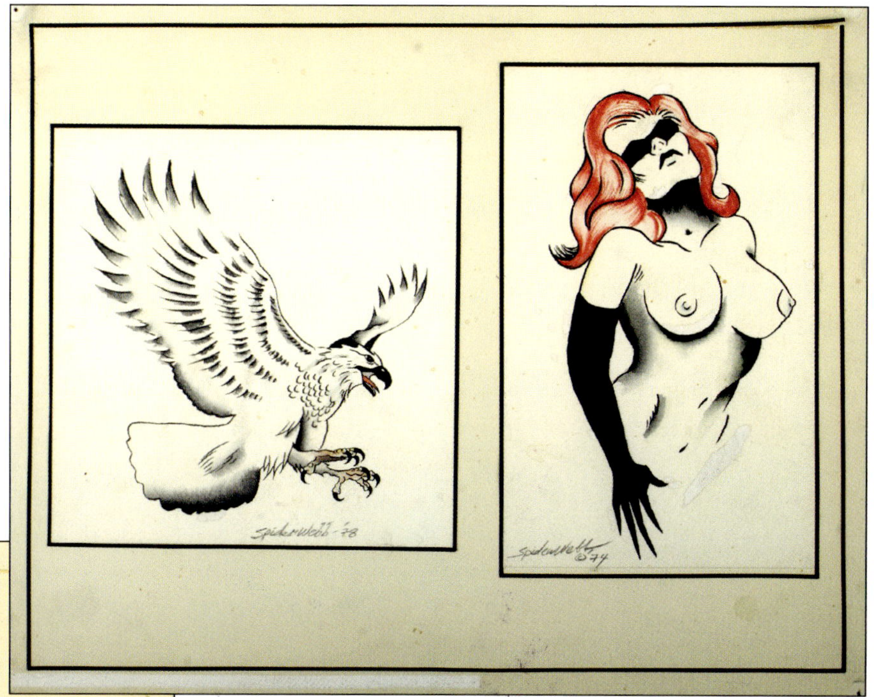


"Without Fanfare." Pencil on board, 11" x 14". 1978, 1974.

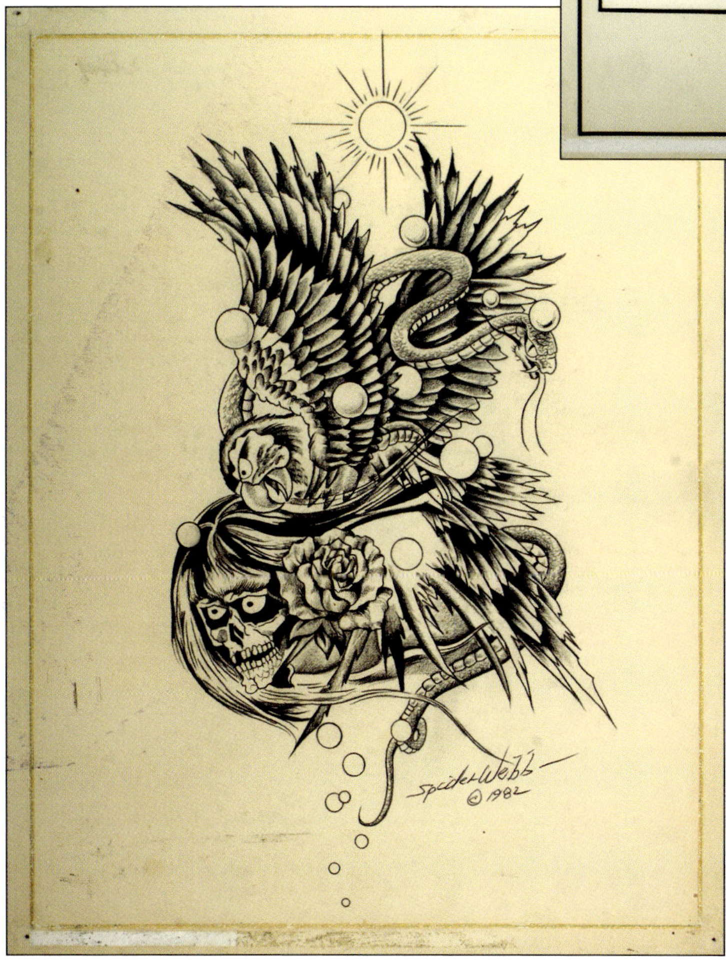


"Ancient Kisses of Teens." Pencil on board, 11" x 14". 1982.

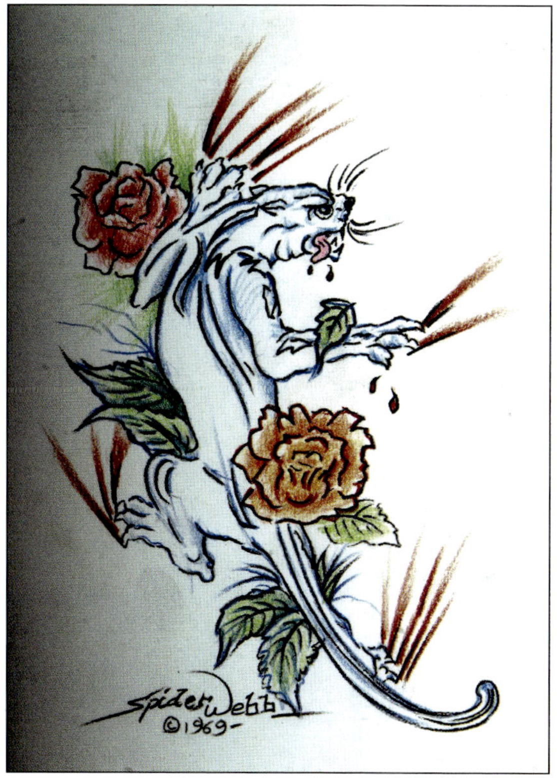


"A Cause to Fight For." Mixed media, 8 1/2" x 11". 1969.

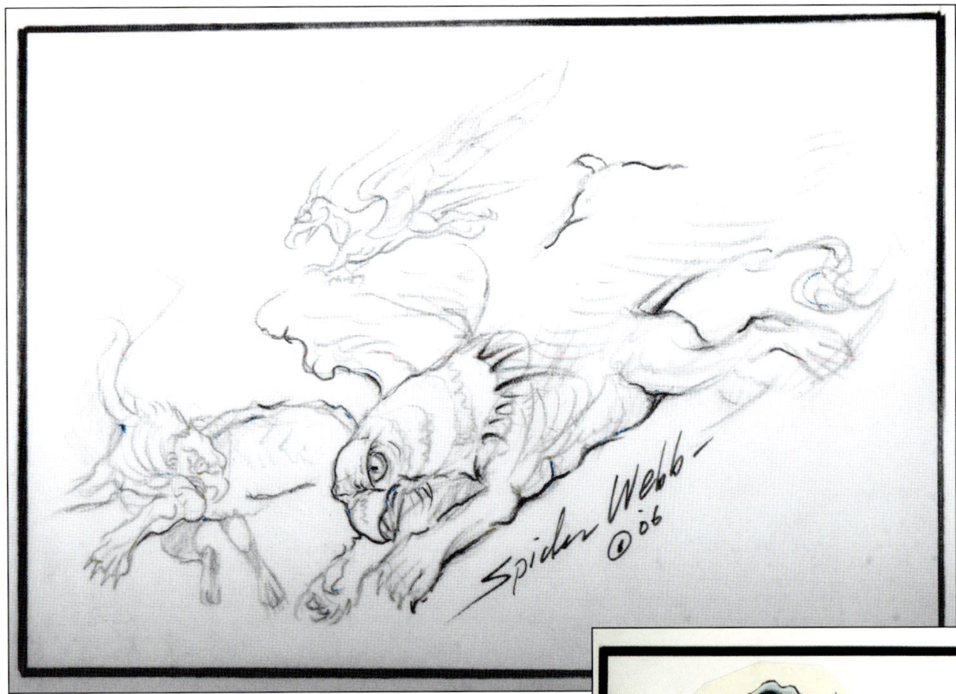

"Eskimo Toe Jam." Pencil on Vellum paper, 11" x 17". 2006.

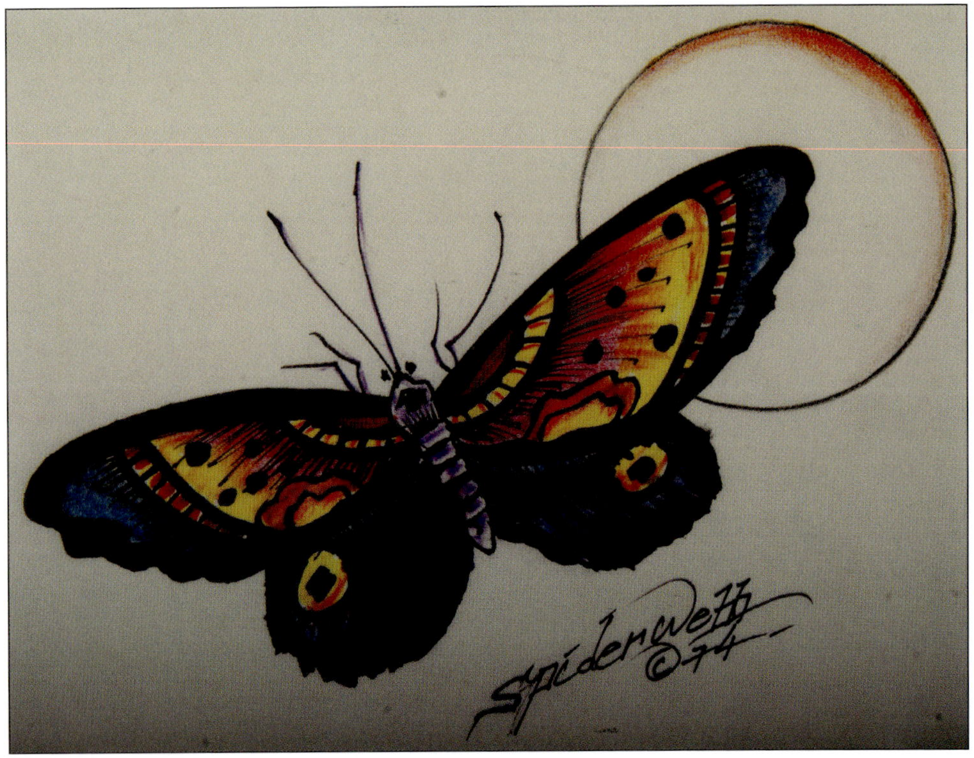

"Lifting a Ballerina." Pencil on Vellum paper, 8" x 10". 1974.

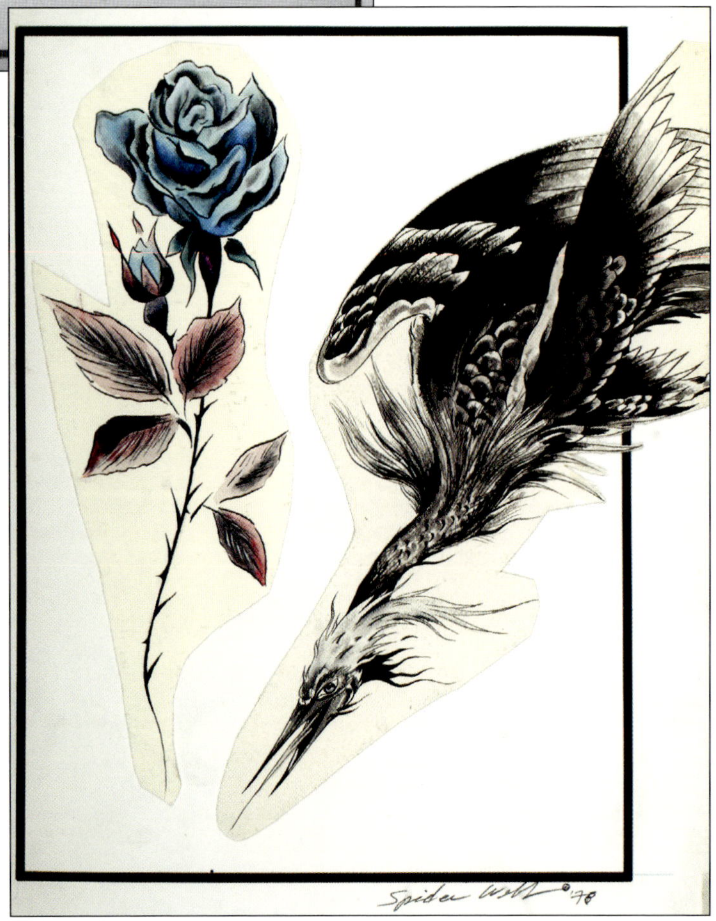

"Pearl in Claw." Watercolor on board, 11" x 14". 1978.

There's more to be learned from the cartoon character's balloon than the medium's ectoplasm.

—*S.W.*

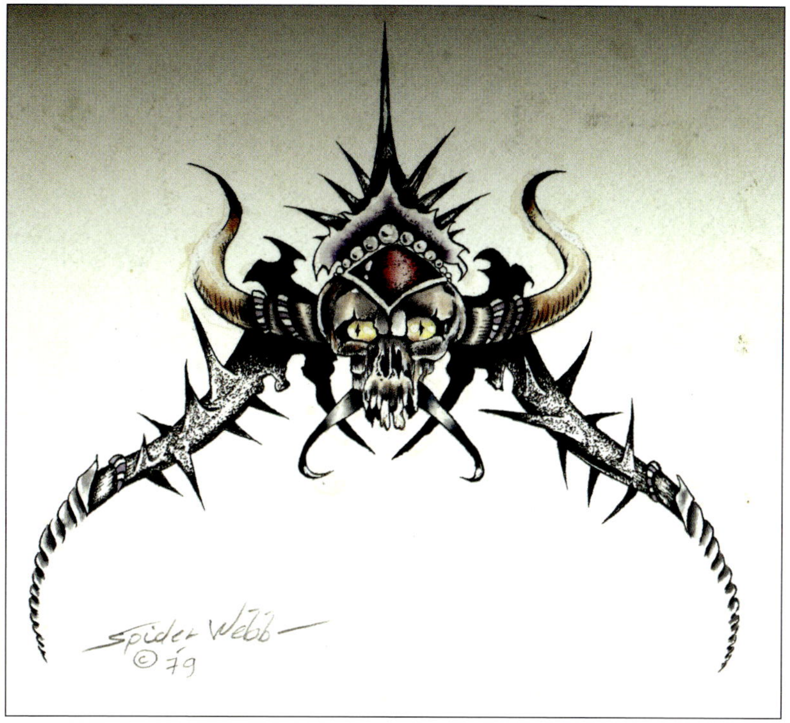

"Distilled Gold Extract." Ink and watercolor on Archers paper, 9" x 12". 1979.

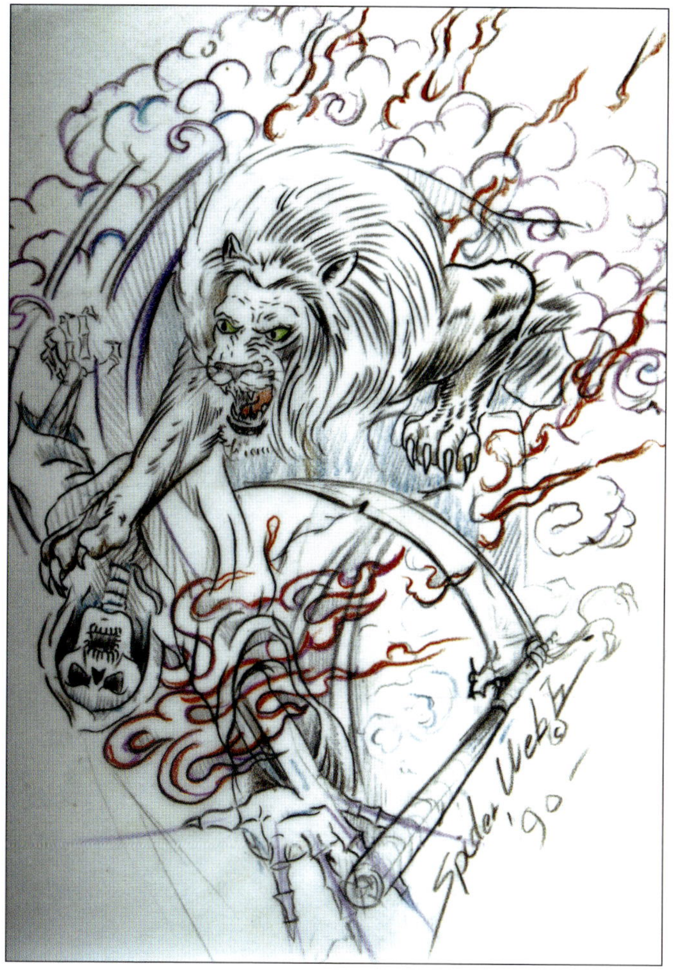

"Smoke Musk." Pencil on paper, 9" x 12". 1990.

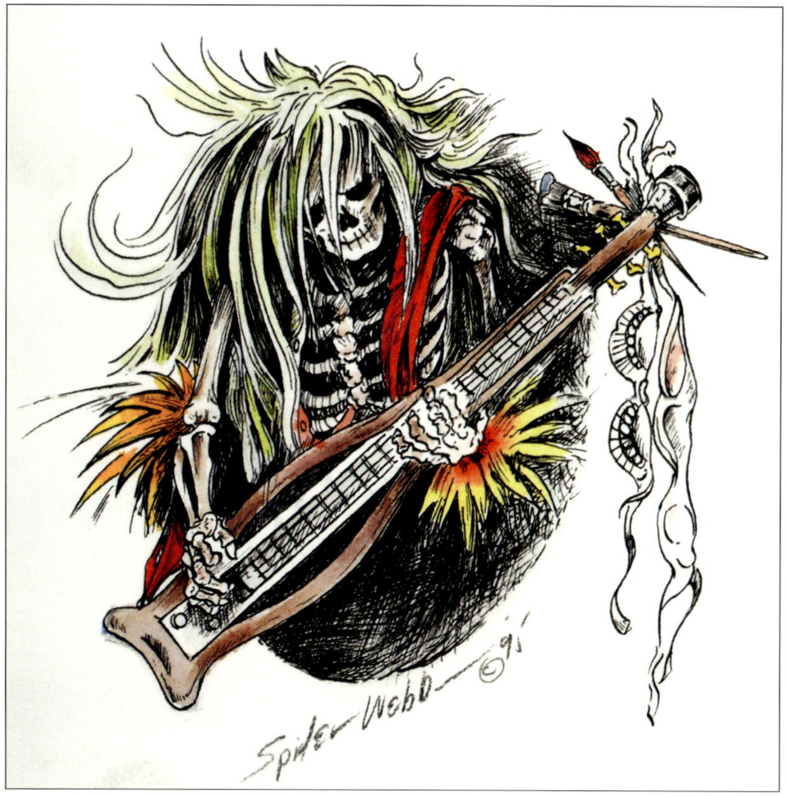

"Imagining Effective." Ink and water color on Archers paper, 9" x 12". 1995.

I hope it's something she can laugh about in the morning or regret when she wakes up.

*—S.W.*

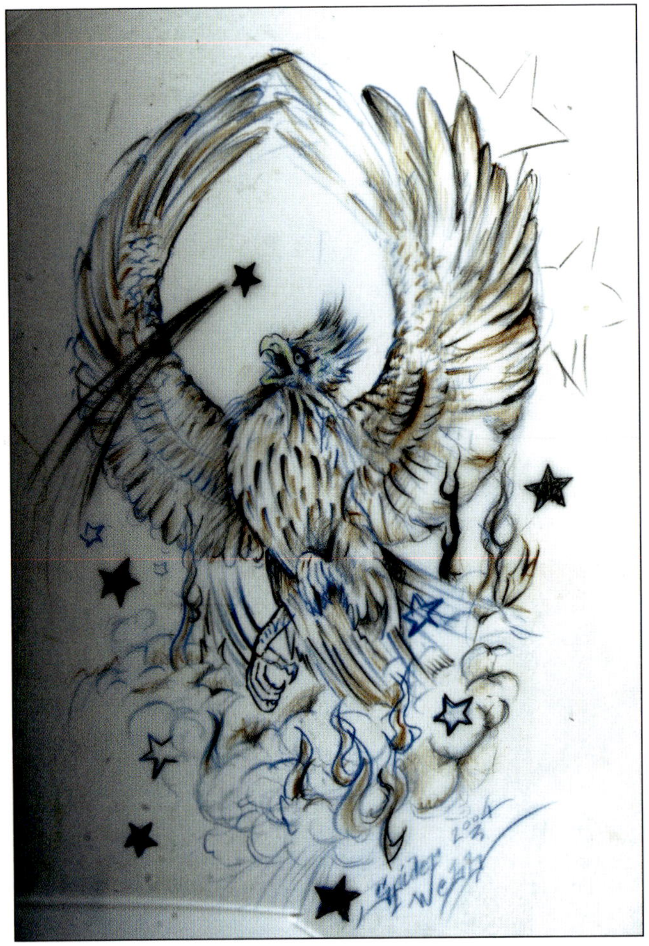

"Essence of Intentions." Pencil on Vellum paper, 11" x 17". 2004.

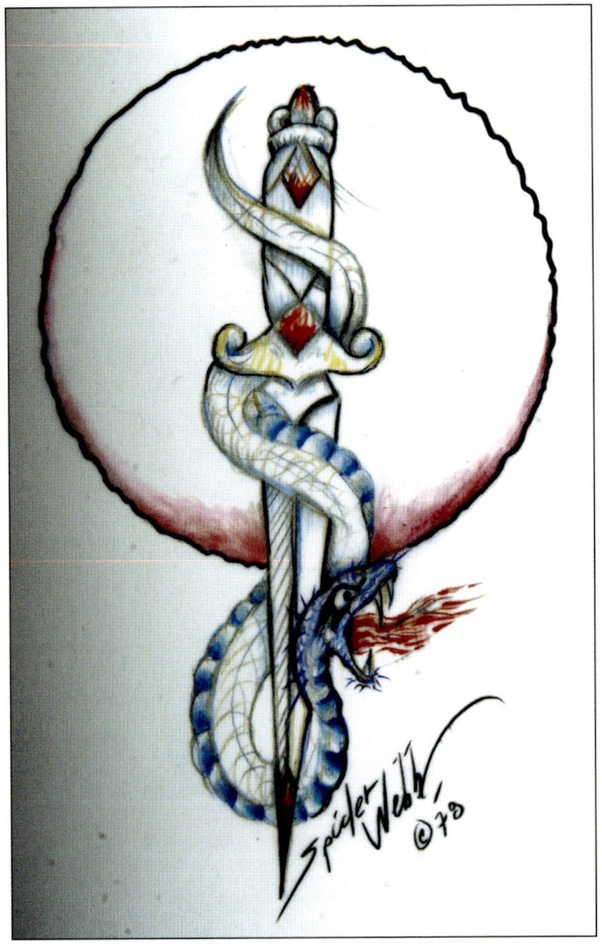

"Justification For Yourself." Pencil on Vellum paper, 8 1/2" x 11". 1978.

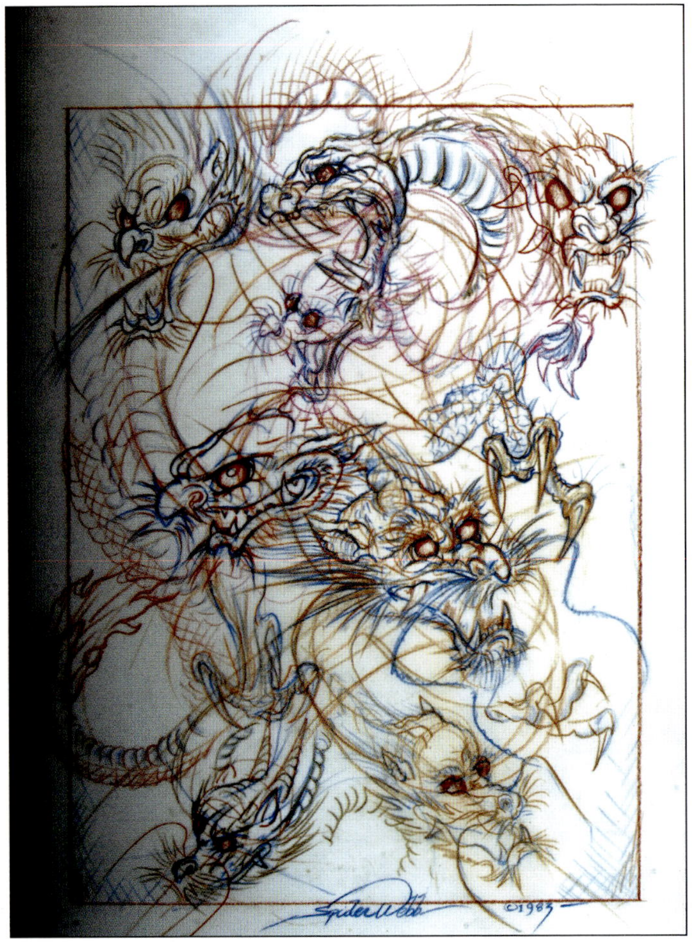

"Check-Mate." Pencil on Vellum paper, 9" x 12". 1983.

Tattoos, a mark of uncertainties and surprises.

*—S.W.*